C000139635

BITING BACK
The Mike Gregory Story

BITING BACK
The Mike Gregory Story

MIKE GREGORY WITH ERICA GREGORY,
STEVE MANNING AND DAVE HADFIELD

VERTICAL EDITIONS

First published in the United Kingdom in 2006 by Vertical Editions, 7 Bell Busk, Skipton, North Yorkshire BD23 4DT

www.verticaleditions.com

ISBN
1-904091-18-0
978-1-904091-18-9

Cover design and typeset by HBA, York

Printed and bound by the Cromwell Press, Trowbridge

To my most amazing blessings in life, my sons, Sam and Ben. You have given me so much, from the first day you were born, your first cry, your first smile, your first step, your first word. I have been there for all of them and I want more than anything else to carry on being there. Each day I see both your faces and that gives me the strength to carry on, so I may have the wonder of seeing you grow. Never doubt that I love you, you are part of my every fibre, my every breath, my every heartbeat. I love you more than you can imagine. My darling boys.

Your Daddy xx

CONTENTS

ACKNOWLEDGEMENTS

This story about my life so far, may not have come about had it not been for the help and encouragement of some lifelong friends.

I knew there was a book in me but it was not until weekly get togethers with myself and close friends, David 'Butty' Melling, Nick Gregson and John Ashton, where we would reminisce about the old times. We had a lot to talk about and stories to tell, although many of them could never be printed. So this was what became affectionately known as my 'book club'.

After a while I decided, why not write some of this down, as I felt I had a story to tell and within weeks we had the 'bare bones and bullet points' (sorry John) of my story which later became the framework of this book.

My wife, Erica, has been the driving force behind the book, so that my sons, Sam and Ben, will know first hand all that their Daddy has achieved in his life. From the friends I have made, the places I have visited and the ups and downs along the way – which have made me the man I am today.

I would also like to thank Steve Manning for his considerable time, patience and efforts in all my interviews in an attempt to put flesh on the 'bare bones'.

To Dave Hadfield, for skilfully making sense of these stories and putting the book together with the assistance of Andy Wilson. And, Vertical Editions, the publishers of this book for being enthusiastic about my story.

I would also like to thank all the photographers: Andrew Varley, Eddie Fuller, Sig Kasatkin, Newspix in Australia and

Phil Wilkinson on behalf of the *Wigan Observer* for permission in using their photographs in the book.

As I draw to a close, I would like to thank Joe Lydon, Paul Cullen, Jonathan Davies, Shaun Edwards, Ellery Hanley, Hugh McGahan, Shaun McRae, Brian Noble and Malcolm Reilly for their humbling tributes. Finally, to Phil Chadwick, Glen Sweeney, Dave Lyon, Billy McGinty and Phil Clarke for helping a rugby player who has taken one too many knocks to remember!

Mike Gregory
August 2006

FOREWORD BY JOE LYDON

'The harder the conflict, the more glorious the triumph. What we obtain too cheap, we esteem too lightly; it is dearness only that gives everything its value. I love the man that can smile in trouble, that can gather strength from distress and grow brave by reflection.'

Thomas Paine

It is far too easy to place superlatives alongside the name of Mike Gregory, as our memory is, on reading or hearing his name, jolted back to his playing days as captain of his club and country. Like so many, I'm sure, I hold a vivid picture in my head of a powerful, somewhat 'unnaturally tanned' athlete wearing a head band, tight shorts and the number 13 jersey. He is carrying the ball in one hand as he enters the field of play with a swagger that borders on arrogance. This distinctive gait is partly due to a troubled knee and partly born out of confidence. Confidence in his own ability, trust in his teammates, an understanding of what's needed and the assurance that comes from the hard work and dedication that has afforded him the opportunity.

In this picture, I'm not sure if I'm a supporter, an opponent or a teammate of the man in my mind, but having had the luck to have experienced all three, I rather hope it's the latter. What I do know is that this is a person with the commitment to give his all in an attempt to gain victory. A natural leader who will demand high standards of himself and his teammates and one who won't quit until the end of the game, the session, the competition or the series. I then wonder if the headband is there to keep the hair out of his eyes or to protect his ears from the conflict to come – either way it's been a waste of good tape.

Suddenly, this image changes as easily as turning the page of a photo album or book; it's time to party as hard as he has undoubtedly played or trained. While some of the traits have changed in this social environment, that same confidence and determination remain, now accompanied by a wicked sense of humour, a streak of devilment and an infectious enthusiasm. Once again, I know which side I want to be on but realise that as so often has been the case, I may have no choice in the matter!

As I smile to myself, and believe me there are many memories and exploits to smile about, reality bites and I see the present day Mike. Gone is the powerful physique that he worked so hard to create, the swagger, the confidence, the banter, but before anger sets in at the cruel injustice, I quickly realise that what remains, what are constant, are the core values, the heart encased in a stubborn shell. Courage, determination, a sharp mind and a love and appreciation of family, friends and laughter. These are the qualities that deserve to be applauded and afforded the superlatives that are too often used without real merit. These are the qualities that define the man I have had the pleasure to play alongside and to call my friend. These are the same qualities that should stand as a reminder to us all of what must be valued in sport, at home and in life.

It's not unusual in any kind of team sport to develop a lasting friendship with the people you train and play with, but I do believe it to be very special to be able to play professional sport with and against a lifetime friend. Rugby league and a certain Michael Keith Gregory have provided me with that opportunity and so much more. Thanks Greg; here's to the future, the fight, the values you hold so dear and the return of the swagger!

Joe Lydon
July 2006

INTRODUCTION

When Mike and Erica Gregory asked me during the 2005 season whether I would write his life story, I was caught somewhere between a quandary and a dilemma.

On the one hand, it was profoundly flattering to be invited to play that role for one of the people in rugby league I most liked and respected.

On the other, I knew I would not have the hours over the next year to do the task any sort of justice. So, over a few beers in Mike's mate's back garden, we hit upon this rather odd way of getting the story told.

The idea was that Mike would commit his memories to mini-disc and the transcript would come to me to be kicked into shape. That was where Steve Manning came into the equation.

He had already volunteered to record Mike's story and he has been the workhorse of this project, carrying out 20-odd interviews covering his life and times.

Apart from organising it and trimming it for length, I have done precious little with the text after that. This was never going to be my book; it was always Mike's. What you get is his voice, which might be indistinct now when you meet him, but which comes through here, I hope, loud and clear.

It is not, of course, your average rugby league autobiography. True, Mike has a distinguished career as player and coach to look back upon; and it might surprise those who misunderstand his condition to find that his power of recall is as sharp as ever, sharper perhaps.

But that is just the start of it. As most people will know, his life has become a struggle against a cruel medical condition; something you would not wish upon your worst enemy, but which seems somehow more unkind when it strikes an individual who has been so fit and vigorous.

And yet there is no self-pity about Mike Gregory. Some anger, yes, and he is surely entitled to that, but the wry humour still shines through. The unquenchable spirit that made him one of rugby league's great competitors is still there.

He would give a lot of the credit for that to the help he has had, from both friends and strangers, in his hour of need. One thing Mike is blessed with is a wide circle of friends, who would do anything for him, and with Joe Lydon at the centre of the network. Too many other rugby mates to mention have rallied to him and I'll admit that there are some that I've seen in a different light through their response to Mike's situation. The depth of the concern for him has been a reflection of his standing in the game.

The same goes for the legions of people who only knew him from the vantage point of the stands and terraces. Rugby league stars stay a lot closer to the roots they sprang from than most sportsmen – it is one of the classic virtues of the game – but Mike holds a special place in the public's affections. I know what a source of strength that has been for him.

His sons have also been a constant inspiration for him. It was when he described this book as a legacy for them that I knew I was going to have to help as best I could.

Most of all, there is Erica. She might not have endeared herself to everyone over the last couple of years, but if you ever struck problems like the ones that have afflicted Mike and you had a fight like his, she is the woman you would want in your corner. Clever, tenacious, combative when she has to be; apart from Mike, she is the heroic figure in this story.

I must say another thank you or two. Andy Wilson of *The Guardian* helped out with some text when the workload was too great for one older and slower. Mike Latham checked the final manuscript with his customary diligence.

Karl Waddicor at Vertical Editions backed Mike and Erica's determination to tell their story from first hearing of their plans. Before this book sells a single copy, his generous contribution has gone into their trust fund and has made a considerable difference to the trust's finances. By buying it, you have made a difference as well and our thanks for that.

Dave Hadfield
August 2006

1

INJURY PRONE

I was born at 13 Mitchell Street, Pemberton, in Wigan on the 20th of May 1964. We didn't have time to get to the hospital so my mum gave birth to me in my grandparents,' Jim and Ann Jayne, front room, so that was a bit frantic. The midwife was there but my Nana said that she did most of the work. So I was born at number 13, unlucky for some but lucky for me.

For my parents, Keith and Joan, I was the middle child. I had an older sister, Christine, and a younger brother, Philip. They always say the middle child misses out but that wasn't the case for me; we were all well loved. We lived with my grandparents for a time, then we moved up to Campbell Street in Pemberton, so really I'm born and bred in Pemberton and I'm proud of my roots. We had a very stable family atmosphere and in that I'm very fortunate.

My grandfather as I was getting older said to my mother that 'you've got to tie that little so and so to the table leg' because I was so mischievous, I think that's the word. I was always on the go and quite boisterous. From an early age I was also injury prone. I was 18 months old when I was standing on the couch trying to switch the light on. You can guess what happened; I fell off the couch, landed awkwardly and broke my collarbone for the first time. I've no memories of going to hospital, but they put my arm into a sling for quite a while. The younger you break bones the better they heal, because they are not as brittle. I suppose that counts as my first injury.

My sister Christine was nearly two years older than me and we got on quite well, although if she did something

16

wrong when we were little I would take the blame and would never say that she had done it. But if Philip and I had done anything we shouldn't have, Chris would tell my mum if she asked her. My brother is five and a half years younger than me so I always took him under my wing, protecting him.

As I said I was a bit boisterous with a bit of rough and tumble outlook and I enjoyed my childhood. When I was four we went down to London, as we had relatives down there. One day my father took my sister Chris, my cousins and I down to the park. Stupidly, I went up the slide the wrong way instead of going up the steps to the top. As I turned around I lost my balance and fell off and this is probably the very first thing I really remember as a child. I remember landing on my face and some people say that they can still see evidence of that injury now.

I couldn't move my jaw. It was just hanging down but my dad said 'Oh, there's nothing wrong with you.' I couldn't speak properly and my dad picked me up and carried me back to the house. They carried on playing in the garden, but I couldn't, because my jaw was aching. Eventually, they took me into the house and my mum, who was a nurse, said 'What have you done?' I said, as best I could, 'I've hurt my mouth.' My mum knew I had broken my jaw, so from there we went to hospital.

Apparently I had shattered my jaw completely on both sides and they wired me up for six weeks. They said that, because my bones were still growing, I should heal okay but I'd never be able to play contact sports, which meant nothing to me at that time. They left a gap between my teeth where you could fit a straw and I was on chicken soup for six weeks. To this day, I can't stand chicken soup and my mum wouldn't ever make it again.

I had to go back to Withington Hospital in Manchester and then to the dental department every year until I was 14. I never had problems with my jaw after that and it's always been quite strong since the repair. I've been told since that I'm a case for students to study at medical school because I healed so well.

I broke my jaw in the summer holidays before I started at Sacred Heart Primary School, Springfield. I had never picked up a rugby ball before I went there and wasn't interested in the game at the time. As a kid you played in the street kicking a football and that was all I did. At Sacred Heart we didn't really play any competitive sports in the infants, but in the juniors we played rugby and football. Before I could get involved I had to go and ask the surgeon if I could play. He said that I could, but that I should wear a gum shield when playing rugby. In 1973 when I was nine, my Year Five teacher, Dave Malin, started me off playing rugby league. I played in the Year Five school team and I also played in the Year Six team. But I got my first medal playing football. I played centre forward and the school team won a six-a-side competition. It was my first silverware and I enjoyed the feeling of winning.

When I started playing rugby league I was quite tall and lean. I played second row or prop as I learned the game. With the rugby team I lost in two finals at Central Park, but won a number of other medals and cups. Really that's when I started to enjoy rugby rather than football. We played St Cuthbert's School and that was when I first got to know Joe Lydon, who played for them. He was only small and skinny but even then he had pace. None of our team could catch him and he scored two tries when they beat us in a Cup quarter-final. If you've got pace to burn you can play our game and Joe had pace even at that age.

In my final year at school, I went for trials for the Wigan Schools Under-11s, together with my teammates Alan Clough, Michael Hall and Michael Hancock. We all got into the squad and Joe was captain of the side. I became real friends with Joe and now I've known him over 30 years. They say that schooldays are the best years of your life. I certainly enjoyed mine but I also had one of the biggest disappointments of my life when I played for Wigan Schools.

Wigan was selected to play in the schoolboy curtain raiser against Widnes at the 1975 Challenge Cup Final between

Widnes and Warrington at Wembley, but I broke my toe and missed playing in that game. I was devastated, as it's every boy's dream to play at Wembley. I've always had injuries at the worst times, but this was a particularly bitter pill to swallow. I wasn't allowed to walk out with the team but I was allowed to sit on our substitutes' bench. We lost the game 8-0 and came back home the same day on the coach with the Widnes lads.

These things are brought to test us, I believe. Wigan had some great players then, but I preferred playing to watching so I didn't go to Central Park with my dad. What I did do was go to Springfield Park with him to watch the football. Even though I played football at school I preferred rugby, but I went watching the 'Latics' and became a ball boy. I enjoyed watching players like Micky Worswick, Ian Gore and Johnny Rogers in the Northern Premier League, which is where Wigan was at the time. I was a ball boy for 18 months and went to every home game, so it was a balance between watching football and playing rugby league. As I said, it was Dave Malin who started me off at rugby and if it weren't for him I wouldn't have achieved what I have so far. I have him to thank for the way that I enjoyed playing sport and wanted to participate rather than just watch. At school, I was an average scholar who only worked fairly hard. My mum said that when I started school they would sort out my mischievousness and they did. I became a bit more disciplined, because a few years ago you could still get the slipper or cane or ruler. I wasn't exactly good, but I wasn't naughty. I just wish with hindsight that I had worked harder, especially at secondary school. I moved on to St John Fisher, and was again not the greatest scholar or hardest worker. At John Fisher you had so much tradition of being excellent at rugby league that you certainly worked hard at that. Nowadays the attitude to sport might be 'Play if you want to,' back then it was a case of 'You will play.' I was fortunate that I enjoyed playing all sports – cricket, athletics, softball, football, swimming and, of course, rugby league.

A big influence on my rugby was Steve McLeod, the PE

teacher, although our coach was Phil Derbyshire, who took us all the way through from 11 to 16. In my five years of rugby league at the school from 1975 to 1980 we only lost one game and that was in the first year when we lost 19-8 to Gidlow High School. That's some feat, but we were a special team. I had some good teammates at John Fisher: Michael Hancock, Paul Minton, Andy Bailey, Adrian Burns, they were all great players. There were a number who went on to bigger and better things, like Jeff Clare, who was a year younger and went on to sign for Wigan, but played for our team. It was a good time to play rugby league, but I've got to emphasise that I was only a good average player until one day I had a training accident and broke my collarbone.

It was purely accidental, when Mike Hancock, our captain, who was only tiny but strong, lifted me up and dumped me on my shoulder in a fair tackle. The colour drained from my face and I felt sick immediately, so we finished training and Phil Derbyshire took me to hospital. It was a clean break, but I now have a deformed left collarbone because of the two fractures. I had six weeks out with the injury. On my return Phil sensed straight away that I had changed. I had a mean dirty streak in my game and I probably became a bit tougher and a bit more resilient as well as a little nastier in my play. I didn't know why, but I was told when I came back that I was a different player. It wasn't on purpose, it's just something that clicked inside me and, from then on, my game kicked on.

I got back into the town team at 15 and in my first game back we played Oldham. Up to then I hadn't been sent off, but a lad called 'JB' and I kicked off and started an almighty brawl. We both got sent off. A St John Fisher player had never been sent off in a town team side before and I was quite worried about what Steve McLeod and Phil Derbyshire would say, but they were fine. By the age of 15, it gets quite physical and maybe at times a bit dirty. There was no video evidence to catch you out and I didn't really take a backward step.

With my game moving up a gear, I was selected for Lancashire Schools, which was an honour for the school and me. St John Fisher wouldn't let you play for an amateur club like other schools would, because we trained twice a week and played a game at least once a week. A lot of us doubled up to play football, but I'd gone off football altogether and I started going down to Central Park with my mates. My rugby league heroes at the time were always loose forwards, like Malcolm Reilly, Ray Price, Steve 'Knocker' Norton and Doug Laughton, so there were quite a few people who ultimately influenced the way I played.

In my final year at St John Fisher I was picked for the English Schools Easter Tour of France, along with Andy Bailey, who was a phenomenal full-back, and Adrian Burns, who had blistering pace at centre or wing. Our captain was my old mate Lee Crooks and Russell Smith was on the wing, although he became a lot better known in his second rugby league career as a referee.

It was the first time I had been abroad and it was a great experience, but quite daunting to be away and not really knowing everyone, although we'd played against one another. Even now, a few of them have remained friends from that trip. We lost the first game 18-8 to Languedoc-Roussillon, who became the first side in France to beat the English Schools, and I played in the second half. I got picked for the Test and, in the first of many tough encounters I had against France, we came from 8-6 behind to win the match 11-8. We won our final two games and I played in the last one, a 38-0 victory over Midi-Pyrenees. I've still got my jersey at my mum and dad's house because I knew that to be picked for England schools showed that I was on track for being signed as a professional.

At St John Fisher, we went into our last-ever game having lost just that one game and having won every trophy available. The game was against Bedford School, from Leigh, who we had never played before, in the Lancashire Shield Final at Hilton Park. There was an intense rivalry between the two districts and because of our record we were favourites to win, but we were behind at half-time and I can't repeat even in this book what Phil Derbyshire said to us at the break. It worked, though, and we won 25-13 to take a clean sweep of all the trophies we played for that year. On my way back to Wigan with my dad we had Phil with us. My dad asked me what Phil had said to us at half-time and I said 'I can't tell you, I can't tell you' and no one will ever know.

During that final year scouts would come to St John Fisher and watch us play. I believed I had the ability to improve and ultimately I wanted to play rugby league professionally.

On leaving St John Fisher at 16, I moved to St John Rigby 6th Form College. Unfortunately I hadn't worked hard enough at school and I only came out with three GCEs, so when I went to St John Rigby I had to re-sit three others and I did A Levels in Human Biology, Art, The History of Art and General Studies. In my first year, there was a lot of work and I passed my re-sits in Chemistry, Technical Drawing and Geography at the end of that year. The following year I passed Art and The History of Art at A Level but failed the others. The second year had a bit more recreation along with the class work and I enjoyed playing sport for the college. In the first year, I played rugby union as they didn't play league there and in the second year rugby league, as well as getting involved in other sporting activities. Also during those two years at college I played rugby union and rugby league outside college, but more about that later.

As I've admitted, I didn't work hard enough at school and I carried on that way at college. I didn't work hard enough for my grades and it's a big regret to this day, because what I wanted to do was be a PE teacher. I should have put more effort into my grades rather than concentrating more on sport and socialising, especially in my final year. I knew that I was good enough to sign as a professional rugby player but it would have been nice to continue my further education at college or university. I really have no excuse for not studying hard enough as education is the uppermost thing in early life and can be something to fall back on if it doesn't work out in the sporting arena. I was fortunate but, even so, with injuries it can be a short career. The kids of today need something in case they don't make the grade. Rugby league is more cut-throat now and all about success. The way the game is going there are loads of kids who don't get the opportunity and plenty of late developers who miss the boat. A very small percentage make it, especially when you look at home-grown talent, even though I think the game is going in the right direction with the emphasis on Academy sides at clubs.

Even on an organised college holiday I managed to get injured. It was on a skiing trip to the French Alps. I had never skied before and again it was a sport I took to quite well. On this occasion, we were following the instructor and he just said those fatal words 'Stick by me'. I was the one behind him as we skied along at quite a speed. With snow there is very little depth perception and the instructor skied over the roof of a chalet on the mountain. He didn't realise there was a 20 foot drop off the roof, but as he turned to shout 'Stop,' I was in mid air and there was no going back. I was the only one who went over; the rest stopped in time. I had done what the instructor had said earlier to do by sticking by him. I landed okay – my knees were good then, not like they are now – but unfortunately I landed with one of my ski poles in my mouth. I went down like a sack of potatoes and I was pumping blood from my lip and mouth. Even though I was insured we didn't contact the emergency helicopter. That would have been ridiculous and the cost would have been outrageous, so it was decided that the group I was in would ski down the mountain. I put snow inside my mouth to help stop the bleeding and I ploughed down the mountain without ski poles.

When we got to the resort I saw a doctor at the clinic and I had a tetanus injection and ten stitches in the wound. I ended up cutting that day's skiing short for the rest of the students in my group and I apologise profusely to them again. John Ireland, the teacher who was in charge, wasn't happy about what had happened at first, but eventually found the funny side of it. He was a rough and tumble hooker at Orrell and also our rugby league and union coach, so he knew the sort of person I was. It was a fantastic holiday – one I'll never forget – and I've got the scars to prove it. I have got a lot of time for John Ireland because he is the one who started the change of rugby codes at St John Rigby and got rugby league played there. We played rugby union with a bit of league influence in the first year, but in the second year we played rugby league. When we played union, it was with league skills thrown in. The only differences were unlimited tackling and two extra men. We only lost one game in that year of playing union, so it wasn't bad considering the majority of the team didn't know how to play or what the rules were. Maybe that came down to having good players. I met up with Joe Lydon again and we had Mike Hancock, Alan Clough and Fran Clough, who went on to play union for England and the British Lions, plus a good coach in John Ireland.

I played blindside flanker for the college and I had begun playing union at Wigan union club with some more players from college, including Joe. Whilst playing union, I went to the trials for Lancashire and the final trial was at St Helens. The coach for Lancashire was Ray French and Joe and I were the only ones from a rugby league background. It was the Possibles against the Probables and I played quite well. In fact, I should have been picked but, because I didn't have a rugby union pedigree, I believe, I was overlooked. I was more disappointed about that than when I didn't make the Wigan Schools team in 1975 because of my injury. I had really worked hard on my game and I thought that, even though I was only 17, I had come really close. Joe got picked to play for Lancashire Schools and he eventually was selected to play for England Schools and toured South Africa. That would have been nice for me, but sadly it wasn't to be.

In the second year, playing rugby league at the college, we didn't lose a game. We were a very talented, well-coached team and seven of us were also playing at the Wigan St Patricks club. It benefited us at college because we were playing together at weekends. I was made captain of the college team and our coach, John Ireland, entered us in the first ever BUSCARLA Cup for schools and colleges. We reached the final at Station Road, Swinton, and we beat Castleford High School convincingly 39-0. We timed it well in the inaugural year of the competition and it was extra special for me as captain of the side picking up the trophy.

As I said earlier, I went to play union at Wigan and again Joe Lydon went as well. We played midweek for the college but every Saturday we played for the Wigan Colts at the club. I went there because some of my mates like Dave Melling already played there and I heard that it was a good atmosphere. It had a good social side and it was just around the corner from where I lived. My coach was my old mate, Frank Morgan, and at the time the club had a good Colts side. I played at loose forward at union and even though Frank coached us about the finer points of rucking, mauling and line-outs we played an adapted form of rugby league. It could be said that we were ahead of our time playing this style of rugby union, but we used to play other rugby league towns that had union sides and we saw the same lads playing the two games. We used to beat most sides with our rugby league skills but when we came up against a side which played rugby union as their first game we struggled and usually lost. For example St Helens had a good Colts side and they played proper rugby union. They had all played at Cowley and I think Ray French and people like that had coached them. When we played them, they would use their specialist rugby union skills to beat us. When we played Orrell Colts, we were the bigger side, with me at loose forward, Andy Platt at blind-side and Joe at stand-off. The side also included Steve Melling, Keith Williams, Andrew Bailey, Ian 'Goose' Gormley and David Jones, who all played both codes of rugby.

Joe, as I have mentioned, represented England Schools at rugby union. He was a good player who could have gone a long way in that code. He had talent, speed and – the main thing – a long boot and could kick goals, as I found out a few years later in a Challenge Cup semi-final against Wigan at Maine Road.

They were really good times there, especially my one and only Easter Colts tour to Torquay in my first year at the club. Frank Morgan organised it with one or two other members of the club and we met at the Gas showrooms – 18 Wigan lads with not a care in the world. We all travelled down on Good Friday, played a couple of games and came back on Easter Monday. I was on crutches at the time with my leg in plaster and I was in charge of 'The Sacred Horn,' which was a foghorn on a gas canister. Every time I blew The Sacred Horn, the lads, no matter what they were doing had to do the 'Dying Fly,' which meant that they had to lie on their backs with their arms and legs in the air. If you didn't do the Dying Fly, you had a forfeit and it was always a drinking forfeit, because that was the spirit of the tour. It probably wouldn't happen now, because the game is a bit more serious. Not so serious then; a few times when we were defending our line I blew the horn and straight away the lads were on their backs, leaving the opposition laughing as we suddenly stopped the game.

Our Colts team also went away with the first team and played in curtain-raisers in places like Jedforest and Swansea. The first team kept their eyes on us until we were close to stepping over the line and at that stage they said 'Hey, come on lads.' We then used to calm down. Who would argue with the first-teamers? Certainly not me and it taught us what we could and couldn't get away with.

The best game I played for the Colts was in the Lancashire Cup against Orrell. At the time the two clubs had fallen out; in union then you only played friendlies and Orrell wouldn't play us because they considered themselves part of the elite. So our only way of meeting them was in the

Lancashire Cup, which was a very competitive knock-out tournament. We got our big chance against our neighbours and rivals and we beat them 4-0 with Steve Melling scoring the winning try. The 'no hopers' had never beaten Orrell before and we did it by playing a rugby league style of game. In the next round, we were drawn against St Helens and they were a good union side with all the skills of that code and they beat us. They were happy days and I had a great time learning and playing union and thoroughly enjoyed the social side.

While I was still at John Fisher, Jackie Melling and Cliff Fleming came to the school disco one Saturday night and asked me about joining Wigan St Patricks. I had no idea they were coming and I was quite adamant I was going to play union on a Saturday and that I may have to study on Sunday when I went to 6th Form College. So I didn't give them a guarantee, I said I'd think about it. It didn't take much thinking; I decided to go down and I'm glad I did. All my friends were playing rugby union but a number were doubling up. I always wanted to play league and turn professional, so really when Jackie and Cliff approached me to play for St Pats it was no contest. They also signed the rest of the Wigan Schools Under-16s although I didn't know that when I made my decision.

I was fortunate that Jackie and Ray Unsworth were the coaches of the Under-17 side and I was proud when they made me captain, because in that team there were phenomenal players. Talent was just oozing out of that team and it was the first time that we were really coached. We were learning about modern set-plays and game plans, who to run at, what moves we were putting on. For an amateur set-up, it was very professional.

We had a great season and never lost a game, but that wasn't just down to me as captain. It was down to all the players and their talent. Teams got frustrated with us because we could play at pace, so they would throw in a few cheap shots. But as well as playing rugby, our team could fight as well. I'm not condoning the fighting, but we looked after ourselves. There was Shaun Wane, Ian 'Goose' Gormley, David Wood and Kevin Egan and all of them could look after one another and look after themselves as well. It was a great season for us. We won the league, the Lancashire Cup and the Inter-Town Trophy.

Nine of the team, including me, got selected for the Lancashire Under-17s – a record that hasn't been beaten to this day. The players from the St Patricks side were Shaun Wane, Kevin Egan, David Wood, David Jones, Conal Gallagher, Ian Gormley, Joe Lydon, Andrew Bailey and myself. I was made captain of the team and I was fortunate that I was at the right place at the right time. If that team had stuck together for years to come it would never have been beaten, because it had all the attributes needed to play rugby league well. Lancashire won the County Championship beating Cumbria and Yorkshire.

During that first season I also doubled up on occasion with 'Goose' Gormley, playing for the Under-19s coached by Tony Scahill. I remember the first time. I played in the Under-17s in the morning and 'Goose' and I were then driven over to Wyther in Leeds to play them in the quarter-final of the Under-19s National Cup. We were the best side in Lancashire and they were the best side in Yorkshire and they had some lads playing who played in the Leeds RLFC Colts side. I came off the bench and played in the game, which was a tough, tense encounter. My lifetime mate, Dave Melling, drove over from close range to score the match-winning try. With that lead, it was 'up the jumper.' We just drove it up through the forwards and everyone took a smack for the side. It was a big game and we won it. I played three more times for the side and we reached the National Cup Final at Blackpool. I was picked as substitute, against our Wigan rivals, Rose Bridge, and I came on early when Dave Melling got injured. We won the final and I scored a try in a close game. That was special, as I didn't score many tries, but it was a team effort and that's what counted.

We had a great celebration as Under-17s at the Riverside

Club, which was part of Central Park. I was lucky that I didn't get thrown out that evening along with the rest of the squad. I had only just turned 17 and I was in charge of the beer kitty. John Martyn, who owned the club, was giving his rendition of his favourite song 'Music was my first love.' He was really belting it out when I just strode onto the stage, grabbed the microphone off him and shouted: 'Right lads, the Under-17s' beer is at the bar. Go and get it.' I gave him the microphone back, strode off the stage and mingled in with the crowd, although that was difficult with a blond mop of hair. Sorry about that, John.

It was a great ending to my first season at St Pats and, because of our success, the scouts were always sniffing around at our games. I was always going to finish my education and play for the Under-19s again. David Wood, Kevin Egan and Shaun Wane signed for Wigan and they were a big loss to us, but Andy Platt had come from St Helens and signed for Pats and played in the second row for us. He had a belting pair of hands, a great engine and was another good player in a very good side.

I moved up with the rest of the lads to the Under-19s and Tony Scahill made me the captain. We had another superb season and only lost one game. That was to Widnes Tigers just before the National Cup Final at Blackpool. I got a sprung shoulder – the one that had given me problems on the two previous occasions – and I had to miss half the game, go to hospital and have an x-ray. My old teammate at Warrington, Billy McGinty, played for Widnes Tigers that day and even now he reminds me that they beat us and that he's the one who did my shoulder. I know different; he didn't, he wasn't quick enough to get me at the time, but maybe now he can.

There were a few games that stood out that season, like the Lancashire and Cumbria Cup Final against Egremont at Central Park. We won, but five players were sent off, two of ours and three from Egremont. The reporter at the match, Ron Girvin, said it was the worst brawl he'd seen in 27 years of rugby at all levels. Two weeks later we had to go up to Egremont and play them in the National Cup and, after the first game, they were telling us what they were going to do to us at their place. We got changed and at that time we had to walk to the ground, with the Egremont spectators shouting abuse at us and trying to wind us up. As we got onto the field, I saw that the pitch wasn't fenced off and it seemed as if the whole of Egremont was standing around the touch-lines. They gave us a mouthful throughout the game, but we beat them 17-13 and it was a pretty clean, hard match compared with the previous one.

I said earlier that we could look after ourselves. We had to when we played at Leigh Miners and created a record for all the wrong reasons. In the first ten minutes of the game, the Miners decided to fight with us. We went down in the scrum and it just broke up into a brawl and we all started fighting. We were waiting for the referee to blow the whistle as he would normally, but no whistle came. Eventually, we all stopped fighting and as we looked round we could see the referee walking towards his changing room. I believe he said 'I'm not putting up with this.' It must have been a record for an early finish to a game and our coach, Tony, came onto the field and said 'Come on lads, we're going home. He's abandoned it.'

We had the re-match with Leigh Miners on the Monday of the week leading to the National Cup Final on the Saturday. Joe Lydon hadn't been playing for us for a while, because he had been away with the England Schools playing rugby union. He showed up against the Miners, played well and we won the game. In the National Final we played a Yorkshire side, St John Fisher – the same name as my old school – and we knew nothing about them. At that time we only played sides in the North West Counties League, and Cumbrian teams in the Lancashire and Cumbria Cup, but before the game began we got the psychological edge on them, as we had been in this situation a year earlier. Both teams lined up and were introduced to the Mayor of

Blackpool and then the announcer would introduce the players individually and they would run to their respective half of the pitch. St John Fisher didn't know this, so as the announcer shouted 'And the St John Fisher No 1 is….' they had all gone. We had stayed in line because we knew what to do and when they announced our side and named our players we ran one by one to our end of the field with loud cheers from our spectators for each player. I believe that gave us that initial edge. The game was played on a hot, sunny afternoon – it must have been a good 70 degrees – we just ran rings round them in an exceptional effort. Platty put me in for the first try of the match after only six minutes, but Joe played absolutely superbly, justifying his selection and scored two tries. The big thing about the team was that we really played for one another and playing a big team on a dry field was always going to benefit our quicker players.

The 21-10 victory saw us win the National Cup for an historic third successive year and completing a grand slam of trophies made up for my only disappointment, which thwarted one of my ambitions as a rugby player and nearly made me pack in the game at 18. I went to Blackbrook in St Helens for the trials for the Lancashire Under-19 side. I had to get into that squad to be considered to play for BARLA Great Britain, but I knew there was something wrong when the Possibles played the Probables and I was on the bench, which was a joint bench for both teams. When I came on, even though I say it myself, I was outstanding and thought I had really made a point. I played a bit for myself. Normally, players up against our St Pats full-back, Andrew Bailey didn't score. I did and when it came to selection in the clubhouse I really thought I had done well. But they didn't name me in the 13, they didn't name me as one of the two on the bench and I wasn't picked as one of the four reserves. Jackie Melling, Ray Unsworth and Tony Scahill said that it was a fix and I believe to this day that BARLA stitched me up. It wasn't a case of me being bitter and twisted, but if I wasn't good enough someone should have told me. Not one

BARLA representative could face me and I really feel it was a case of 'You pick my lad and I'll pick yours.'

We went to the Ben Jonson pub on the dual carriageway near Wigan and every player from St Pats who had got picked said they were refusing to play for Lancashire. I said: 'No, we're all bigger than this.' But I was going to give up playing rugby. It was a major blow, because I had always wanted to play for my town, county and country. I can still picture those BARLA reps now, even with the game long gone. I hope it's not as political now as when I played. I would have held my hands up if I wasn't good enough, but I was good enough and they did me an injustice. I decided to prove them wrong and be successful after I had spoken to Jackie, Ray and Tony. It was a case of pick yourself up, dust yourself down and start all over again. I was fortunate that I had good people around me who at the time gave me sound advice and I got on with playing.

Injuries are all part of the game and, as you know, I had my share early in my playing career, although I was always able to return to fitness and continue playing. We had a player in our team at St Pats called Glen Marsh and he was a really solid prop or second row. We were playing at Hull and Glen broke his neck, although at the time we didn't know how severe it was. It was the first time that I had seen a really bad injury and it brought home how fragile the human body is. Thank God, Glen is up and about again now, but he couldn't play any physical sport again because he needed major surgery on his neck. Thankfully, he can walk and now has a family. When you are young, you think you are invincible and especially when you're a young athlete, but things like that put it all in perspective.

As I finish recalling this part of my career, I want to say that I've got nothing but respect for Jackie, Ray and Tony. They not only taught me how to play the game, they also taught me how to be humble in victory and never to accept mediocrity, but always try to improve and find that extra level. Those three are all special people. In fact, all my coaches, from Dave Malin to Steve McLeod, Phil Derbyshire, John Ireland and Frank Morgan, played a massive part in the way I became what I am today.

2

WIDE AWAKE AT THE WIRE

The team at St Pats had enjoyed another great season and, with the talent we had, there were always scouts and coaches from professional clubs watching our games. The one who really impressed me was a feller from Warrington called Snowy Rowlands. He came to the house and met my mum and dad and really sold us on Warrington. At the time it was Salford who really showed interest in me. Saints did a little later, but, at that time, there was absolutely nothing from my home-town club, Wigan.

At the National Cup Final at Blackpool, Tony Barrow was watching the game and he was assistant coach to Kevin Ashcroft at Warrington. He approached me after the game and wanted to speak to Andy Platt and me to persuade us to sign for them. Our coaches, Tony Scahill and Jackie Melling, said: 'No, not yet. Let them think about it, let them enjoy today and we'll meet you next week.'

Tony Scahill had played at Warrington for a while, as had Jackie Melling and Ray Unsworth, so they may have been a bit biased towards Warrington, but it was Salford who offered me the best deal in terms of money. I met John Wilkinson, the chairman, who was nothing but professional in the way he spoke to me, and he invited me to the end of season 'do.' I was most impressed with the club, but I was always impressed with the way Warrington dealt with me as well. Snowy was very persuasive in selling the club to me and I had also spoken to Tony Barrow, but they gave me a bit of space so that I could prepare for the games I still had to play with St Pats that season.

I went with Platty to the end of season 'do' at Warrington, where we were shown around and well looked after. Platty and I met all the players and we were in awe of them. We'd heard about them, but didn't dare to dream of speaking to them. But it was the players themselves who were talking to us, players like Dave Chisnall, Steve Hesford, John Bevan, Ken Kelly, Alan Gwilliam, Mike Kelly, Derek Finnegan, and Derek Whitehead, who was coaching with Tony and Kevin. The chairman at the time was Brian Pitchford, who spoke wonderfully about the club and where he wanted to take it.

I arranged to meet Tony Barrow and Kevin Ashcroft in the Greyhound pub on the East Lancs Road at Leigh the week following the Cup Final. I had just turned 18 and I was out to impress them so I only drank orange juice at the meeting. Andy had arranged to meet them at the same time but came a bit later.

I took Jackie Melling with me as he had been around the block time and time again. He advised me on how to work the deal and really it was Jackie who persuaded me to sign for Warrington. He did that because he thought I'd have an earlier chance of playing first team there, because John Bevan was playing loose forward and John was really a winger or centre playing out of position.

When I met Kevin and Tony together for the first time, my impression was of two larger-than-life characters, both loud and very animated. I was a bit scared of them. I knew that they had both played for Leigh and Warrington at the same time as the all-time great, Alex Murphy. They had played for Alex at clubs he had coached and, if Alex moved to a club, they both moved with him, so all three of them knew what they were getting. I think that was a big recommendation, plus with Kevin and Tony what you saw was what you got – big, hard, honest men who told you straight. I've got nothing but respect for both of them for guiding me towards becoming the player I was to be.

As for the deal, in those days players talked in terms of a

couple of thousand pounds when they signed, with more due on birthdays and after playing so many first team games. I was quite happy with the offer; it was below the terms that Salford would have given me, but I've always maintained that I never signed for the money. That's a bit of a contradiction in terms, because players do literally sign for the money, but that wasn't my main reason. The real reason was to play in the first team, be successful and win trophies. Every professional player, whatever the sport, wants to win and I was no different. My motivation for playing was I wanted to be the best I could be, to play in big games and win. So with Jackie's advice about my first team prospects at Wilderspool, I signed on that infamous dotted line in the Greyhound on the 8th of June 1982. My mum and dad, who have always been supportive throughout my life, didn't try to influence which club I signed for. They just wanted me to be happy with whatever decision I made.

I bought a car with the signing-on money because, with my mother and father both working, they couldn't carry on taking me to training forever, as they had done up to then. Even though I had passed my test a year before I signed, I didn't have the money to buy a car. Now, as long as I could buy a decent car to take myself off to training, they were happy with whatever decision I made. Ultimately, they had also liked the way that Warrington dealt with my situation.

That was the time still when, once players signed, they were at that club until they decided that they had had enough. Basically, players signed for life and, don't get me wrong, the money came in handy. £2,000 could buy quite a bit in 1982. If I played for the 'A' team I got £50 for a win, £20 for a loss and in the first team it was £250 a win and £25 a loss, even if a player was on the bench and didn't play. The difference in winning and losing pay was a big incentive, so it was all about winning. In the contract, there were bonuses for playing in finals, for playing for the county and for playing in internationals. I was fortunate that I had a good bonus scheme, but the problem with bonus schemes is making the grade. A contract could be worth £50,000, but there was no guarantee that a player would ever see it. My contract was roughly what I wanted, thanks to Jackie, and he was happy with everything that was offered. The £2,000 up front made me a wealthy man for a time and I took the family out for a meal as a 'thank you' for all they had done. One thing a player can forget during his career is how the family is put through it all as well: mood swings, the tension when building up for games, and the injuries, when a player's mood is the worst it can be. So I've got to thank my parents and my brother and sister for putting up with me being a moody bastard, which I know I was at times.

Before I signed for Warrington, St Helens showed a bit of interest. They came to a few of our games but primarily they wanted Andy Platt. Andy was offered a contract with Warrington on the day I signed, but he said he wanted time to think about it. He rang them back later that day and told them he had signed for Saints.

Although I was Wigan born and bred, I was happy to have signed for Warrington. The Wigan club hadn't shown any interest in me, but the week after I signed, would you believe it, they phoned me up and to say 'We've heard you've signed for Warrington, is this true?' I admitted it was and they said: 'Well, we would be wanting to talk to you.' Unfortunately, I told them, it was a bit too late. I could only play the cards I had been dealt and all I had in the way of definite offers was Warrington and Salford. When my home-town club came in for me too late, I was initially disappointed, but at the time Wigan were only just out of the second division. Despite that, I would have loved to have played for my home town, but I was a Warrington player. I had made my decision, I stuck by it and to this day I've no regrets about it.

What I wanted now that I had signed was a big off-season, training to get up to professional standards of fitness. I can still vividly remember doing the terrace work, running up and down the terrace steps at Wilderspool, with players like

Bob Eccles. He was a seasoned pro and I remember him saying: 'Slow down, young un – you'll learn quicker that way.'

Also doing their terrace work were two other young players – Billy McGinty, who had signed a few weeks after me, and Mark Roberts from Oldham. We knew all about each other, because we'd played against one another for years, and we developed a good, strong bond. We were the new kids, so when we trained we pushed ourselves and each other. Also training with us were Paul Cullen and Ronnie Duane, who had come back from the Great Britain Colts' tour to Australia. There was only a year's difference in age between us and we were all fit, young lads who wanted to impress.

When everyone trained together in the pre-season, we'd have 50 bodies on the field and the track, first-teamers and 'A' team players. There were a lot of bodies out there and we had great players in John Bevan, Neil Courtney, Ken Kelly, Mike Kelly, Alan Gwilliam, Bob Eccles, Carl Webb, Steve Hesford – the list was endless. Once I had signed and was training with them, my ambition was to get into the first team but I was a bit in awe of the players I was training with. I mean, I had heard of the name Chisnall before and we had David Chisnall playing at Warrington – a legend of a player. Again he was one who came to me and said: 'Slow down, you're making us look bad.'

At this time, the new players or 'A' team lads got changed in one changing room and all the first team squad in another. There was this hierarchy of players and 'never the twain should meet,' except on the training field. I accepted it, because that's the way it was, but it wasn't something I would have wanted to change. They were all approachable and you could ask them questions about big game situations. My biggest strength was probably that I did want to learn, not only on the field, but also by asking what I thought were relevant and pertinent questions to players and coaches.

So I had my big pre-season, trained with the first team, and made my debut playing for the 'A' team against

Workington Town at Wilderspool, in the August of the
1982–83 season – this was still winter rugby, don't forget –
and we won 56-10 or thereabouts. In the first team
programme the following week it said that this team was the
fastest, hardest, slickest 'A' team at Warrington for a few
years. Also making their debuts in that side were Billy
McGinty, Mark Roberts, Steve Morris, another young kid
signed from Leigh Miners, and Peter Halpen from Widnes.
We were just a pretty good team.

I still needed to work to supplement my income, as it
wasn't full-time then like now. I was fortunate that, until I
became a full-time professional in 1987, I worked for Peter
Higham, who was a director and later chairman of the club.
I started off as a scaffolder, which was hard work and then as
a scaffolding co-ordinator, before I was moved to the office
as an estimator. That was easier, because I used more of the
grey matter rather than the brawn.

Whilst I was in the 'A' team, players could be picked to be
a 'squaddie,' which meant that they would be one of two
players to travel with the first team and give them their rub
down before the game. After two 'A' team games, I was
picked as a 'squaddie' for the game at Post Office Road
against Featherstone Rovers. Kevin and Tony always said
that we had to dress smartly and I had my club blazer, shirt
and tie on; not recommended for trips to Featherstone in
any season. Mark Roberts and myself had been selected for
rubbing down duties and, as you can imagine, we'd got 15
players to take care of between us. Also there was our kit
man, Roy Aspinall, always known as 'Ocker' – what a
character he was. He could get players anything, even
though he usually wanted something in return. I was quite
fortunate that he liked me.

This time, we stripped down to our undies to do the rub
down. There was oil everywhere and, as we were about to
start, Ocker said to us 'You're getting new tracksuits for
rubbing down. I'll need your measurements.' We said: 'We'll
give them you.' But Ocker said 'No, we do it with string.' So

he tied string around our chests, down our arms, around our wrists, down our legs. We thought to ourselves 'No, this can't be right,' but we said nothing because we didn't want to appear daft. Ocker put string all over us; imagine the two of us with string everywhere. We realised that the boys and Ocker were taking the piss out of us as they were doing their stretching and couldn't keep their faces straight.

That was Ocker's humour for you. He was a hell of a character around Warrington, but, if he didn't like you, you'd have either tight shorts or holes in your socks. You would go and say that things didn't fit and he would reply 'I've got no more.' You had to wear them; you had no choice, because they were hung up on your peg before the game. If Ocker liked you, you were okay; if he didn't, you were in for a tough season with a lot of ill-fitting kit. I always brought him some cigs or whisky back from holiday. I knew where my bread was buttered and Ocker was a good friend to me for the 14 years I was at the club.

Anyway, we began the rub-downs – me in my undies and bare feet because I didn't want any oil getting on my gear. With the likes of Dave Chisnall and the size of his legs, it was a training session in itself. We had 15 players to do and the sweat that we got on in that changing room was unreal. We couldn't even wipe our eyes, because we would get oil and Fiery Jack in them. Mark and I decided to get our own back and we put Fiery Jack on everyone. We thought if we did that they won't need as thorough a rub-down, but the boys made us work twice as hard. All of them had a rub, all of them wanted a shoulder rub or a back rub and Mark and I were completely knackered by the end of it. Even though we had tried to get our own back, the senior players had done us again. I never wanted to be a squad player again. It was hard work, although it was an experience. They paid us £20 and we worked harder than some of the players on the pitch.

I played four or five 'A' team games before a day I will always remember. I made my debut for the first team on Sunday 5th of September against Huyton, in the first round of the Forshaws Lancashire Cup at Wilderspool. I was nervous, but more about going in the first team changing room, not about the game itself. The week before, I'd been told by Kevin and Tony that I was selected at loose forward against Huyton, so I had been training with the first team, but I still got changed in the 'A' team dressing room. For some reason, I still remember to this day going into the changing rooms not knowing where to find my peg. Ken Kelly, the captain, said: 'You're playing loose forward. Number 13 – go and get it.' I knew all that, but I was in awe of these players, and I didn't want to get my jersey until Ken told me to go. Despite those nerves, I knew then that that's where I wanted to be – playing loose forward for the first team. I had my own peg and own jersey and that was quite an achievement at such a young age, as I was still only 18. I had always wanted to play at 13, as I enjoyed getting the ball in my hands and doing a bit with it. Mind you, I considered myself fortunate to play anywhere I was told. Believe me, the way Kevin and Tony coached, players were told to play in different roles quite a bit.

The game I was coming into was a far dirtier, rougher game than it is now. Although the game today is faster, it is not as tough. I think the game now is physically more demanding, but back then what it demanded was pass and cover up. It was a rough and tumble type of game. In the early 1980s, it was already six tackles, but we still had the five-metre rule as opposed to today's ten-metre rule. We couldn't get away now with what we did then because of all the technology that is concentrated on the game these days. Over 20 years ago, we could get away with murder.

We won the game 43-5 and even playing Huyton in the Lancashire Cup seemed so fast to me that it went past in a blur. I don't remember a lot about the game apart from getting changed at my precious peg and scoring the first try of the afternoon and how good that felt on my debut in front of those Warrington fans. There was no score and we were awarded a scrum ten metres from the Huyton try line. It was our head and feed and as Ken Kelly put the ball in, it came to my feet and I just picked it up, went up the blind-side and scored near the sticks with not a finger laid on me. I guess that's the type of try that you would like to score on your debut. To open the scoring for Warrington and score on my debut was so special that I had a feeling of ultimate exhilaration and euphoria all blending into one. I remember the players jumping on me in celebration, because they obviously knew it was a big moment for me. Bob Eccles, John Bevan, Steve Hesford – these were names I had only heard of a few weeks earlier, but now I was actually playing with them. No wonder it meant so much to me. I don't remember the game being over-physical, but what I do remember is being completely whacked at the end of it. Kevin and Tony said that I was like a chicken with its head cut off – chasing everything that moved. I soon realised that I couldn't do that if I wanted to play for the full 80 minutes, but that was the way I'd approached my first game and I'd enjoyed every minute of it.

I kept my place in the Warrington side for the game against Widnes and my big mate, Joe Lydon. He had signed for Widnes at the start of the season, as had 'Goose' Gormley. Goose had to wait for his first team opportunity, because Keith Ellwell was the team's hooker at the time. He never seemed to get injured; he was phenomenal.

The game was played at Wilderspool and the first time Joe and I clashed, I tackled him fairly and then he gave me a kiss! A few of the spectators noticed it but, more to the point, Ken Kelly, our captain, did too. I got a roasting off Ken and I said 'What can I do?' Ken really gave it to me. 'Don't let him kiss you,' he said. 'Knock his fucking head off.'

I think Joe got the same riot act from his captain, Mick Adams, but even though he knew he shouldn't have done it, he must have decided that surely he could have a laugh in a game. Throughout my playing career, I had a laugh on the field, because, when I played against mates, the game would be serious but with a light-hearted edge at times. I think that was what was going on when Joe did that, but he didn't do it again.

We won the game against Widnes and this was an era when they were the team to beat. They had Kurt Sorenson, Kevin Tamati, Emosi Koloto, Mick Adams, Mike and Steve O'Neill, Stuart Wright, Eric Hughes, Mick Burke, Joe and Dave Hulme – another I knew from before. It was an awesome team they had in the early 1980s.

We played St Helens in the Lancashire Cup Final at Central Park, which was special for a Wiganer, who had played there as a schoolboy and an amateur and stood on the terraces as a supporter. I remember Ken Kelly going under the sticks from 40 yards out, outpacing everyone, which wasn't like Ken.

The St Helens scrum-half was Neil Holding and I knew he was going to test me out early in the game. He came blind from the base of the scrum and I read the play. I hit him with the lot and blood, snot and everything flew off both of us. I'd hit him with all my might and he just got up as though nothing was wrong with him. I'm in for a tough career, I thought, not just a tough day. I realised there and then that I had a bit to learn. On a few occasions I got it wrong, but we won the game 16-0. To 'nil' a team like St Helens was something special. Part of my job, playing with Bob Eccles and John Fieldhouse in the back row, was to be a tackling machine and early in my career I did more in defence than offence. I knew all my family and mates were at Central Park watching and that they would be under the press box on the Popular Side, where I used to watch Wigan. Sure enough, the boys were there hurling abuse, but wanting us to win rather than their dreaded rivals, St Helens.

So I had won my first trophy and medal as a professional; I remember Ken going up for the Lancashire Cup and then us all doing a lap of honour for the fans. I realised then that what Jackie and Tony had told me about getting an early chance to play in the first team was true. I had played in a Cup Final in my first dozen games and the feeling was one of euphoria at achieving something like that so soon.

As we came around to where my family and the boys were, I could see that they had a few beers in their hands and I knew what was going to happen. As we got to them, the boys tried to soak me with beer, but I was too quick for them and it hit John Fieldhouse, who is another Wiganer. He knew a few of the lads and took it in good spirit.

During that first season, I remember going to Thrum Hall to play Halifax. There was a lad there called Gary Van Bellen who was about 6ft 5ins and 18 stone. The ball was on our try line and I had gathered it and was on the floor waiting to get up and run when this monster hit me with everything he had. Again blood, snot and everything else came out of me and I got my first serious injury as a professional. I didn't know it at the time, but I had a slipped disc. I couldn't move my legs for a couple of minutes and when I eventually I got to my feet I couldn't straighten up. They tried all sorts in the dugout to get me right, but I couldn't straighten my back. The journey home was horrendous and I was in agony all night when I got home and went to bed.

I made an appointment with Dr Morris, our club doctor, and was told to drive to Warrington General Hospital to see him. I couldn't get in the car as I was in such agony, but my brother helped me get into the driving seat with a shoehorn and I had to drive there. To be honest, I was in no fit state to drive; the pain was unreal, especially when I changed gear and put my foot on the clutch. I know it sounds soft, but nowadays players are more looked after. I walked into the hospital like the Hunchback of Notre Dame and Dr Morris knew what I had done. He was talking to me and, all of a sudden, he ripped my shoulder one way and my hips the other and I heard this enormous crack. The relief was immediate, I could move and walk normally and I thought that this man was God. He had sorted out all the agony and pain I had been in in less than a minute.

In the 1985–86 season I got a shoulder injury and Tony Rothwell, our physio, said that I needed to build up my shoulder, so what a few of us did was meet at six o'clock in the morning at O'Malley's Gym and train. Walter O'Malley would train with us and Tony would take the session. We would train for an hour on the weights and that was the start of the Wide Awake Club. The reason we did it at that time was that we all worked. On a Tuesday and a Thursday, we would train in the morning, go to work and go back training at Warrington for the 'A' team after work. This was all done voluntarily. What I'd realised was that to become a better player I needed to train harder and two or three sessions a week wasn't good enough.

The sessions were intense and non-stop from six o'clock; then Tony got a new job so we had to train from five o'clock! I look back on it now and I'm glad I did it. I trained at the Wide Awake Club for five years. I was fortunate that in 1987, when I came back from a spell in Cronulla and signed a new contract with the club, I could become a full-time player. I still trained early in the morning, getting up at half past four; I'd have breakfast and then a 20-minute drive to O'Malley's. He would have a coffee for us all before the onslaught of training. It was the hardest training I've ever done; it was full on for an hour. We would blitz the legs and shoulders one day, chest and biceps another day and back and triceps another. It was a complete burn, but I felt the benefit. I put it in, gave it my all and made a lot of sacrifices. It was tough when I was working as well, but I and a few others were able to go full time – Paul Cullen, Billy McGinty and Bob Jackson – before it became the norm. It meant that after the session, it was back home and to bed at 8 o'clock. I believe that the extra training made me a stronger, better, more disciplined player and I reaped the benefits when it made me an international player.

3

WHAT MADE MILWAUKEE FAMOUS AND OTHER MAYHEM

Having established myself in the Warrington side, I had to wait another three years, until 1985, to reach another final. That was once again the Lancashire Cup Final when we met my nemesis, Wigan, at Knowsley Road. We had beaten St Helens in the semi when the notorious Australian bad boy, Les Boyd, had made his debut for Warrington. It was his first game for 15 months after he had been banned in Australia for gouging.

Boydy was such an inspiration. In 1982, he had been a member of the 'Invincibles' who had toured Great Britain and changed the way the game was being played all over the world. He was 5ft 9ins tall and 17 stone when he was at the club. I wouldn't say that it was all muscle, but he was so powerful and guided a young team really well. He couldn't help us in the final, even though we were leading 8-2 with a try from Brian Johnson and two Brian Carbert goals. That turned out to be as good as it got and we lost 34-8 in front of over 19,000 fans. Alan Rathbone and Andy Gregory played for us that day. Alan got sent off early in the second half and Andy followed later, so it was backs to the wall. If I'm honest, we were outplayed on the day and Wigan were about to dominate rugby league in this country for the next decade.

In March 1986, there was a change of coach, with Tony

Barrow made caretaker following the resignation of Reg Bowden, who in turn had taken over from Kevin Ashcroft. Tony made Boydy his assistant and we got to the Premiership Final at Elland Road against the Champions, Halifax, under their player-coach, Chris Anderson, who later coached Australia. They were a great side, with players like Colin Whitfield, Tony Anderson, my old mate Paul Dixon and the former Wigan forward, Mick Scott.

By the time we reached the final, Boydy had taken over the captaincy and we had defeated Wigan at Central Park in the semi-final. We beat Halifax quite convincingly, 38-10, and Boydy got two tries and had a fantastic game, whilst Brian Johnson got one direct from a drop-out. We were a good, hard-working outfit. Billy McGinty, Mark Roberts, Gary Sanderson, Paul Cullen and Ronnie Duane were all young lads who had come through the ranks at the club together. Then we had a front row which was unreal – Boydy, Kevin Tamati and Bob Jackson – with Andy Gregory and Paul Bishop at half-back. We could play football and, with a team like that, we could fight as well if required.

To beat the number one team in the league and win silverware for the first time in three years was a great achievement and made up for the Lancashire Cup defeat to Wigan earlier in the season. There were photographs of us going around the field after the game and we looked so young. We looked like kids. I remember going back to Warrington after the game and the clubhouse was full. The Warrington people hadn't had success for a few years, but there's no speccy in the world as good. They are very knowledgeable and very appreciative of hard work. What they like is honesty. They want the team to try; if they fail they fail, but they expect honesty. They know when players don't put it in. I can always say, even when I was a crock coming to the end of my career, I always gave it everything. Whether or not it was good enough, I can't say, but I hope it was.

The following season, we started really well and, on the end of a 12-game unbeaten run, we met Wigan in the John

Player Special Trophy Final at Burnden Park, Bolton, on the 10th of January 1987. We played well that day and the game was deadlocked at 4-all after an hour, following Mark Forster's first-half try to level the score. Henderson Gill scored for them to give them a four-point advantage and, as we attacked on their 25-yard line, Brian Johnson tried to chip over the defence. Unfortunately, it didn't come off and Andy Goodway caught the ball above his head and raced under the sticks to score. That changed the complexion of the game. At the time we were matching Wigan stride for stride, and there wasn't too much in the game. We gave it everything to get back into it, but a final Wigan try in the dying moments by Dean Bell gave them an 18-4 win and us another final defeat by them.

We finished third in 1986–87 and we reached the Premiership Final at Old Trafford, the first final to be played as a 'double header.' Swinton, the club I later coached, beat Hunslet in the Second Division final. We arrived at the ground early and most of us watched the game, because we knew players could be too intense going into a final. We were playing Wigan again; they had finished the season as the League Champions. Yet again, we came up short, losing 8-0, with Joe Lydon scoring the only try of the game and also being awarded the Harry Sunderland Trophy as man of the match. Wigan had done us again in a major final, but I believe to this day that we had a good try by Gary Sanderson disallowed. I've seen it time and time again on tape, and I still don't know why it was ruled out, but we had to take it on the chin. That season, we played Wigan in the John Player Special Trophy and the Premiership and we lost both games. Funnily enough, we tended to beat them in the league, but never in the big games. They had the players who could raise their games on those occasions.

It wasn't all about the glamorous occasions. I remember one Christmas we had a fixture at Hull KR. It was never nice going up there in the best of weather with that east coast wind blowing, but on this particular day it was so cold that they called off the horse racing at Pontefract. So the valuable horses wouldn't run, but us, we travelled up there for the game. They had a hell of a pack, with forwards like Mark Broadhurst, David Watkinson and Len Casey, and we played at Craven Park on four inches of solid snow, like playing on concrete. It was so bad that Phil Blake, the Australian who was playing for us, got hypothermia.

In the 1987–88 season, we started off well and got to the final of the Lancashire Cup and once again we were pitted against Wigan at Knowsley Road. It was a memorable game, played in front of over 20,000 spectators, and a great physical contest. Mark Forster scored a couple of tries, I got one and John Woods kicked two goals, but, although it was a great performance, we once again lost to Wigan. Although I had scored the try, it didn't mean anything to me as we had come second again.

At the end of that season there was a British Lions tour to Australia. We were playing Salford at The Willows and I was told by Les Bettinson, who was then the Great Britain manager, that I had a good chance of touring but I needed a big game. Malcolm Reilly and Phil Larder were the coaches and the week after this game was the selection meeting. Les had told me this and the pressure was on to perform; he had done me a favour by telling me, but it was a case now of how I reacted. We won and even though I say so myself, I was outstanding. I think it was the performance in that game that got me on the tour.

In the February of that season, I was appointed as captain of the club. Tony Barrow, I think, was grooming me as a potential captain. When Boydy was playing he was a natural leader, but at times when he was unfit I captained the side and really enjoyed the responsibility. I didn't consider myself a great player, but I was a thinker about the game, who understood how to get the best out of players on the field. Players react differently to motivational techniques. I knew that if I gave Paul Cullen a rocket for doing something wrong, he would make up for it by 'killing' someone. It is important to know how to talk to players and I think that helped me going into coaching later in my career. It is possible to learn the intricacies of how a player works and how to bring the best out of them. It was a great honour to be made captain, especially when I thought of the captains who had gone before me at such a prestigious club, and I took my responsibilities very, very seriously. It had always been my ambition to captain the club. All the way through my amateur career I had captained my club side, so I knew how to do the job. We had a great spirit at Warrington and a fantastic work ethic, but, most of all, all the players were my friends. I think that showed in the way that we played and the way I captained. A coach can only say so much; when you get over the whitewash it's down to the players and I thought the job of the captain was to pull everyone together for the same cause. If it wasn't going right then again I could sort the problem out, but we had great players at Warrington who helped me immensely.

When the rest of the team found out I had got the captaincy, I think they knew that it was a natural progression for the team, the club and me. I think, well, I knew I had the respect of the players, because, if I was asking a player to put his head where it might get kicked off, I'd got to be able to do that myself. I think a captain has got to lead by example, to do whatever it takes, keep his head and direct traffic when needed. Let everyone do their job – the half-backs controlling the game, the pack taking the team forward. My job was the link between the forwards and backs and to make sure that we had a common goal. The goal was to win; unfortunately, we didn't do that all the time but we won more than we lost. A captain needs good troops and I was very fortunate as I had an abundance of very good troops. We were quite a young team in the late 1980s and early 1990s, so the captaincy was a demanding job but one that I thrived on and enjoyed.

In the 1988–89 season, we took part in the British Coal Nines at Central Park – a mid-season knock-out tournament played to a conclusion on the night. The previous year, we got to the final and once again met Wigan and lost, but this time we defeated the Rest of the World in the final having beaten Wigan and St Helens along the way. We beat the Rest of the World 24-0. They had a very good side including Allan Langer and Ronnie Gibbs.

In the final, Gibbs was wearing goalkeeping gloves, as it was so cold and he had come over from Manly to our nice climate. He had a bit of an altercation with me and stuck a cheap shot on me on the rim of my eye. Because of the gloves, my skin split really easily and it was quite a bad cut. They were big goalkeeping gloves with a grip around the knuckles for punching the ball away and that's what caused the damage as the punch twisted in the skin. In those days, you carried on playing and I had a bit of Vaseline put on the cut, whereas today players go in the blood bin and sometimes replace the shirt. The injury wasn't as bad as it looked. My main concern was winning the game and we were on top at that time, so it was probably caused by a bit of frustration on Ronnie's part. As a result of the incident, the rules changed so that you couldn't wear a full glove. That was my first trophy as captain of the side, which included Dave Lyon, Mark Roberts, Billy McGinty, Ronnie Duane, Brian Carbert, Robert Turner, Mark Forster and Gary Sanderson. I got an authentic miner's lamp and this was my one contribution to the game's rule-book: I got a smack in the face off a daft Australian and forced the rugby league to ban gloves.

We had a good season and we were 80 minutes away from Wembley when we met Wigan in the Challenge Cup semi-final at Maine Road. Again we were the underdogs, as Wigan was a full-time side, but we were quietly confident that we could defeat them. We had beaten them in the league on a number of occasions and we thought it had to be our turn in a big match. So we went to the semi-final quietly confident, without any shouting from the roof-tops. Unbeknown to my teammates, though, the ultimate professional had been totally unprofessional the day before.

I went to Blackpool with a few friends and ended up at the Pleasure Beach. I went to one of those punch bags they had there and took a swing. As soon as I hit it, I knew I had hit it wrong and that I had broken my hand. So, on the day of the game, I had a few injections in my hand and I had it taped up quite rigid. That meant I couldn't grip with my right hand, so all through the game I was frustrated at being so stupid the day before and not being able to perform the way I knew I could.

During the first half Joe made a break down the left flank and chipped over our defence. I weighed things up and hit him off the ball on the shoulder. As he wasn't expecting it, he fell like a bag of spuds. I said to him: 'Get up Joe, you've made the most of it.' His mum, Nancy, wouldn't talk to me after the game nor for about a month until I apologised to her, although not to Joe! It was all down to me being stupid the day before and getting injured.

The team, which included Phil Blake and Les Davidson, played well and Steve 'Blocker' Roach probably had his best game during his time with us. Shaun Edwards had scored a try for Wigan and the game was very close when my mate Joe got his own back on us and on me for the cheap shot earlier in the game … the bastard! We thought, and Joe says to this day, that he was just going to kick it 'downtown.' But he said to himself 'What the hell' and went for it. He dropped the goal from 61 yards out, the longest drop goal in the modern game and in Challenge Cup ties. Although Ellery Hanley scored a try afterwards, that drop goal broke our hearts and changed the game completely.

Joe was a special player, but at the time, Wigan had 13 of them. We gave them a game, but I had come off at half-time because I was neither use nor ornament during my time on the field.

After the game, our winger, Desi Drummond, invited us back to his pub in Moss Side, a short distance from Maine Road. We all went, including the chairman and directors.

One of those was Brian Pitchford – a lovely fellow, a very well-spoken and well-to-do guy. He was in this pub among all these big Rastafarians and he looked stunned. His expression seemed to be saying: 'What am I doing here?' It was something outside his experience, but Desi's welcome there was fantastic and it was another show of how somebody within the team commanded such mutual respect. It eased the blow of the semi-final defeat and again showed the camaraderie within the team.

I thought I had kept the reason for my injury secret until I turned up a couple of days later with my hand in a pot, but Brian Johnson, our coach at the time, knew everything. The doctor had told him and I had to apologise to the coach and the players. When I had been getting the jab before the game, Johnno knew that there was something wrong but he didn't know how I had done it. I don't regret many things in rugby but that was my biggest regret. I always thought that I was a total professional but I had been dumb trying to impress my friends at the time. It never happened again.

At the end of the season, it was decided that we would go to America and play an exhibition game in Milwaukee. Mike Mayer was trying to develop the game over there. Mike said there was a market for it and the clubs were promised it wasn't going to cost them anything. He wanted two established teams who would put on a good show. At the time, Warrington and Wigan were big-name teams and we both went on the trip of a lifetime. I think we were there ten days, and trained maybe two or three times at the maximum. We had to sell the game, so a lot of our job was to go out and meet people. We got picked up in a fleet of stretched limousines. We were all standing up through the roof as we went down the streets. They would take us to a shopping mall and they had us all up on the stage selling the game and talking it up. We had to go and meet a lot of people in a lot of bars and have a lot of drinks. It was a hard job, but someone had to do it!

We were told that we were all going to get gold rings for playing in the exhibition game and the Most Valuable Player would get a Harley Davidson. Nothing ever materialised and it cost the clubs £200,000 each. It was a good idea on paper; they were going to do this, going to do that. But nobody got what was promised. The field we were playing on was another problem. It was on a baseball diamond. There was a big grass area but part of it went over the gravel of the baseball running area. When we arrived to look at the ground, we told them: 'We can't play on this.' They said: 'No, it's okay, we're going to sweep the gravel off it.' We said: 'Hang on a minute, we don't wear padding.'

The pitch was going to be a maximum of 55 yards wide and we told them that we had to play on grass. The negotiations went on about the playing surface and we weren't that far from having the game called off. We were saying: 'Forget it, cancel the game.' We were all happy for it to be called off, because we were having a good holiday courtesy of the Rugby League.

They were told that what they had to do, which was to bring in turf and lay it over the area which was going to cause us damage. They managed to do it in just in time and we played the game. There was a crowd of over 7,000, although a lot of them had been given free tickets to generate an atmosphere. They did interviews with the crowd and they were saying 'These guys are crazy. There's no padding.'

The game itself was just a bashathon, with the field being as narrow as it was, and it was a really hectic, physical match. There were several battles, mainly between Ellery and Les Boyd, that the crowd really enjoyed. Boydy had left three months earlier, but he was flown in to play what was supposed to be his last game before he retired. He was one of the hardest players I have ever known, but when we knew he was coming, we said it was a pre-retirement holiday for him. Andy Gregory and Ellery Hanley were also flown in from Australia and Les and Ellery were at it for the whole 80 minutes. With it being Les's swan song, he had nothing to lose – and it showed! I sat next to Les Boyd getting changed and he was saying about how much he'd changed, how much he'd mellowed. This dressing room was like nothing I ever experienced; you all had your own individual cubicle – typically American, bigger and better.

The game hadn't been going five minutes before Les and Ellery were ripping hell out of each other. I immediately recalled his earlier statement about how mellow and calm he was. In another life, I thought. There were plenty of high tackles and Wigan kicked early a lot, because it was a narrow pitch and they were trying to dominate field position. I remember Mark Preston broke and in my head was the way he did me like that in a game the previous season. Mark was quick but, because of the narrow pitch, I closed him down and I took his head off his shoulders. His legs came straight out from underneath him. I thought: 'I'm on my way here,' but the referee, to my amazement, didn't send me off.

There was only one try and that went to Wigan as they beat us yet again, 12-5. I was awarded the Most Valuable Player and won the Harley Davidson. I was imagining myself on the bike, like something out of *Easy Rider*, my blond locks blowing in the wind as I rode through the streets of Warrington and Wigan. It would suit me down to the ground. I thought about the logistics of shipping it over and what a great prize I'd won. Unfortunately, it never materialised at the game and I was told that I would get it when I arrived home. Every day at the club, I asked the club whether it had arrived, but, alas, no Harley Davidson was to be seen. I probably would have sold it to Joe Lydon, because Joe was riding one at that time. Wigan had told him to give up his bike, because it was an insurance risk, so maybe it was a blessing in disguise. I didn't win many man of the match awards and I believe Mike Mayer was last seen riding my Harley Davidson into the sunset, doing wheelies!

Mike was very good with the organisation of the trip and he was really enthusiastic about selling the game to the Yanks.

The Americans love a contact sport and I thought that our game was something they could get into. The problem was that they already play everything from American football, soccer, baseball, basketball, and ice hockey to track and field.

Although our game is now played over there and they played in the last World Cup, it has never really taken off, which is a shame. There must be so many players who don't make the grade at American Football who would be suited to rugby league. Our game isn't as technical as theirs; they have a 'play book,' which is the thickness of an encyclopaedia, whereas our game is a lot simpler to learn and is played to a principle of 'play what you see.' I think it would be easy for American footballers to change to our sport, once they got rid of the padding and helmets.

After the game, it was suggested that with all the altercations between Ellery and Boyd, that they refused to fly back to Australia on the same plane, so you couldn't say it was played without feeling. We had a great time and, apart from still waiting for my Harley, it left me with some good memories.

The fun and games had started before we went away when we got called in quickly to get measured up for suits. Our kit man, Ocker, was a hard man and a difficult person to deal with sometimes. He was virtually threatening this tailor 'Don't forget my left leg is two inches shorter than my right leg.'

He had had an accident when he used to work on the fairgrounds when he nearly lost one leg and it ended up shorter than the other one. He was a character, Ocker, and a tough bloke, but Tony Rothwell and Phil Chadwick, who were our physio and conditioner, decided to change the leg measurements around so it was the left leg that was longer, completely the opposite of Ocker's instructions. We picked up the suits at the airport. Most of the lads knew what had happened, but Ocker had no idea.

When we arrived, we had an official function, and had five minutes to get back to the hotel reception. I've never seen a team get changed so fast and two minutes later we were all sitting at the foot of the stairs. Ocker's room was at the top of these stairs and all of a sudden we heard this 'You bastards!' Ocker appeared, his right leg was short and his left leg was long; it was unbelievable. Everyone apart from Ocker burst out laughing. It was a sight and a pity that video cameras weren't available. Ocker looked as if he was ready to kill somebody. He couldn't wear the suit and he wore something else for the Mayor's reception. It has never come out until this book, although he tried his best to find out, because I would imagine that he would have literally ripped the culprits' heads off. Well, Ocker, the long or short of it, or is it the short and long of it, is that it was Tony Rothwell and Chaddy.

Ocker isn't very well these days, but still lives next door to the old club. He was well known in the town and was also head bouncer at Wigan Casino. He was a very hard man; although he was 5ft exactly, he was as wide as he was tall. He was also Alex Murphy's minder when he was at the club and he was the only kit man in the country to sell players back their kit. When we got our playing shirt at the end of the season, he wouldn't give it to us, unless we gave him something. He wouldn't give players their own shirt, which they had sweated blood and guts for; we didn't question it, it was just done. His kit room was like Aladdin's cave.

Whilst in Milwaukee, a few of us were in a bar and there was a gay fellow tapping up Billy McGinty. Billy said to me 'Follow my lead and be effeminate when you speak.' I had blond locks then – yes, honestly, locks. I hope I didn't look gay, but Billy said that I was his boyfriend. Billy was coming on to this fellow and the guy was quite infatuated with Billy and said 'What do you want to drink?' Billy said 'Two Budweisers and two chasers for me and me boyfriend.' This went on for most of the night. Billy was leading him on and he was buying us drinks. I made a scene about Billy two-timing me and stormed out. Billy chased after me, but it was only to get away. I think we had taken it as far as we could, but not as far as this guy wanted. Probably to this day he's waiting for Billy to come back in, playing that Diana Ross and the Supremes record, *'I'm Still Waiting.'* I don't even know what the fellow was called. Billy did all the talking; I just sat back and watched a good pro at work.

The day after the game, we went to the beach. Believe it or not, Lake Michigan is as big as England and we couldn't see across the beach, which just keeps going and going and going. We were all friends by this time, the Wigan and Warrington players, 'Boydy' and Ellery apart. We were on the beach and it was a glorious day. We were a bit battered and bruised, but now it was time to relax even more than we had before the game.

We got these massive coolboxes, packed them with ice and beer. It took two of us to carry them and we had three or four of them. It was great everyone being together because we didn't mix socially that often. Apart from British Lions tours, we just didn't get a chance. After a game we normally got changed, had a quick bite, had a drink and got on the coach and left.

So we were on the beach, larking about relaxing, Desi Drummond and Rocky Turner were throwing a rugby ball, just messing about, and two big Yanks came over and said 'Would you guys like a bit of two-on-two?' I thought, 'Oh no,' but Desi said 'Yeah, why not.'

So they marked a pitch out in the sand and Rocky kicked the ball to them and you could see this lad catch it. They were two typical beach bums and he looked at Rocky who was about 15½ stone and looked good, and looked at Desi who was 13 stone maximum. You could hear the lads on the touch-line as the Yank with the ball looked toward Rocky, saying 'Don't run to him.' Pound for pound, Desi was the biggest hitter ever. He ran straight at Desi who wasn't even blinking. He straightened his back and his head and put his right shoulder into the lad's sternum. There was blood, shit and snot everywhere and the Yank couldn't move. That was the shortest game of two-on-two that I've ever come across. As he was on the floor, Desi kicked a bit of sand over his back and said: 'Pull me another beer.' What that young man will now realise is not to mess about with people who are smaller than you but quite lethal. Desi was; he had this ability to snap in the tackle. I haven't seen anyone who can compare with his head tackling, because Desi used to hit with his head first, not his shoulder. Physically, he was an awesome specimen of a rugby league player and I'm just glad I played with him rather than against him.

Before we flew out for the game, a competition had taken place with a prize of a lifetime – tickets to travel with the teams, stay in the team's hotel, VIP tickets to the game, all that sort of thing. This couple from Wigan won the two tickets, but they had a daughter as well, so they paid for a third one. We got to the airport and everybody was chatting, trying to make them feel welcome, but they found out when we arrived that that their bags had been left in transit and they had nothing to wear. Wigan didn't really help them and it ended up being Warrington who gave them all a club tracksuit apiece, because they had only got the clothes they had come in. The fellow who I'm going to call 'Lucky' still had his wallet with him. A couple of nights later, he was in the lift at the hotel in his Warrington tracksuit when these two girls got in. As the lift was going up, one of these women pulled a gun out of a bag and they rolled him for his wallet, the only thing he had left. No clothes, no bags, no money. A Wigan speccie with a Warrington tracksuit on and they roll him for his wallet and disappear. So he had an absolute nightmare start to what should have been a trip of a lifetime.

After the day on the beach, we still had loads of beer left, so we went back to the hotel. It was quite late, but no one would have a party in their room, because they knew how it would get trashed. I was rooming with Billy McGinty and I said 'We'll have the party in our room, setting a good example as the captain and leader of men.' The room was massive and the lads came in and got started. The telephone went later on and it was probably someone complaining, but Tony Rothwell got to the phone before anyone else, pulled it out of the wall and said 'It's for you.' I thought I was better off getting out of there and I slept in another room.

When I came back in the morning the maid was just shaking her head and Billy was in tears of laughter. I said 'I told you we shouldn't have had a party in the room.' We had double beds, one on top of the other, and we had a table, a TV, curtains, every light fitting and a phone on top. Everything in the room was piled up to the ceiling. I said 'Billy, what have you let them do?' He said 'I had no control.'

I told the maid it was the latest Warrington open-plan hotel bedroom design. We got around it by paying the maid 50 dollars to clean the room and she did a hell of a job. No one could tell afterwards, because she did such a good job. When I got home, I thought about going into interior design for hotel rooms …

The following season we reached the Lancashire Cup Final against Second Division side Oldham at Knowsley Road and we were odds-on favourites to win the game, although they did have a good side. During the game, Dave Lyon was knocked out after a clash of heads with Desi, which split his head open. He had to have stitches and didn't come around until the second half. It just showed how hard and strong Desi was; he just carried on. Desi would take no prisoners.

It was a tough game and a close one, although the final score doesn't look that way. Towards the end, Oldham was putting a bit of pressure on and Bob Jackson scored a try against the grain which actually won the game. We were only leading by two points when Bob scored the vital try, his second of the game. We won the game 24-16 and Bob, who had an outstanding game, was named man of the match. It was the first major trophy I lifted as captain of Warrington and was the first the club had won since the 1986 Premiership Final – a long time between drinks.

We were always the bridesmaids, never the bride, because a lot of the time we met Wigan in finals, but we were always an honest team with lots of good individuals. I always thought that we probably deserved a bit more than we got, but it wasn't a level playing field, because Wigan was the only full-time side in the league. When they say what a great team Wigan was in the late 1980s and 1990s, I have to ask whether it's fair to put that tag on them when it wasn't an even contest. We were the most successful side in that era, apart from Wigan of course, when it came to reaching finals.

At the end of that season, I achieved the special dream of every kid who picks up a ball and plays rugby league. We got to the Challenge Cup Final at Wembley and, just for a change, we were up against Wigan. I was more nervous going out to an empty stadium on the Friday; the last time had been 15 years earlier, when I was injured, but was there with Wigan Schools.

I had no nerves on the day. I had been building up for the game and I was just excited that I had the chance of playing on the biggest occasion in the game. 80,000 fans, with the sun shining on the stadium and the twin towers of Wembley – the atmosphere was unreal.

The game itself was disappointing for the way we let it slip, but the Wigan team was a bit special and we had quite a few youngsters playing. Everyone gave a good account of themselves, but we were just outclassed. It was two Wiganers who scored against Wigan, me and Dave Lyon. I was proud to score against them, but I just don't think we were good enough on such a big occasion.

It was red hot that day and during the game Ellery Hanley made a break down the middle and I chased him. He gave it to Shaun Edwards, who had it tough, as he had broken his cheekbone in the game and carried on. He continued the break down the left. I managed to tackle him, but he turned the ball back inside for Mark Preston and his momentum took him over to score. To run all that way and not get a result was a bugger.

I nipped in for my try just before half-time and it brought us back into the game, within eight points of them. We were on a move, going left about 20 metres out, Paul Bishop popped out and passed it back inside for me and I threw a dummy to Adrian Shelford – now gone, God bless him – and I sidestepped Andy Gregory. Steve Hampson was a bit out of position and fortunately I scored under the sticks.

Dave Lyon scored in the second half. I made a break from the base of the scrum and Dean Bell came over and got me, but I offloaded to Dave, who outpaced Joe Lydon, who could only ankle-tap him as he was going over. At the time, it meant nothing, because we lost the game, but they are memories we will have forever.

It's true what they say about Wembley – it's no place for losers, but we gave it our all and I have to say our Warrington fans were great after the defeat, when they cheered us off the field. Wigan, who had been there many times before, lapped us on the lap of honour, because we were absorbing it and taking it all in. We were last off the field and we thanked the Warrington people for supporting us. They made the defeat bearable, the way they treated us after the game and on our homecoming.

It was as if we'd won the Cup. It was all the way from the M6, quite a few miles, and the welcome was fantastic. At the 'Golden Gates' of Warrington Town Hall, you couldn't see a blade of grass; it was jam packed in there and it's a big area. All the roads in were chock-a-block with well-wishers and, from having a really downbeat feeling of losing at Wembley, it eased the blow quite a bit. It made us feel like we'd won. We thought we'd let them down with the way we had played, but they are special people. I have an affinity and friendship with the Warrington fans that will last forever.

One of the most disappointed players at the club was my teammate and now Wolves coach, Paul Cullen. 'Chachi' had hit Sean Devine of St Helens with a head high tackle with his forearm and he went down in a heap. Unfortunately the referee saw it and 'Chachi' went for an early bath. The Rugby League were clamping down on 'head highs' and 'Chachi' paid the price with an eight match ban. He appealed to the Rugby League and got more games. Paul was an uncompromising player throughout his career.

On another occasion he got sent off with Andy Goodway when we played Wigan at Wilderspool. Andy hit Paul off the ball; he took a bit of a dive and Andy was sent off immediately. As he was walking off, Paul was still on the floor and 'Badway,' as we used to call him, stood on Paul's hand. He flew up and set about Goodway as he went into the tunnel and there was a big brawl. Tony Barrow, our coach, got involved and threw Paul down the steps, but Paul got sent off as well for retaliation. After that game against Wigan we called Paul 'Pantomime,' as in 'He's behind you.' That stuck for a while.

I'll never forget the state we got into in the aftermath of that Challenge Cup defeat. We had just come from one of the most prestigious games you can ever play. We wanted to create an impression and look very professional at the Town Hall reception. As we were on the motorway approaching Warrington, Chaddy came up to a few of us at the back of the bus. There was Tony Thorniley, Billy McGinty, Mark Thomas and I. We had nothing on, not a stitch, and we were covered in champagne, beer and sandwiches. Our feet were black from the coach floor that was soaking wet. We started larking about with Chaddy, throwing things at him and throwing him onto the floor. Brian Johnson had told him to tell us to get right for the homecoming and clean ourselves up. We must have looked a sight as we got off the coach at Knutsford Services and piled into the toilets to clean up and make ourselves look presentable. When we made it into the Town Hall, the Mayor and Mayoress were unimpressed with the way we all stank of drink. They were even less impressed when Chris Rudd turned up three quarters of an hour later and fell on his face in the reception. He nearly pulled the Mayor's chain off and demanded to know where all the cucumber sandwiches were! But a great weekend had been had by all, in a great Warrington team that had failed on the day but had given their all for the club and the town.

From the next season, 1990–91, until I left the club in 1995 it was a stop-start period for me and a very frustrating time in my career. I came back from the British Lions tour with a finger problem that took a while to heal and I missed the start of the season.

My first game back for the club was against the 1990 Kangaroos who had come for the Ashes series. I played well after being out for so long, although I got sin-binned for talking to the referee. As captain of the side, I was questioning a decision, not swearing, and I'm annoyed to this day that the referee sin-binned me. I didn't like letting my teammates down, but as captain I thought I had a right to question the decision. It was hard enough playing Australia with 13, never mind 12.

We were leading 6-0 when Tony Thornily our centre went inside Mal Meninga for a try – and that doesn't happen very often. On this occasion, Tony, who was a strong individual with a great turn of pace, surprised Mal and we were level at 6-all. It didn't last very long and they went further ahead before half-time and finished us off with another 12 points late in the game. With a team like they had, we gave a good account of ourselves and the match was a lot closer than the 26-6 score-line suggests. Bob Jackson, Gary Sanderson, Dave Lyon and Billy McGinty were immense that night, in fact all the team was.

In November, I played against Runcorn in the Lancashire Cup, which we were defending, and got seriously injured. It was a nothing tackle, in fact I think I did the damage before the tackle was made. I remember planting my right foot and I twisted my body to give the ball out to my right. As I twisted, I felt an explosion in my right knee and then, after I had offloaded the ball, I got tackled. As I went down, the pain was excruciating. I got up after a few seconds to play the ball and I knew there was something wrong with my knee. Tony Rothwell, our physio, came on and had a look at it and thought there was maybe a bit of ligament damage, so he took me off. I can remember trying to jog up and down the touch-line for a while, but it was unsteady. I found out later that it was my anterior cruciate. It was a complete rupture and, at the time, the thought was that, if you could build your quads and hamstring up, maybe you didn't need an operation. That's where I probably got the wrong advice, because with a cruciate injury now they operate straight away after the swelling goes down.

I did it in November 1990, but I got operated on in March 1992 and in between I had extensive physio. I went to a place in the Brecon Beacons, where you lived and had full rehab treatment. They got my leg so strong, but with a cruciate it is always unstable. In 1991, I made my first comeback at Widnes and I felt good, but I hadn't taken a big hit on the leg. A minute into the game, I tackled Kurt Sorenson and again my knee exploded. This time I couldn't get up. My cartilage had shattered into bits and my knee was the size of my head. I went into hospital and they removed all the pieces of cartilage. I came back from that with a few more games under my belt, but again I had cartilage damage. I went in again for repairs, but I only needed an arthroscopy this time. As a result of that, the Doctor decided I needed a patella reconstruction. That's where they take the middle of the patient's own patella tendon and place it behind the knee to compensate for the anterior cruciate and drill into the bone. In theory, that stops the movement of the knee, which in my case it did. They did a fantastic job, but like a couple of friends of mine said, my knee was like a cheap Easter egg, with nothing in it.

My physio was David Fevre, who was working at Fairfield Hospital as well as for Great Britain. Dave was the reason I got through the 1990 British Lions tour. At the time, I had a chronic Achilles problem and Dave worked on me three times a day. Because of my knee and me putting extra weight on my good side, my Achilles problem flared up again. I played a handful of games before I tore the Achilles and that is what really knocked me back after being out for so long with the knee surgery. To come back and snap the Achilles was devastating. I was always quite strong mentally, but this really set me back and I thought I would never play again. During those comeback games, I was not playing to a level I was happy with, but when it went again I was the never the same player.

I'd had problems with my Achilles since 1990 and I'd gone into the Challenge Cup Final as a big doubt. I got through the game and it was one that I wasn't going to miss. Hindsight, that wonderful thing, tells me that in 1987 I played for a full 12 months with Warrington and Cronulla, in 1988 I again played for 12 months with the club and the tour. In 1989, I played for the club, went to America and we had the Kiwis touring over here. In 1990, I played for the club and went on the British Lions' tour to Papua New Guinea and New Zealand. That was four years of back-to-back rugby league, giving 100 per cent all the time. Soccer players get through a lot of games, but our sport is a bit more physical. Ultimately, my body gave in, but you know I wouldn't change a thing if I had time to do it again. To play for your country and have a chance to play in Australia was a goal I was allowed to achieve. I am proud of what I achieved in my career and proud of the way I did it, although now it does cause me a lot of trouble with arthritis. Most sportsmen deal with arthritis day in day out; the nature of our game is impact and unfortunately the impact told on me.

I had started at the club in 1982 and my testimonial should have been in 1992, but there were quite a few players who had signed for Warrington around the same time, including Mark Forster and Paul Cullen. So I had to wait for my testimonial for another year – a year that consisted mainly of rehab from my injuries, building my strength up for my first game back – the pre-season Locker Cup game against Wigan. There was no such thing as a friendly against them and it was a really good return for me. Kevin Ellis put out a long ball and I hit it on the angle and outpaced Joe Lydon. Only in my dreams, you might think, but I had the angle on him and went on to score a try. I was so elated after being out for so long that I jumped over the advertising billboards at the Fletcher End and gave everyone high fives. I thought if my knee and Achilles can do that and hold out, I'll be okay. We won the game 21-12 after trailing 4-0 at half-time and I was awarded the man of the match. The day after, though, I couldn't get out of bed, my body had seized up because I wasn't used to the impact after being out for 15 months and my body had gone soft. I'd got through it, but my knee was aching and my Achilles was killing me.

I can honestly say that I was never the same player after that long lay-off. It would have been nice to do it again week in week out, but my body just rebelled against the demands of the modern game, so it was hard work. I keep thinking back to the players who have had far worse injuries than me and I know it's part of our game. You never go onto a rugby field fully fit, except maybe in the first game of the season if you've got through the pre-season unscathed.

After the Locker Cup, it was a bit up and down. I had put a bit more weight on because I realised that my game was changing. I went from a good playing weight of 14 stone 10lbs to 15 stone 10lbs, so I was playing more in the second row, but not at a level I was always happy with. I played a few games okay; I guess the word is mediocre, as I had lost a yard of pace in bulking up.

My body was crying out for a bit of relief. The dilemma was that my body was telling me to pack it in, but my head was telling me to carry on, because the game was in me and I loved it. I got advice from pros and ex-pros like Jackie Melling and Tony Scahill. They said to play as long as you can, because you're a long time retired and that's what I did; I realise now that it was a mistake.

In the 1994–95 season, I left Warrington and that was so hard to come to terms with. It had been part of my life, the Warrington people had been a massive influence on my career and they were great for me. They had supported me throughout, but I realised that the club didn't want me or need me any more; I was surplus to requirements. As an experienced pro, I knew and accepted this. The longevity of a player is based on how well he is playing and my body had taken enough. I played my last game for the club in the 5th Round of the Challenge Cup on the 12th of February 1994 in the 38-4 defeat against Leeds at Headingley, going out with a loss, and a big loss at that.

It was then that Salford and the Keighley Cougars came in for me. Keighley was coached by Phil Larder and I was so close to signing for him. He was going to make me captain and use my experience, as they had quite a few up-and-coming players. At this time, the atmosphere at Keighley games was unreal; it was the time of Cougarmania. The only reason I didn't sign was the travel; I wasn't prepared to move and living in Wigan and travelling to Keighley was not an easy route, especially in winter. I realised it was a lot of travelling time and I wasn't prepared to do it. I have got to thank Keighley for coming in for an old crock, though. They must have thought I was a player who had quite a bit of knowledge between his ears.

During my career at Warrington, I had scored 43 tries, but there are a few other outstanding ones apart from those that I have described earlier. One was the try that the photographer, Eddie Fuller, won a competition with. You can see me scoring by the sticks at Wheldon Road or The Jungle. There are four bodies in the background on the floor and it looks like I have beaten those four and scored. Actually, Ken Kelly had beaten two and I was in the right place at the right time to score so I can't take all the credit. But it's one hell of a photograph and Eddie won the competition because the players on the floor are so animated. I think one is Bob Beardmore, a great player and character. They say that the camera doesn't lie and I'll take credit for looking as if I have left those Castleford players in my wake; only the knowledgeable Warrington supporters who were at the game know what really happened.

Another was when we were playing at Central Park. I

always loved playing there; it was my favourite ground, being a Wiganer. John Fieldhouse had sent a long ball out on the halfway line and again I met the ball. I timed it right and went through and there was Steve Hampson and Henderson Gill. Hampo was coming on one side and Gilly was chasing down behind me and I had momentum on both of them. I came in and out on Hampo and managed to fend him off. I just outpaced Gilly, but I did have a good start on him, and scored beside the sticks. I didn't score many from the halfway line and the other pleasing thing about that try is that we won the game as well.

Another I remember scoring from the halfway line was at Leeds when Andy Gregory put me in for one. It's more the long-range tries I remember. I scored so few, but I was always about being busy and setting them up for others; that's my excuse and I'm sticking to it.

When I think of other memories from my time at Warrington, I often come back to training and the camaraderie of all the lads working together – something I really loved about the game. Our conditioner, Phil Chadwick, was a bin-man during the day for Warrington Corporation, but he always made it to training on time. This one session we were training at an all-weather track. It was a dark, cold night and a few of the boys couldn't be bothered; they were leaning on the fence and when Chaddy shouted 'Let's get round,' there was no movement from some of them. He read the riot act to us and promptly lay on the floor. He said 'If they can't be bothered to train I'll take the session lying down to make a point.'

The guys never did that again. Even though we had a laugh and a joke at times, we always took training quite seriously and we would often come to blows in contact sessions because of the intensity.

When the club brought in new international players like Gary Mercer and Duane Mann, we would introduce them to the club spirit with a team-building exercise in mid-Wales. A lot of clubs did it and we decided to do the same. We went to a centre at Llanberis, where everything was very well organised, all with a planned agenda. Gary was very impressed and said 'I've not been here five minutes and I know I've made the right decision.'

The weekend involved splitting into teams and building rafts out of oil drums, ropes and anything that came to hand. We had to get it across the water with six people and an observer. Chaddy, Dave Lyons, Tony Rothwell, myself and two other players made a superb raft. We had a little place at the back for the observer and he said 'I will just board the raft now along with the six of you.' He did this little hop, skip and jump and disappeared right under the raft and the last we saw of him was him disappearing down the stream covered in mud, followed by a shoal of fish.

We continued with the team-building exercises and the next one involved Mark Roberts, who had diabetes. Someone had decided that it was a good idea to get a gallon tub of tomato sauce out of the kitchen, open Mark's bag and pour it all over his insulin and needles. One or two players who had contact lenses also discovered them soaked in tomato sauce. Mark Roberts wasn't happy with what had happened and decided to get his revenge. He opened a door into a television room and threw a three-gallon tub of rice pudding all over the lads.

The following evening, Chris Rudd volunteered to be lashed to a banister rail. He had a fire extinguisher put down the top of his shirt and the whole canister emptied onto him. Then there was a crashing sound from outside; Paul Bishop had thrown a huge plant and pot out of his third floor window onto someone's car. These were the sort of things that brought professionalism into our club and helped the team prepare to win the Challenge Cup and the Premiership!

During the day, we kept up the serious part of the team building. One day, our coach saw that there were only five on one raft and that someone was missing. That player was one of the best players in the world and one of the best ever at the club, Desi Drummond. All the players loved Desi, but he was on the riverbank and wouldn't get on. Brian Johnson went across to him and Desi said 'Listen Jonno, there's no way you are going to get Desmond on a raft. Are you looking for rugby players or do you want us all as shit smugglers?' Brian Johnson knew when he was beaten and said 'You just stay where you are, Des.' So I went across with Desi in a little canoe and he was happy with that. When we got to the other side, I enjoyed a nice bottle of juice, Desi had a smoke and a good time was had by all.

The owner of the centre where we had done our team building was not very impressed with how we had behaved. He had told us to treat it like our own homes and the boys certainly did. Brian Johnson learnt a lot about us, as did Gary Mercer. We got fined £1,000 between us to repair the damage and we were ordered 'Don't come this side of the border again.'

Funnily enough, we didn't do any more team building in Wales.

Back home, we used to train in an area to the west of Warrington between some railway lines. It was out of the way and it had everything you needed for flat work and hill work. We went there two or three times a week with the club and some of the lads would come up on their own for extra training. On one occasion I said to Chaddy, 'Whatever would you do if this land was taken away from you? It's not the club's land and you would be lost, wouldn't you?' I thought he was going to burst into tears, but he smiled and said 'I've got something here that means there's no way that they can ever take this land away from me.' He walked over to a nearby pond, bent down and put his hand in the water and then came back to me. 'This is a crested newt and the pond is full of them. I stock it up; I go here and there and I get the crested newts and they are protected. If they try and take this training land off me there'll be me, the Prime Minister, someone from the Environment Agency and a crested newt on my shoulder putting two fingers up. If the owners of the land try, all you'll hear is bulldozers slamming into reverse.'

We had some great times training up there; he really flogged us, but they were great sessions. The lads who lived in Wigan and St Helens used to come up on Saturday afternoons to run on that old land between the railway lines. It showed the commitment, spirit and respect they had for each other when I was captain of the club.

4

PRIDE OF A LION

I gained my first international honours as a professional when I was selected for the Great Britain Under-21s to play France at Albi in 1984. The coach was Maurice Bamford, a great character in the game, loved and respected by the whole squad. He had been there, done that, and one thing I learned was that you don't mess about with him.

When I was selected for the squad it was another step on the ladder I had been on since I started playing professionally. I was good enough to sign from the amateurs, I made the A team, the first team, I got recognised as a potential Great Britain player. This selection was the biggest honour for me at the time.

Maurice gave us his team talk about the side we would be playing and it really had us motivated and ready for the battle ahead. Both sides went down some steps and walked through a concrete tunnel underneath the ground to the opposite side of the grandstand. Maurice went up the steps, but we waited and started fighting with the French players in the tunnel. When Maurice came back, we stopped as if nothing had happened. As we emerged from this tunnel, we looked impeccable. France came out with torn shirts, cuts and bruises and blood and snot everywhere. The first psychological and physical battle had been won.

Typical of the French, they had put an Under-24s team out. Some of them had full beards; I was only 20 and hadn't started shaving! We led 4-0, through two Dave Creasser penalties, at half-time, but France pulled it back to two points. Dave Creasser and Deryck Fox then combined to put

Vince Gribbin in for the only try and we won the game 8-2.

To win on your debut, even though it was for the Under-21s against France, was fantastic and after the game we decided to go and hit the town. I wasn't dressed appropriately and the late Roy Powell, who I was rooming with, lent me a jumper. He was a fantastic guy, Roy – a man mountain and his jumper dwarfed me.

We went out and had a few Kronenbourgs and a drop of wine and a few of us tried to get into a nightclub. The bouncers wouldn't let us in, so we had a bit of a 'to do' and some of the lads took a bit of a beating. We didn't end up getting in, but went back to the hotel to get the other lads to assist us by ramming the door. Maurice intervened and that's when we saw the other side of him. He stopped us from doing what we wanted to do, just by saying 'Be careful.' Perhaps it was the way he said it, but we understood what he meant and cancelled the ram-raid.

Later on, a few of us slipped out of the hotel, as we were quite hungry. It was late and Foxy and I went into a restaurant to see if they would serve us with a beer and something to eat. The next thing, I heard the sound of breaking glass behind me. Paul Round had come through a plate glass window at the front of the restaurant. Roundy picked himself up, not a scratch on him. The window must have been 10ft by 8ft and the waiters tried to get hold of Foxy and me but we ran out of the door with Roundy close behind us. To this day, he says he just leaned on the window. I know he was a big second row from St Helens, but not that big. Foxy and I are adamant that he and Lee Crooks had been messing about outside. You just don't fall through a window; he wasn't that drunk. I later asked Crooksy about it and he said it had nothing to do with him.

Even in a small town like Albi, we got away with it. The police didn't come to the hotel and we didn't get a bill at reception to pay for the damage. Somehow, Maurice knew all about it, so we didn't hide anything from him about what had happened and here, for the first time, the incident has become public knowledge. I'm just hoping that there isn't an international arrest warrant out for me after 22 years!

The following May, Maurice selected me in his Great Britain squad to play France at Limoux for The French Chairman's Trophy. Although the game was an international, it was a non-Test match and caps were not awarded for the game. It wasn't a full Great Britain side; there was a mixture of senior players and youngsters like Lee Crooks, Garry Schofield, Shaun Edwards, Nicky Kiss, Ellery Hanley, Bob Beardmore, Kieron O'Loughlin and myself. I started on the bench, came on as substitute for the last half hour and enjoyed the step up from the previous year's game. We won the game by over 40 points and to play with players like O'Loughlin and Jeff Grayshon was an awesome experience.

After the game we were based in Limoux. In the middle of Limoux there was a fountain, very idyllic. Kieron – that great Widnes centre whose son Sean was appointed Wigan captain for the 2006 season – had gone into the fountain and after a few of us joined him, we were all wet through. Kieron went back to the hotel and got changed but the rest of us didn't bother. We were joined by Schoey, who had kept himself quite clean and hadn't gone into the fountain. But that was about to change as the next moment we saw that Kieron was on a moped riding towards us and he began going around the fountain. All of a sudden he jumped off the moped, ran at Schoey and carried him into the fountain with a superb full-on tackle. We then had a great night of celebrating in Limoux as we dried off.

Just over 18 months later on the 15th of January I was included in the full Great Britain squad for the first time, to face France in the Whitbread Trophy Bitter Test – a World Cup game. So I made my Great Britain debut at Headingley on the 24th of January 1987 – a very proud young man. But then you had to play in two Tests in the same series to get your cap, so to me this was just the start. Although I didn't receive a cap Mal Reilly, who had taken over from Maurice

Bamford as coach with Phil Larder as his assistant, presented me with my jersey in the camp preparing for the game. My Warrington teammate Mark Forster made his debut in the same game, and made the perfect start with an 80-yard interception try. I was supporting all the way to the line hoping that Mark would pass it, but there was no chance of that. I did score my first try for my country on the hour when Schoey and Andy Gregory combined to put me in, and they did it again with two minutes left. We ended up winning 52-4, a record, and that feeling of scoring on my debut was unreal.

A few days later I received another letter informing me that I had been selected in the squad for the return Test in Carcassonne on the 8th of February – the day I bumped into Jean Luc Rabot and saved money on future Christmas cards to him.

My parents came out to watch, but whereas we flew to France they made the journey by coach. It took them about 23 hours. Before the game we were each presented with a bottle of wine as we were lining up for the national anthems of both countries. Hearing the anthem away from home is even more special, and if you don't have a big travelling support it's up to the players to sing their hearts out – and we did. I don't understand people who don't sing the anthem – it's got to say something about them. I guess it's each man to his own, but it was quite emotional for me.

After the anthems we lined up for the game, with the bottles of wine placed at the side of the dugouts. My old school mate 'Knocker' – Ian Nolan – had also come over, and I believe he came down and helped himself to all the bottles for him and his mates. They all had a good time via the French hospitality, although how they improvised without a corkscrew I don't know.

As for the game, the Australian Mick Stone was the referee, and we knew it was never going to be another 52-4. It was a big, physical, ugly encounter, and we were trailing 10-8 at half-time. We took a 14-10 lead through Henderson Gill's converted try, but a few minutes later my game was over as it descended into French thuggery. I had made a tackle on a French player with Chris Burton – a no-nonsense forward from Hull KR. As I was getting up, Rabot – a prop – came steaming in and threw an unexpected flying punch that connected with my cheekbone and nose. It was a cheap shot, something they call a king-hit now. I was out for the count, but I believe a melee took place between the boys and the French.

When I came to after a minute or so I knew that things were wrong with my face because I could see my nose in the corner of my eye. I was feeling blood streaming from my nose, and had pins and needles all across my face. I eventually stood up in extreme pain and Mick Stone called me over to one side and said to me 'The French touch judge has come on and said that you were gouging in the tackle.' I have always worked hard, played hard and tackled hard but never during my playing career did I gouge or spit at any player – the French players were renowned for that. I told Mick Stone, 'That's bollocks,' but although he hadn't seen it he sin-binned me for ten minutes. I couldn't believe it, all for a lying little French touch judge – I was so annoyed.

As I said, I feel I was quite a fair player and I only got sent off once. There were no complaints about that, as it was for a flying head butt in a Warrington-Widnes derby. What a great job Widnes's scrum half Dave Hulme had done on me that day, needling me to the point where I lost it completely. The butt didn't even connect, I just glanced off him and didn't do him any damage. Dave's a good lad, and unlike the incident in France, I can laugh about it now.

Back in Carcassonne, I walked groggily to our dugout and saw the team doctor, Forbes Mackenzie, who took me into the dressing room. I was blocked full of blood up my nose and did the worst thing possible, blowing all the snot and blood out of each nostril – within 30 seconds both of my eyes were almost completely closed. I went back out but Malcolm Reilly took one look at me and said 'You can't go back on.' From that day I was looking forward to meeting Monsieur Rabot again.

After the game none of the France team or officials came in to see me or apologise for the incident. To be honest I wouldn't have accepted an apology anyway. I had a constant headache, pins and needles in my face, and breathing difficulties. So no, I was in no mood for even a beer that night.

The great and positive thing that happened as result of playing in this second Test against France was that I got my Great Britain cap. You only get the one no matter how many games you play, and it means more to me than any trophy that I ever won – not that I won that many.

All that night the boys were calling me Panda. I would have liked to laugh but I was in so much pain. I couldn't drink and I was on painkillers. My mouth and the side of my face had swollen and I couldn't breathe except through my mouth, and to this day my nose is the result of the work of Monsieur Rabot.

I was out of the game for three months with a broken cheekbone, broken nose and broken sinus bone. The blood just kept coming. Fortunately the cheekbone wasn't depressed, so I guess I was lucky that I didn't need an operation. But I kept reflecting on the way it was done: why should I be out for three months because of Rabot and the French Rugby League? I considered taking legal action, and asked Warrington to take advice on my behalf. But given the state of rugby league in France at that time, I was advised I'd get nowhere. So I had to take it on the chin.

What the incident did do was make me more aware of everything that was going on around me, a bit more streetwise, I suppose. I turned it into a painful learning curve. The game was so much dirtier in the early 1980s than it is now – not harder, but there were thugs about. Now the game is now too fast to be dirty.

By the start of the 1987 season, I was ready to play again, in the knowledge that there was a Great Britain tour to Papua New Guinea, Australia and New Zealand the following summer. I'd played for Lancashire against Yorkshire in the War of the Roses the previous autumn, and won two more Lancashire caps in 1987 – another loss against Yorkshire, and a draw against the Papua New Guinea tourists. I played well in that game, but not well enough to make the Great Britain team who beat PNG 42-0 at Wigan, and I also missed out on the two Tests against France early in 1988. At that stage I feared that Monsieur Rabot had cost me a tour, but things changed after I'd bumped into Les Bettinson before Warrington played at Salford. Les, who had already been appointed as manager for the tour, told me to have a good game, and even though I say so myself I did. But it was only when I read Ceefax on the 5th of April, a Tuesday, that I knew I was in, with a letter of confirmation arriving later. There were no phone calls in those days, with the letter going into detail about being measured up for a blazer, tracksuit and training kit, and the itinerary prior to leaving. I can't describe the elation of seeing my name in the squad on Ceefax, and then again when that letter arrived. I think touring is every player's dream in so many sports, and certainly for me to be a British Lion, with all the great history of Great Britain rugby league tours of Australia, was the ultimate accolade.

We had a good squad, although it could have been even stronger if Des Drummond and Joe Lydon had made it. They were both withdrawn after controversial incidents towards the end of the season. Desi blotted his copybook in a Premiership semi-final against Widnes at Naughton Park, after a big brawl started and spilled into the crowd. A few kids were knocked off the perimeter wall, but eventually things calmed down – as Warrington captain, my involvement was trying to pull our players away. Then a spectator came on to the field and started wagging his finger and shouting at Desi. Des didn't get the first one in, but it takes two to tango and the spectator was flattened. The police came on to the field, the referee was called, and told me as captain that Des would be arrested after the game.

Des's reaction was that he was only defending himself. But that brawl, which also led to Warrington being fined a record £10,000 and four more players (David Lyon, Barry Peters, Mark Roberts and Paul Cullen) being suspended, cost Des his tour place.

It was a similar story for Joe in a game against St Helens at Knowsley Road. There was another pitch invasion, Steve Hampson was hit by a spectator and Joe took matters into his own hands. He was seen to be the aggressor and lost his place. The Rugby Football League didn't back him or Des, and knowing both players so well I was saddened that they had to withdraw. Both of them had been on the last tour in 1984, so their experience would have been invaluable to us. We were always going to need all our best players, and maybe things would have been different if they'd been out there with us.

I suppose the Rugby Football League had their procedure to follow, but I reckon the Aussies would have bent any rules if there was a danger of someone like Wally Lewis or Peter Sterling missing a tour.

I think today's player is getting a bit of a bum deal not to be able to tour. I know we have the Tri-Nations Series, but that's only a few games at the end of a long season – the key is to play in New Zealand and Australia, and to experience the sights and sounds of another culture. On that 1988 tour we played in places like Gympie and Toowoomba, against big farmer boys who just wanted to take your head off or break your jaw so that they could go in the pub and say that they had injured Mike Gregory, Ellery Hanley or Garry Schofield, and stopped them playing against Australia.

I don't think we could ever go back to those days, with the switch to summer rugby in England meaning our season runs parallel to the NRL in Australia. But a couple of games against NRL sides before Tests against Australia or New Zealand would be better than nothing – and crucially, would mean that rugby league was offering young stars like Sean O'Loughlin, Danny McGuire and Jon Wilkin the sort of experience that might help prevent them looking to rugby union, with its structured international programme.

That 1988 squad were such a great bunch of players, and I'd count them all as friends to this day. On meeting we knew a bit about each other, but the camaraderie we developed from living together for eight weeks was impossible to match. I don't think that our full-time players will revert to winter again after ten years of summer rugby. The days of snow, frozen pitches and ankle deep mud are long gone and the supporters want to see a fast open game on playing surfaces like carpets. I want our best modern-day players to play against the best, but I think the people in charge of our international game are thinking about the time and money, rather than the players from both hemispheres.

In 2008, Australia will be celebrating their centenary and will be holding the World Cup there. The last one took place in this country in 2000 so it's a long time between drinks. It will be interesting to see how they market it, but hopefully it will be a success and catch the imagination of the public like the last Rugby Union World Cup Down Under – when England became World Champions. Should Great Britain or England triumph and win the World Cup, given the precedent set by the rugby union and cricket sides, will we have an open-top parade in London or is this just a dream? We have the talent coming through and to play the best in the world is a challenge for them and a challenge for the administrators to do what is best for those players rather than the interests of the respective competitions.

I really feel touring is the best thing that a player can do, to go overseas and test oneself against the best the other countries have got to offer. It's not just the playing, it's the places they will see and probably never see again; it's meeting new people from these countries and making friendships that will last a lifetime.

In 1988, our first stop was Papua New Guinea. That meant flying from Manchester to Heathrow, Heathrow to Bahrain,

Bahrain to Singapore, Singapore to Sydney, and finally Sydney to Port Moresby, the capital of PNG. That took 33 hours. All through the journey we'd drunk water, eaten salads and changed our body clock to Papua New Guinea time, so that we could be up and running when we landed. And as soon as we got there, our coaches Malcolm Reilly and Phil Larder told us that we had ten minutes to get our kit on, ready for a run. The heat and humidity was unbelievable, something we'd never experienced before. I also found myself elected to the social committee with Lee Crooks, Andy Gregory, Andy Platt, Paul Dixon and Phil Ford – a good crew.

We only had a couple of days in Port Moresby before the Test, and again I was proud and honoured when my name was read out for the team. It was 90 degrees and the humidity was something else, but we won the game 42-22 in front of a packed crowd. We had led 28-6 at half-time, with a rare try for me, but the heat and humidity got to us and with five minutes left they had come back to 30-22, before two late tries clinched it for us. PNG were tough opponents, especially in those conditions – all about 5ft 9in, and unbelievably strong, with pace as well.

Just going to the place was a great experience. PNG was what you think of as a Third World country, and when we went out into the sticks to places like Goroka, basically one-horse towns, we were mobbed everywhere we went. It could be frightening at times but they love their rugby league.

Our short stay in Port Moresby also gave us an early insight into the competitive character of Malcolm Reilly. We were staying at the Travel Lodge, where they had a small 20-metre pool, and Malcolm was told that Roy Powell had swum six lengths under water. 'I can beat that,' Malcolm insisted, and dived into the pool to do seven lengths. He came up puce, his eyes nearly popping out. We were all amazed because we'd only been geeing him up, nobody had done six lengths or anything like that. For Malcolm, and Phil Larder too, the fact that they were both very fit and did all the training that they asked us to do earned them extra respect from us. It was great fun, and meant the management team bonded close to the squad.

Along those lines, we came up with a call 'hit the beach' for when things weren't going our way – a call for the war-time spirit, I suppose.

After PNG it was on to Australia, and socially things definitely started looking up. There still weren't that many times to relax with all the travelling and training, but before the first Test in Sydney we had a golf day at Manly, organised by the International Board. It will always be remembered for what happened at a dinner afterwards. I'd been playing with Andy Platt against Phil Ford and Andy Gregory, but Phil wasn't a great player so by the time we all sat down to dinner he was already the worse for wear. So when Platty told him that he was much funnier than the comedian up on the stage, Fordy went straight up there and after a bit of heckling took the microphone. He messed up completely, and Malcolm and Phil were livid.

We got flogged the next day in training, the old-fashioned 'beasting'.

In the lead-up to the first Test I'd played well in a tough 28-12 win against Newcastle Knights, and hoped that would clinch my spot. Sure enough, Malcolm announced that I'd be in the second row with Platty, my old Wigan St Patricks teammate. My first game against Australia – I was speechless.

It was at the Sydney Football Stadium, and we were 6-0 up at half-time after a Paul Loughlin penalty and a superb try from Ellery Hanley, our captain. Australia's great scrum-half Peter Sterling went off holding his shoulder but it didn't stop him weaving some magic as we were beaten 17-6. I still think we deserved better than that, especially as Kevin Ward had a try disallowed when Australia were 12-6 ahead, with the French referee Francis Desplas ruling a forward pass against us. Still, it was a top effort considering the pace of the game which was frightening for us, still semi-professional in those days, against the Aussie superstars and their big pack, with Bella, Backo, Lindner, Gillespie and Fullerton-Smith. That took its toll in the second half.

It had been a couple of notches higher, harder and faster than any match I had played in before. After the defeat I was totally floored physically and emotionally, because the whole team had put so much into the game only to come up short.

My next game was against Toowoomba, a side of farmers. Playing teams like that was a backward step even though I understood the philosophy of the tour. They just wanted to take our heads off – maybe the Australian Rugby League had a hidden agenda. Having said that I scored two tries in a 28-12 victory, and always quite enjoyed that type of game, even though I was taken out without the ball and the referee let them get away with murder.

Then it was on to Brisbane for the Second Test at Lang Park, when I switched to loose forward because of injuries. We had to win to have any chance of regaining the Ashes, the whole purpose of the tour. We came out to a barrage of beer cans being thrown at us – hostile, but an adrenalin rush that I'll never forget. A couple of incidents involving Garry Jack, Wayne Pearce and Wally Lewis were equally memorable. Jack was notorious for kicking out on the floor after you'd tackled him, and caught me under the chin with his studs. It was cut down to the bone leaving the fold of my skin just flapping about. But our physio Geoff Plummer just put on a bit of Vaseline and tape, and I carried on. It was an Ashes Test!

In the second half, with Lewis controlling everything and the Aussies winning fairly comfortably, Pearce brought an elbow up and cut me. It may have been an accident but I thought 'Fuck it, why wait? Let's get it on.' I swung a few punches and connected with a couple, so did he, and the next thing Lewis came flying in and shoulder charged me in my back. All hell broke out with all 26 players at it hammer and tongs. When peace was restored, the referee, Monsieur Desplas, spoke to me. I don't know what he said because it was in French, and anyway I didn't get sin-binned or sent off. I'd won my fight, and as a team we won that battle. But we lost the game, and with it the series – Australia were 2-0 up, so they had retained the Ashes.

Like the whole of our squad, players and coaches alike, I was devastated. It needed Platty to point out the state of my chin, so the doc stitched me up as I held his hand, because there wasn't any anaesthetic.

Injuries were really hitting us hard now, with Platty joining a long list which also included Paul Dixon and Lee Crooks ruled out of the tour. Before they went home we had a leaving 'do' for them in Sydney, and I'm told that Lee had his false teeth pinched – Andy Gregory and Phil Ford were the prime suspects, a brave move by two backs against a prop forward.

Those of us who stayed had to pick ourselves up for a game against the Western Division in the backwoods of Orange. I was loose forward again and we made hard work of it, hanging on for a 28-26 win. That did nothing to tone down the way the Australian press were writing us off ahead of the third Test, but that allowed Malcolm and Phil to instil a real bulldog spirit, asking us if we were going to just take it, or come out fighting.

The injuries kept coming, with Kevin Beardmore the last to go, forcing Paul Hulme to play hooker for the first time in his life with his brother Dave at stand-off. I was injured myself but wanted to play, and when Malcolm named the team the night before the match, I was in. But I was restless that night, and I wasn't the only one. Andy Gregory knocked on my door, we arranged to meet in the hotel foyer – by that time it was about 10 o'clock at night – and David Stephenson and Phil Ford were there as well. All four of us were playing but at Greg's suggestion we went for a walk and ended up having two pints of Guinness the night before the game. I had never ever drunk before a game – apart from at Joe Lydon's 21st birthday, but that Guinness helped calm the nerves, and didn't seem to do any of us much harm.

I'll never forget the rallying speech Malcolm gave us in the dressing room. 'What are you going to do when your back's against the wall with nowhere to go, are you going to go forward or are you going to sink and get the shit kicked out of you?' Australia hadn't been beaten at home for about 16 years, but we knew we had to be at least capable of giving them a game. The spirit we had was unreal, everyone thinking 'Let's give it a go and show them all.' As captain, Ellery led by example, and the way the little pocket battleship Andy Greg played was awesome. If you didn't do your job Greg was on you like a ton of bricks. Paul Hulme might never have played hooker before, but I'll tell you to this day, I would have him in the trenches with me.

We fought, kicked, hit and did everything that was needed to win a Test match. From Fordy at full-back to Brian Case on the bench everyone delivered that day. We all had a job and we all did our jobs and more.

At half-time we were 10-0 up after Greg set up a try for Martin Offiah, and Fordy scored a cracker himself. Malcolm just told us 'Have faith, have belief.' Three minutes into the second half Wally Lewis used his strength and forced his way over by the posts, and I think the majority of the crowd in the stadium thought it was the start of the Australia comeback. But Ellery and Greg were saying 'It's against the run of play, dig in for the next ten minutes, get field position and do whatever it takes.'

We did as they said, and when Henderson Gill nipped in for a try from another Greg kick we had the ten-point cushion again. But Australia continued pounding our line and prop Sam Backo went over our try line to score and put them back within four points with 18 minutes left. We hit straight back when Paul Loughlin's majestic break set up a second try for Gilly. We still had to defend for our lives on our own line as Australia came at us again. But then came the moment for which I'll probably be best remembered.

It started when Greg drove the ball up from dummy half and evaded four Aussies with his nuggety strength. He ducked under a few swinging arms, drew full-back Gary Jack, and gave me the ball. I was still on our 25-yard line, but I knew I had the fitness and strength, and I just went for it. Wally Lewis and Wayne Pearce, two of the greatest players ever to wear the Green and Gold, were chasing me down, but I did have the step on them and I knew Martin Offiah was supporting me. I could hear him at the side of me, shouting 'Just give me the ball.' But I could see Lewis giving up as I glanced behind, after trying to pull Martin back, and then out of the corner of my right eye I could see that I could hold off Pearce as well. Thinking 'If I'm going to run all this way, I may as well score,' I just pinned my ears back and made it to the sticks – a special moment.

Inside I was feeling 'We've done it, it's not going to be a whitewash,' just trying to take it all in as I lay on the ground realising what I and the team had just done. I was physically and emotionally knackered, I couldn't even get up. But Ellery had come over with the rest of my teammates and said, 'Get up, don't show them that you're tired.' I was totally gone, I was drained. Along with the Wembley try, it was the most important I'd ever scored, and this meant a bit more because it was the beating of Australia rather than in defeat against Wigan, even if Greg still insists he did all the hard work!

On the Australian television commentary Jack Gibson, who had coached me at Cronulla 12 months earlier said 'It's Gregory to Gregory' – it sounded like a law firm.

The game still wasn't over, even at 26-12 ahead after Lockers kicked the goal. We were playing the world's best and we knew they could score three tries in no time. But my try had broken them – they were beaten men. One thing I noticed in those closing minutes was the travelling army of supporters, who had been right behind us all through the series. When the game was over we went over to thank them, and they were almost as delighted, ecstatic and tearful as us. There's a picture from those celebrations of me wearing a floppy Union Jack hat that was given to me by Jack Roden, a

Wigan St Pats lad who now scouts from Wigan. It was on the front cover of every paper. These were special moments that make you realise what a good sport rugby league is, both for the special people you play with, and the people who support the game and their country.

The win and the try against the world's best was one of the defining moments in my sporting career. It still doesn't rank with the birth of my two sons, Sam and Ben, but in sport that occasion has to be number one.

Back in the changing room afterwards, every one of us basically collapsed. We were physically and emotionally shattered. We'd lost nine players injured during the tour, including Shaun Edwards right at the start, in addition to losing Andy Goodway, Joe Lydon and Des Drummond before we left. So, although I admit I'm biased, to defy the odds as we did lifted it up there with Great Britain's two most famous against-the-odds wins, the so-called Rorke's Drift Test of 1914 and the Battle of Brisbane in 1958.

I think it's worth remembering that team in full: Phil Ford at full-back; Martin Offiah and Henderson Gill on the wings; Paul Loughlin and David Stephenson in the centres; David Hulme stand-off and Andy Gregory scrum-half; loose forward and captain Ellery Hanley; myself and Roy Powell in the second row; Hugh Waddell and Kevin Ward the props; hooker Paul Hulme; and replacement Brian Case who came on during the game for Waddell.

Darren Wright was an unused sub, a great player with Widnes who had been called out to Australia as an emergency replacement, and played consistently well in the midweek games. And the rest of the squad who didn't play in the Tests were all part of the bigger picture – like the Three Musketeers, we were 'All for one and one for all.'

But still the tour hadn't finished. We had another game in Australia, then two in New Zealand including a Test to decide who would play Australia in the World Cup Final. We lost the last game in Australia, against a President's XIII who were the young up-and-comers – Phil Blake, who later played for Warrington, destroyed us. It was a real slog of a game in the rain in Canberra, but another great test for us. I scored a try, but we lost 24-16.

So we moved on to New Zealand for a Test at the Addington Showgrounds in Christchurch. It was raining again, which meant a low-scoring match, and I'm convinced we would have won it if Greg hadn't had a perfectly good try disallowed for a so-called forward pass, after a run-around move with Kevin Ward that they had perfected during the tour. Instead a costly mistake just before half-time allowed their substitute stand-off Gary Freeman to score his second try, and they hung on to win 12-10. I still believe we were better than the Kiwis then, but that result meant it was them who played Australia in the World Cup final. They switched the game to the rugby union ground at Eden Park, but lost.

Before that we had one last game against Auckland, when we went down 30-14, bringing the tour to an end. It had been an unforgettable experience, and it got even better for me when I was selected to play for the Rest of the World against Australia to celebrate the Bi-Centennial celebrations. Andy Gregory, Ellery Hanley, Kevin Ward, Henderson Gill and I were all selected to play with a couple of players each from France, Papua New Guinea and New Zealand – including Mark Graham, who was captain, with Wigan's Graham Lowe as coach.

We were staying at Rushcutters Bay in Sydney, and because we were taking the game seriously there was quite a bit of training to do. You could tell it had been a long tour because all I wanted to do was curl up and sleep. I was rooming with Darrell Williams, a Kiwi who played full-back for Manly. But when he got injured in a club match he was replaced, in the team and as my room-mate, by Gary Mercer – that's the first time I met Ming the Massive, and we went on to become good friends.

It was a great experience being in the same team as guys like Mark Graham and Dean Bell. Graham is an immense guy, 6ft 5in tall, 17 stone and built like granite. I was his second row partner at 6ft tall, 14½ stone – it was like the Little and Large show. During the training sessions we worked together on a planned move, and it worked perfectly during the game for me to score the first try – not many players can say they've scored for the Rest of the World. Australia still won the game, 22-10, but there was further evidence that the tour had established me as an international when I was voted with Paul Sironen as the two best second rows in the world. I consider 1988 to have been a perfect year for me – a lot of hard work, but a lot of reward from it.

The next international also involved the Rest of the World, but this time I was playing against them for Great Britain in another commemorative game, this time at Headingley, to mark the opening of the Hall of Fame. Great Britain won 30-20, good preparation for our Tests against France the next year.

The first Test against France was special for me because it was at Central Park – and also because my old mate Jean Luc Rabot was playing prop for them. I was a bit older, wiser, bigger and nastier, I had learned a lot since 1987. I didn't go out to get him, but like an elephant I have a long memory, and within the rules of the game I kicked him all over the field. Whenever I could get to him I did. Maybe I was a bit over-zealous once or twice. On the first crunch on him I didn't whisper anything but he definitely knew who I was – the first hit must certainly have jogged his memory. Funnily enough he didn't last the game, which we won 26-10, and we beat them again 30-8 in another tough game in Avignon the following month.

As you've probably gathered I'd never seen eye to eye with the French, and I wasn't the only one. Having said that I'm a good friend with Gilles Dumas, who was a scrum-half for his country and recently coached their Test side, and I recognise the importance to the game of France becoming strong again.

The following 1989–90 season New Zealand were coming

over on tour for a three-Test series against us – when I fulfilled another of my ultimate ambitions by captaining my country. Ellery Hanley was injured, and in the end I think it was between me, Andy Gregory and Garry Schofield. I was already captain of Warrington and took the responsibility very seriously, so I knew how to speak to players and get the best out of them. When Malcolm and Phil told me that I was the man, it was the proudest day of my rugby league life. Captaining my country has to be the ultimate accolade – I'd come a long way since being left out of Lancashire Under-19s.

I can't describe how it felt leading the Great Britain team out for the first time, at Old Trafford on the 21st of October. But the game didn't go well, as we lost 24-16, and I wasn't happy with my own performance. The captaincy affected me, I was a bit more concerned with the way the team played and lost focus on my own game.

The pressure was on for the second Test, we had to win to keep the series alive, and Shaun Edwards replaced his Wigan teammate Andy Gregory at scrum-half. We got off to the worst possible start when our full-back Steve Hampson was sent off by the Australian referee Greg McCallum in the first five minutes of the game. He went for a head-butt after a bit of an altercation with their scrum-half Gary Freeman – although Hampo still claims he was going for the ball. But the sending off made my job as captain so much easier, all the players really rallied together and came up with a terrific 26-6 win. I was happier with my own game but Andy Goodway scored two tries and really made the difference that day, with an outstanding 80-minute performance.

So it was off to Central Park for the decider on the 11th of November. Great Britain hadn't won a home series against the Kiwis for 25 years, and there were also two crucial World Cup points up for grabs, as well as the previous year's defeat in New Zealand to make up for. It's a game that I'll always remember for the performance of Paul Newlove, who had made his international debut as an 18-year-old in the previous Test, but really came of age in this one. After Martin Offiah had scored the first try, it was Newlove's break that set up a second for Alan Tait – who had replaced Hampson at full-back – to put us 10-0 ahead. But they came back through a Kelly Shelford try, and it was backs-to-the-wall stuff for us for the whole of the second half. Somehow we held them out for a 10-6 win, a huge effort to keep such a good side scoreless for 40 minutes, and a special moment for me as I went up to collect the trophy – and at Central Park as well, with all my Wigan family and friends watching.

The way we'd come back in the series showed just how focused we were, helped by the fact that there was so little to do at Shaw Hill, the golf club where we were based just outside Wigan. Believe it or not, hide and seek was one of the most popular options.

When the job was done we took the chance to let our hair down, although I will always remember it for a faux pas which came back to haunt me 12 months later. The post-match function was at Upholland Hall, and the New Zealand management team and their captain Hugh McGahan had stood up and spoken eloquently. Malcolm Reilly and the British management responded, then it was my turn. I congratulated all the management, coaching staff, everyone concerned and especially my team, and thanked the Kiwis for the way they played in good spirit. But then I said, 'But tough shit.' I meant hard lines, but that wasn't the way it sounded, and it didn't go down well with the Kiwis and their staff – not helped by the fact that our lads were pissing themselves. Even when we went over to New Zealand a year later, they were still bringing it up.

When the next Great Britain team was picked for two Tests against France the following spring, I wasn't captain – although that was no surprise with Ellery Hanley returning to the team. No complaints from me, Ellery was always the number one choice as one of the very few Englishmen to be voted the world's best player. He was a great player, great coach, great character and a friend for life.

Ellery led us to a tight 8-4 win in Perpignan, but when he was injured again for the return match at Headingley, Shaun Edwards took over as captain – for a shock 25-18 defeat. Then when the squad was picked for a tour of Papua New Guinea and New Zealand that summer, both Ellery and Shaun were injured – and I received the greatest accolade of my career, captaining a British Lions tour. I'd been playing most of the 1989–90 season with a chronic Achilles problem, including in the Challenge Cup final at Wembley just before the tour, but there was no way I was going to pull out with an injury.

Because of the loss of Ellery, Shaun and some other guys, it was a very young squad – guys like Bobbie Goulding, Phil Clarke, Gary Price, Ian Smales, Denis Betts and Ian Lucas were at the start of their international careers, and it was also Jonathan Davies' first Lions tour. So not many people gave us a chance in New Zealand.

The bloke who I have to credit for getting me through that tour is Dave Fevre, our physio. Dave, who was also the Wigan physio, worked tirelessly with all the squad, but he was treating my Achilles three times a day. We started in Papua New Guinea, with the flight time now down to 24 hours via Thailand, a big improvement on 1988. We had a 40-18 win against the Southern Zone in Port Moresby, the capital, but the first Test was in Goroka, up in the hills. That was a daunting experience for all of us, especially the young guys who were in PNG for the first time. We stayed in the only hotel there – it reminded me of Stan and Hilda Ogden's place in Coronation Street, with the three ducks on the wall.

The game was played on a dust bowl, with hundreds of locals hanging from trees outside the very basic stadium, and I became the only Great Britain captain to lose against Papua New Guinea. But there were extenuating circumstances. As well as the heat and humidity, we had to cope with the distraction of people diving out of the trees when a big branch broke, and inside the stadium there was a riot. The local police fired tear gas into the crowd, but the breeze blew it straight back over the pitch. That's when I discovered that tear gas burns your eyes, makes your nose run and burns the back of your throat. The referee Denis Hale from New Zealand postponed the game for a few minutes until we could actually see and talk. We'd been 6-0 up before the interruption, but after it Papua New Guinea threw everything at us – not all legally – and led 14-8 by half-time. They knew we were a young side and came out to intimidate us. I told the referee we needed a bit of protection, but he told me he just wanted to get off the pitch in one piece. We ended up losing by two points.

One of the features of a trip to Papua New Guinea is the red spit on the pavements, and the red teeth of a lot of the people you meet. That's down to the betel nut. I'm not 100 per cent sure where it's from, but it acts like a natural form of cocaine, sending people a bit crazy.

For the second Test we were back in the more familiar surroundings of the Travel Lodge in Port Moresby. The pressure was on, with World Cup points at stake as well as our need to bounce back, but there was a great friendly atmosphere with no riots or tear gas. I was forced off after an hour because of the Achilles, but by then we were 34-2 ahead, and ended up winning 40-8 with seven tries. Revenge was sweet.

Flying to New Zealand meant we met up again with Kelvin Skerrett, the soon to be Wigan prop who had been my room-mate at the start of the tour, but was forced to fly from PNG to Sydney for a knee operation. Kelvin had a reputation as one of the more tough and uncompromising players in the game, but off the field he couldn't have been more different. He phoned me up from Sydney, waiting in a hotel for his operation, wondering what to do. I suggested he went downstairs for a beer and a chat in the bar, but Kelvin couldn't face it. He was all right in familiar surroundings, but hated speaking to people he didn't know. He was just a good, quiet lad like me. Before he left Kel had a press-up and sit-up competition with David Bishop and he did about 500 press-ups. But Malcolm Reilly came in and saw what they were doing and he beat both of them, which was just the way that Malcolm was on tour as I had seen previously.

On the tour the staff had arranged some events and days out and one of them was white-water rafting. This was a fantastic idea and we all got kitted up with headgear, life jackets and paddles. There were eight of us in each raft and Malcolm didn't want to do it, in the raft that is. What Malcolm wanted to do was go down Gradient 5, which was quite steep. He wanted to run down on a body board and he put his flippers on. The organisers and owners of the raft told him not to do it, it would be too rough for him, but Malcolm being Malcolm saw this as another challenge for him to conquer because of his stubborn competitive streak and ignored them. So off he went on his own on the body board and started down the river. We followed him in the raft and you could see him going under the rapids, coming up, going under, coming up, the waves were knocking him about to some tune. He was hitting the rocks in the water at speed and I thought there is no way he will survive this, even though I knew his competitive streak. I mean it was hard enough in our raft with eight of us in. As Malcolm went under the water we wouldn't see him for a few seconds and then he would burst out, kicking and using his flippers to ride the rapids. He carried on doing this all the way for what seemed like hours until we came to the end and Malcolm loved it. The man's crazy; he just wouldn't be beaten by the rapids.

When we went to Avignon in 1989, we were training over there and things were not going too well. A few of the players were messing about but Malcolm was putting it all in and he told us in no uncertain terms, 'If you don't pull your fingers out, I'll take you all outside.' I can tell you this we got things right in that training session and we won the game 30-8, with Peter Williams from Salford scoring a try on his debut. That was Malcolm's winning attitude; he hated losing in anything he was involved in. Malcolm and Phil were great for the country and they were great for me, as they brought my game on no end.

But we didn't start well in New Zealand. As well as losing both the games before the first Test, we had an off-field dilemma involving the former Wales rugby union international David Bishop, and plenty more on-field drama for my old friend Joe Lydon. The trouble with Bish, or Champagne Charlie as we knew him, came because he'd gone for a drink the night before the first game against Canterbury, which we lost 18-10. He'd gone with Keith England, the Castleford prop known by everyone as Beefy, who ended up needing stitches after they'd smashed a marble bust in our hotel. At five o'clock that morning, I was woken up as captain with Garry Schofield, my vice captain, to see our tour manager Maurice Lindsay up in the penthouse suite – perks of the management! Beefy was okay because he wasn't playing in the Canterbury game, but Bish had broken the curfew and the management wanted to send him home. After a long discussion, Schoey and I persuaded them to give him a chance to redeem himself in the Canterbury game. Even though he'd done wrong, he was a good player – and we were on tour to win games. But if he didn't play well, then fair enough, he would go, and that's what he was told when he was called up to the penthouse suite. He'd let himself and the squad down by going out the night before the game, but during the game he didn't let me and Schoey down, giving everything to earn a reprieve.

I'd been a sub in that game but started at loose forward against Auckland, when a 24-13 defeat meant we would go into the first Test without a win – and without a chance, if you read the local press. It was after that Auckland game that Joe was called Lobster, because he'd behaved like a lobster in boiling water. He'd been blindsided by Auckland's Stuart Galbraith, and although his knees buckled he didn't go down, allowing him to catch up with Galbraith and start an all-in brawl. As captain, I tried to calm people down, but with

Joe that was impossible – he was snarling and livid, a side of him I'd never seen, even when I took him out in the Challenge Cup semi-final defeat at Maine Road. He wanted Galbraith's blood, and was delighted that he was sin-binned rather than sent off so he'd have another chance to get at him.

Once the dust had settled, however, the pressure was on the whole squad, especially me, Schoey and the other senior players who realised how much we had to do before the Test. It was then that the character of the squad shone through – young guys like Phil Clarke, Bobbie Goulding, Shaun Irwin, Gary Price and Ian Smales just got on with the job.

We went behind inside three minutes of the Test series kicking off in Palmerston North when Sam Panapa scored a try. But we hit back quickly when Schoey and Goulding put Jonathan Davies in, so even after they scored again through Tawera Nikau, we were still in the game. I was furious about that try, and had words with the Aussie referee, but our defence dug deep and we pulled level again just before half-time when Schoey, who was having a fantastic game, combined with Paul Dixon to put Carl Gibson over. It got pretty tense in the second half, real bodies-on-the-line stuff for our young guys, until Schoey put us ahead with a drop goal in the 57th minute. I thought we had clinched it when Martin Offiah intercepted on our own line, but the referee blew against us and after that it seemed like an eternity until the hooter went. We'd won the match 11-10, Great Britain's first win in New Zealand for 11 years.

Up next were the Maori, and it was touch and go whether I should play. My Achilles wasn't right, but Malcolm Reilly told me he needed me for what was effectively a fourth Test. Part of my job was to lead the troops by example, so it had to be done. I wasn't the only one battling against injury, and as I've said I couldn't have done it without Dave Fevre's treatment three times a day. Malcolm and Phil Larder were smart enough to let me ease off in training, and I was ready for what turned out to be an immense physical battle.

At St John Fisher school with Andy
Bailey and Adrian Burns, Under-16s
Great Britain Schoolboys.

Wigan St Pats Under-17s (1980-81). What an awesome team to captain, never losing a
game with six out of the squad signing pro.

Early days at Warrington. A good blend of experience and youth.

Let the good times roll!

What a try against Castleford at Wheldon Road in the 1980s, but don't be fooled by the picture.

'Ocker' – Warrington's kit man. The
toughest, shrewdest businessman ever.
© Eddie Fuller

At Cronulla in 1987, I used to meet up with
Joe who was playing with Easts.
© Newspix/News Ltd Archive

The try I am remembered for – going 75 metres to score. GB v Australia 1988.
© Andrew Varley Picture Agency

The World's Strongest Man. No, not me, Jamie Reeve who had won the title in 1989.

The Lancashire Cup, my only major trophy at Warrington as captain.

The 1989 squad that beat New Zealand 2-1 at home. The greatest moment of my rugby league career – captain of Great Britain for the first time.

Captains meet. My good friend Hugh McGann.

It doesn't get any better. Winning a test series with Paul O'Loughlin and Shaun Edwards.
© *Wigan Observer*

Great Britain v Rest of the World at Headingley. Shaking hands with Warrington legend Brian Bevan.

On tour in 1990 enjoying a bit of R and R with two great mates, Kelvin Skerrett and Karl Fairbank.

At Central Park, Wigan. Great team, great memories.

David Hulme did a good job and got me sent off for the only time in my career in the match against Widnes at Naughton Park. Dave and Paul Hulme are the ones I'd always want in the trenches with me.

The British Coal 9s and my very first trophy as captain.

The Maori had seriously big men, every one of them wanting to batter us and knock us off our perch after winning the first Test. Not much was asked of us football wise, but physically we took a bit of a battering off them, myself included. I needed treatment to my Achilles and ankle all through the match, but even if I'd wanted to go off we'd used all our subs so it was grit your teeth time. We came back from 8-2 down at half-time and were leading 16-12 when a couple of minutes from the end I picked the ball up at the base of the scrum, dragged my Achilles 30 metres and sent Paul Eastwood under the sticks for the clincher. It was a great win, with Graham Steadman's experience making a vital contribution, as it did all tour. But at the end of it I could hardly walk, so I knew it would be a big job to be fit for the second Test in seven days time.

I really shouldn't have played, but I knew I had to with us having such a young side. That cliché about putting yourself through the pain barrier would be the right one. We were back in Auckland by now, with another Aussie ref – Bill Harrigan – who did us no favours, caning us 15-3 in the penalty count. It seemed that everything and everyone was against us, especially as we were trailing 14-12 with only nine minutes left in the game. Then Martin Offiah, who had been denied by a few harsh refereeing decisions all through the tour, finally got his just reward with a superb try that won us the match and the series. Kelvin Skerrett's break started it, Schoey – who was a giant on the pitch again – carried it on, and Daryl Powell provided the final pass for Offiah to curve around Kevin Iro to the corner. To be honest, I was in complete agony by then, but when the hooter went and we'd won 16-14, the pain disappeared. The feeling of joy and satisfaction was indescribable.

Not many Great Britain players, and far fewer captains, have won the first two Tests in a series in recent times – in fact at the time of writing it still hasn't happened again. Despite the odds against us, generally low expectations and a dodgy start to the tour, we'd done the job we set out to do. All the squad deserved huge credit, but Schoey was a bit special. I know I keep coming back to him but the way he played, bossing it from stand-off and playing with a young half-back in Bobbie Goulding, with all his personal problems in the lead-up to the Test, was outstanding.

Those personal problems of Bobbie's were undoubtedly the most talked-about part of the tour. Paul Dixon tells the story best because he was there with Bobbie when it happened, in Auckland in the week between the first and second Tests.

The two of them had gone out for a quiet drink in a bar and a few Aussies were in there taking the piss out of them. Bobbie didn't like it – that's his nature – and Dicko had to calm him down. Then one of the Aussie lads went to the toilet, Bobbie gave Dicko the slip, and a matter of seconds later there was a loud commotion coming from the gents. Bobbie had poked this fellow in the eye and laid into him. Dicko and the other Aussie rushed into the toilet, only for Bobbie to start on the other guy as well. Even as a kid, he was a tough little half-back who could fight – these two Aussie lads didn't stand a chance. Dicko pulled Bobbie off them both and everybody returned to the bar, but two police officers arrived. Bobbie still hadn't finished, because when they told him they were arresting him he shouted 'It'll take more than you two to put me in the back of a car,' or words to that effect. Lo and behold, a few more police officers turned up, pinned him down on the floor, handcuffed him and took him away to spend six hours in a cell.

That meant the incident was all over the papers the next day, so Schoey and I had another meeting with the management, just as we had over the David Bishop affair, with the same danger that Bobbie would be sent home. Again, we argued that he should stay, basically pleading youthful insanity on Bobbie's behalf – he was only 18. With the players we were missing, we really couldn't afford to lose him.

The management deliberated about the incident, and it seemed to me touch and go whether Bobbie stayed. They realised it took two to tango, and that there had been provocation, but Bobbie had finished off the dance in his own inimitable style. Fortunately, we won them around again, and Bobbie stayed – after a court appearance when he was fined £500 for assault – had a fantastic game in our second Test win, taming and taking control over his opposite number Gary Freeman. He more than justified the faith Schoey and I showed in him, and remains a great friend of mine – still a big character, as he showed most recently with the amazing job he did as player-coach of Rochdale Hornets. He's got the will, determination, passion and character to get the best out of players, and in time can make it to the very top of the tree as a coach.

The Auckland incident had a weird postscript when Bobbie received a letter from the Black Power Gang. They sent him a copy of a newspaper from 1969 with a report of Malcolm Reilly being involved in a bar room brawl in Sydney when he was playing for Manly. For reasons that remain a mystery, this Auckland gang seemed to take Bobbie under their wing, and followed his progress for the rest of the tour.

Winning the series meant as much to our coaches, Malcolm and Phil, as it did to us. Even though we'd beaten the Kiwis at home the year before, no-one had given us a chance on tour because of all the players missing, so it was a different and special feeling. They'd put so much effort into preparing us, and I was proud that we'd given them what they deserved. Everyone in the squad did their bit, and Maurice Lindsay looked after us the night after that Auckland win – we had one hell of a party. We all stayed together, and you could say we painted the town red, white and blue.

There was still a third Test to play in Christchurch the following week, with the chance of completing a 3-0 whitewash and with two World Cup points also riding on the match. It was a game we could and should have won, with a rare error by Martin Offiah when he dropped the ball after a super length of the field move costing him a second try that would have got us home. That would have been the icing on the cake, but it had still been a great tour. Players like Kelvin Skerrett, Martin Dermott, Phil Clarke, Denis Betts and Bobbie Goulding had come of age as internationals, and leading the team was a pleasure as well as an honour, despite the odd sticky situation. We'd started as no-hopers, with a first defeat in Papua New Guinea, but went home heroes.

Winning that series as captain would have to be the high point of my international career, although it's hard to compare these things and, as I've already said, beating the Aussies in Sydney in 1988 was a great moment as well.

I'd had the odd tricky moment as captain, notably after the first Test win when the New Zealand press brought up my ill-advised 'Tough Shit' comment from the previous year. At least that allowed me the chance to explain I hadn't meant to be cocky, and should have chosen my words better, but the fact they were so interested in it was a backhanded compliment I suppose, showing that we'd got the Kiwis a bit rattled.

That great series win did come at a personal cost for me. As well as the Achilles and ankle problems which I'd been playing through all tour, I badly dislocated my finger late in the third Test. It was pulled and put back, set up and strapped and I carried on playing in the game, but because I didn't look after it properly in the aftermath of the tour it ended up costing me the chance of playing in the first two Tests against Australia the following autumn – and has never been right since.

The management had arranged for us to have four days' R and R in Hawaii, which was a great way to end such an enjoyable and successful tour. It was absolutely stunning, one of the most beautiful places I'd seen, and I had another treat after that – not Wigan, but Mauritius, where I was heading for a fortnight's holiday. But I'll always regret not having an operation on my finger before I went. I thought that when I took the strapping off after four days, it would be okay, but I still couldn't bend it fully and when I came back home from Mauritius the joint had deteriorated so much that I needed to have it pinned.

Missing the start of the 1990 Ashes series was especially hard to take because the first Test was played at Wembley, where Ellery Hanley led Great Britain to a famous 19-12 win. I was still out when the British Lions went so close to securing the series in the second Test at Old Trafford, only to be denied by Mal Meninga's last-gasp try, so it was all to play for when I returned as a substitute in the third Test at Elland Road. Sadly we lost 14-0 and the Ashes went back once again to Australia, a massive disappointment after such a close series – and unbeknown to me at the time, my last Great Britain appearance.

I ended with 20 caps, nine of them as captain – a record I'm proud of, although obviously I would have liked to have played the extra games for my country that injuries denied me.

5

LIFE'S A BEACH – CRONULLA AND SALFORD

My move to the Cronulla Sharks came about after speaking with my teammate Paul Bishop, who at the end of the 1986–87 season was going back home to Australia. He lived over there with his parents – his father was the great Tommy Bishop who played with distinction for Cronulla, St Helens and Great Britain. Paul said that the club needed a back-rower so I thought, why not? I'd love to play over there. I put my name forward and the Sharks were quite keen.

I told Warrington what I wanted to do and, after an initial reluctance, they agreed to let me play in Australia. The only drawback was with Joseph Naden Contracting, which was owned by the Warrington director Peter Higham who was later to become chairman at Wilderspool. I had worked for the company since turning professional and was an estimator by trade. I asked them for six months' leave whilst I went over to play for Cronulla, but they wouldn't allow me that length of time off. I had enjoyed working at the company but wanted to pursue my ambition of playing rugby league in Australia, so I decided to leave the firm. When I came home I would have no job to go back to, but this was a once-in-a-lifetime opportunity to play in the best competition, against the best players in the world and test myself.

I played for Warrington in the Premiership Final at Old Trafford when we lost 8-0 to Wigan and the following day, with my bags and boots packed, I flew out to Australia. Paul should have been flying out with me but he had to sort some things, so I made the long journey over on my own. I had flown before but not for the length of time that it took to arrive in Sydney, where I was met by Cronulla's chief executive, Peter Riley. It was my 23rd birthday. Peter drove me to the ground and showed me around; it was very different from what I had been used to. They had what is called a Leagues Club on one side of the ground, with thousands of poker machines, the profits from which provided a lot of funding for the football club.

I had done some research before coming to the club and knew that they were a relatively young side and were coached by the legendary Jack Gibson and assistant coaches Ron Massey and Allan Fitzgibbon, the father of current Sydney City Roosters and Australia second row forward Craig Fitzgibbon. They had an Under-23 side, a reserve side and a first grade side playing in what was then the Winfield Cup.

Even though I had been at Warrington for five years and had played for Great Britain, I knew that it was going to be tough, as I had spoken to Gavin Miller, who had played for Hull KR and was also coming to Cronulla. Gavin had said that they were a good young team and that the game in Australia was a lot more intense than in Great Britain. I had always loved challenging myself and I was prepared to do the hard work to succeed.

I was put in a hotel for a couple of days and then Jack Gibson put me in an apartment with another player they had signed, Errol Hillier. Errol was a top fellow, a big, tall prop forward. It was a second floor apartment and was right on the esplanade and looked over the ocean. The view and the apartment were unbelievable; I lived there for five months and had a great time.

It was also the start of four years when I would play back-to-back rugby league in the close season. I had arrived at the club on the Tuesday morning and I had my first training session that evening. All the players trained together and had other jobs, like I had at home, but what I noticed immediately was how professional they were. That's not to say that Warrington was unprofessional; I just thought that the players had more discipline. In Australia, rugby league was like football at home; it was the number one sport and the papers were full of rugby league news.

During that first training session I met all three coaches and I was in awe of Jack Gibson. He was very inspiring and when he talked you listened, you didn't interrupt. In fact 'Gibbo' was the first rugby league coach to go to America and watch the NFL. Those clubs were full time and he studied the way that they trained, their conditioning sessions and eating patterns. Jack was the first coach to know about aerobic and anaerobic training and use that in his sessions.

Jack was big on defence and that intensity was the biggest difference I found in Australia. The hits were more regular and consistent; defensive attitudes were all about hit and collision. At home we could always play skilful rugby league; over there they were not as skilful but were conditioned defensively. The big difference was how enthusiastic the players were about defence; it got to the stage where the left side would try and out-do the right side and it was good healthy competition. Jack knew the game inside out. He was articulate, smart, a good man to play under and a good man to know.

On that Tuesday, about 50 of us all trained on the first team field and the coaches split us up by position. We did a monster session on defence and although I had done bag and shield work before this was about positional defence. We did inner-tube work, bags, shields and on occasions players coming at us. This was a training technique that I pinched when I became a coach, because all coaches are thieves really. We all borrow ideas and use them for the strengths and weaknesses of teams we are coaching. I got a lot from Jack's training methods.

Over here in training we would work at running with the ball, working on attacking plays, where in Australia there was the emphasis on defence and how you always finished up controlling the offence. It was eye-opening for me and changed my outlook on the game. At home I could defend but now I was given structure and breakdown on the way to defend, which I had never previously been taught to that degree.

After that training session the first team had a review with Jack and the other sides had reviews with their respective coaches. They would look at the video of the previous weekend's game and then preview the forthcoming game. Again this was relatively new to me. Jack was ahead of his time in using the video review and preview. I also pinched that and used the same system when I went into coaching. We hadn't done a great deal of video analysis at Warrington and certainly hadn't gone into great depth on how the team had played the previous game. I later found out when I made the Cronulla first team that this was what it was all about – improving on the review that the team had got the previous week.

What Jack did with the club's new signings was to invite them for dinner at his beautiful house on the bay at Cronulla. Dan Stains, Mal Wheeler, Paul Bishop, Glenn Coleman and I all went round in our second week at the club. What we did was listen to Jack's stories and the way he put them over. What he did for the game of rugby league is phenomenal.

I can remember being on the field at one training session that Allan Fitzgibbon was taking. It was an unopposed exercise when all of a sudden he saw Jack come onto the field with his sheepskin coat on and his big Alsatian dog with him. Jack came on slowly and deliberately and training stopped while he told players where they were going wrong, corrected everything and gently sauntered off the field. On this particular occasion Jack was talking to us and the dog shat on the field, but no-one said anything – not even Allan Fitzgibbon – and we all just listened to Jack regardless. He commanded that kind of respect.

The thing about Jack was that he would say something

with one word rather than a sentence, a sentence rather than a paragraph. He was very much to the point – almost abrupt – he knew exactly what he wanted from his team and got it.

During my time at the club I worked with a woman called Donna Burke who was the first female development officer at Cronulla – the first in the world, I believe. I agreed to it because I wasn't working during the day and this way I would be paid a retainer as well as match payments. We went into schools and this certainly opened my eyes, as it would be with kids as young as seven and as old as 17. The 7-year-olds would have pads, head-guards and mouth-guards and there were hundreds of them playing. Again the comparison is with football over here, where the kids all kick a ball. They kick a rugby ball, pass, hit and tackle. I learned quite a lot from Donna and her staff in the way that they coached kids.

My first game for Cronulla was in the reserve grade side and, although I didn't think I'd a God-given right to play in the first grade, I thought that with my previous experience and having just played in a major final at home I might get straight in. Although I had trained really hard and well since arriving it was not to be. Although I was disappointed, I didn't want to upset Jack. He was very intimidating for a young man like me. He had won Grand Finals and John Monie had been his apprentice, so I just did as I was told, listened and learned as I had done when I began at Warrington.

Our coach was Mark Shulman and we beat Illawarra by 40 points. I played as a ball-playing loose forward and I scored a try on my debut. We played well as a team and after the game we met in the Piano Bar in the Leagues Club and were later joined by the first grade squad after their game. Rugby league in Australia was a full day out for the fans, because the Under-23s, reserve grade and first team all play after each other. The substitutes for the first grade side were picked from the reserves, who had played earlier. My first night out with the boys after that first game was good; they were a great social club as well as being good players.

The following week at our video review I thought I had played really well. What they had at Cronulla was a marking system, where they marked players on offence and defence and, for my first game, I had done okay.

My second game was again for the reserve grade against Balmain at the Leichhardt Oval. They were one of the big teams in the competition. They had Wayne Pearce, Garry Jack, Paul Sironen, Kerry Hemsley, Benny Elias and Ross Conlon, all great players. I played all the game, played well and we just won, so it was a great start for me in reserve grade. The day got even better as I was selected to be on the bench for the first grade against Balmain. Five minutes into the game, my flat-mate Errol Hillier was injured so on I went. It was a lot earlier than I had expected as I had already played 80 minutes and there was only a 30-minute break between games. So it was a bit of a shock; although I wanted to get on I hadn't anticipated it being so quick. In between the games I had drunk quite a bit of Gatorade as well to try to replenish lost fluid. Even though reserve grade was quite fast it was not as fast and as physical as I had been used to with the first team at Warrington. I could live with that, but then – bang! – the step up to first grade was unbelievable.

Craig Diamond, a big second row forward, moved up to prop and I went into the second row with Dan Stains. Dave Hatch was at loose forward and Gavin Miller hooking.

Because I had taken so much fluid I had to get rid of it and at the bottom of the scrum I was sick. The game was so quick and physical that it was a shock to the system. As soon as I got on I knew that I had to make myself sick because I just didn't feel right. I made sure none of the players or fans saw me, because I didn't want this to be my first and last game at the club. I was very discreet but got rid of everything and felt much better.

The game was a blur to me at times, it was so fast. Towards the end we were trailing and I got the ball passed out to me in mistake on the last tackle. The ball should have been for our stand-off, who looked similar to me – blond hair, good looking. I wellied it as far as I could down field and believe it or not Garry Jack knocked on. From the scrum we scored the try that gave us a 36-31 win and I couldn't believe at the time that my kicking skills had won us the game.

At the final whistle I felt like a bit of a hero, playing 80 minutes for the reserve grade and then 75 for the firsts. All the players in the dressing sheds came over and said 'Well done,' even Gibbo the master coach. But I was collapsed on the floor and I bet I didn't move for ten minutes. I had played in two fast physical games and I was completely out of it. I remember Paul Bishop, who had earlier played for the reserve grade, coming over and saying that he had never seen a player do that as well.

So that was a big pat on the back but, come the review, I obviously hadn't played as well as I thought I had, because I was back in the reserve grade. The first team had players like Andrew Ettingshausen, Mark McGaw, Jonathan Docking and Dane Sorenson – a load of talent. The video review basically picked out your mistakes and the coaches thought I had a bit of work to do following my first team appearance from the bench. I was disappointed but after my third reserve grade game the following week I was selected for the First Grade and I stayed in the side for the remainder of the season.

My full debut was against Canterbury and they had a huge pack, the way the Bradford Bulls have now. Warren Ryan coached them and it was the toughest game I had been involved in up to that stage of my career. The standards set by Jack Gibson were tough and the physical demands on my body were awesome but I enjoyed it; I was playing rugby league at the highest level in the best competition in the world.

Socially the players certainly knew how to enjoy themselves and on one occasion we were invited to a 'Jumbo' Tennis charity event in Sydney. It was their version of Wimbledon and also at the event were Joe Lydon, who was playing for Easts, Ellery Hanley, who was at Wests, and Garry Schofield and Lee Crooks, who were attached to Balmain, as well as representatives from other sports. Unfortunately it was raining and the organisers called off the tennis. I had had a few drinks with the Brits and we decided that we would have a go at playing Jumbo tennis with these huge rackets they use. We had a few more beers and got so drunk that when we attempted to play we couldn't because of the state we were in. It didn't go down too well at the event and I don't think rugby league players were invited again. We Brits certainly made an impression but for all the wrong reasons.

I made nine first grade appearances for Cronulla and I scored my one and only try for the team in Round 19 of the competition. We were playing Wests at Endeavour Field, our home ground, and a bomb was put up. All I did was read it and I was at the right place at the right time. I ran 30 metres towards the ball and the defender in the in-goal area let it bounce away from him and I fell on the ball over the line. Not much to it so I can't say it was a sensational try, but I had the satisfaction of scoring against Ellery. Wests were coached by Tommy Raudonikis and were a big, nasty, biting and spitting team. Although I scored a try, Ellery had the last laugh as his team won the game. At least I can say that I've scored a try in the NRL; not many British players can lay claim to that. My win–loss ratio at the club was 50/50 and we just missed out on the play-offs. During my time at Cronulla we had a great team: ET, McGaw; one of the best players there, a little, stocky scrum-half called Barry Russell and his half-back partner, Mike Speechley, who was an awesome defender and always tackled low. He had to retire early because he kept getting concussed. They were fabulous players to play with and to have a good time with. I think that, at the beginning, like anyone new you have to prove yourself to the players and the crowd, but both accepted me straight away. I knew that I had done well in my stint in

Australia and the experience there helped me to become the player I wanted to be.

I never really thought about staying in Australia. I was happy and enjoyed the lifestyle but I had used my stint over there as a learning tool. I do regret not being able to go over again, but Great Britain tours or injuries put paid to that.

During my stay I tried to beat the law, but was too honest for my own good and found out I wouldn't make a good criminal. I drove to a club called Baxters, owned by Peter Tunks, who later came to play and coach over here. I was following Joe Lydon who knew the way and it was a 45-minute drive from my apartment. At the club we got separated and when it was time to leave I couldn't find him. It was throwing it down as I got into my car and when I was driving down an unlit road not knowing were I was, I clipped a parked car. I carried on driving as the weather was getting worse and I ended up in the Kingsford area of Sydney, where Andrew Bailey, who I had played with at Wigan St Patricks, lived. I got him out of bed and slept there overnight.

Before I drove to my apartment the next morning I looked at my car and saw that what I thought would be a small dent was in fact a big dent. I hadn't been there long when Peter Riley rang me and asked if I had been involved in an accident. I thought for a second and told him I hadn't, believing that no-one had seen the glancing blow in the early hours of that morning when it had been dark, wet and I was lost.

I went to training that evening in my dented car and we were doing the video review when Jack Gibson called me over and asked me what I had done. I blurted it all out to him, but Jack wasn't referring to that; he was asking what had I done that weekend. I thought, it's too late now; Jack knew everything and I came clean with Peter Riley. They contacted the police station as someone had witnessed the accident and reported it to them.

I thought the club would get rid of me as a troublemaker; I was a 23-year-old delinquent. Anyway, the club were great about it and I had to pay the owner of the car for the damage

I had caused. The police officer who was dealing with the accident was a big Cronulla fan so I got a signed squad photograph and gave it to him and he sorted out the accident report and I fortunately just got my wrists slapped. It proved that crime doesn't pay and I always played the game after that and to this day.

One of the members of the team at Cronulla was a lad called Michael Wicks and on this particular day he had a meeting with Jack Gibson at Jack's house on the waterfront. He knew he was late and decided to swim across the bay to Jack's house. From one side of the bay to the other it was about a mile and he turned up wet through. Wicksy knocked on the door which was answered by Jack, who looked at him and said, 'Come back when you are appropriately dressed,' and shut the door on him. I don't know whether he walked back or whether he swam back. The thing is that Wicksy was a bit unstable and Jack took him under his wing. He was a phenomenal athlete, probably the hardest hitting player I've ever seen and mad as a hatter. On a couple of occasions he went AWOL for some reason, but he had no regard for his own body or the players he creamed. He just cut opposition players in two and I think if he could have sorted himself out off the field he could have been the next big name in Australia.

On one occasion during training we had a 12-lap time trial around the field and it was a very cold evening. We started at a good pace but Wicksy began sprinting all the way around and he had no shirt on. He sprinted round for four and a half laps and collapsed onto the field and no-one went to him. We carried on with the time trial and Jack and Ron Massey knew what Wicksy was like and left him there. They could see his breath in the cold night air, so they knew he was alive.

He would have been a giant of a player but I think a lot depends on your background. Some players fall by the wayside and some others see it as a lifestyle that they want and drive on to succeed.

I decided that when I returned home without a job to go to,

I wanted to be a full-time professional rugby league player. At the time I was in negotiations with Warrington for a new contract and I told the club my goals and that I wanted to be full-time player. We had our overseas players who were full time, including Bob Jackson who had his own business. It would make it a lot easier for me to train in the Wide Awake Club. Go there in the morning at six, go back to bed for about nine and then train with Chaddy in the Health Club or at the club on training nights. Wigan came in for me whilst I was in negotiations but Warrington came up with what I wanted and I signed a two-year full-time contract with them and felt very fortunate to do that.

On completing that contract at the end of the 1988–89 season I signed a further full-time contract with Warrington, although Wigan again tried to sign me after the 1988 Great Britain tour 12 months into the first contract. With hindsight, I would have made more money going to Wigan and I would have won a lot more trophies at Central Park. But I think loyalty is a big thing; I'm a loyal beast and Warrington had looked after me. I wanted to repay them so I showed faith by staying and I was always happy at the club. I was with a good coach, a great set of lads, and good office staff. I guess you could say that by staying at the same club I wasn't challenging myself by getting out of a comfort zone, but that certainly wasn't the way I saw it.

I don't regret not playing for Wigan but hindsight is a strong tool and everyone could see that Wigan were the team. When we played them I always had a big game and we had a good record against them in league games. The only problem was that when we met in major finals or semi-finals they had the wood over us and always won.

When I parted company with the club at the beginning of the 1994–95 season, I wasn't the same player that I had been. Warrington had been loyal by supporting me when I was injured, but the good things were coming to an end when Keighley and Salford approached me.

Salford came in as John Wilkinson had done in 1982 when

I was ready to turn professional and chose Warrington. John was a gentleman. The coach, Gary Jack, had already signed Sam Panapa from Wigan and he was putting together a good team at Salford: Phil Ford, David Young, Richard Webster, Steve Blakeley, Scott Naylor and Nathan McAvoy – good young lads with a bit of experience thrown in. I agreed to sign for them on a two-year contract on the 2nd of August 1994.

With Gary Jack as coach I thought I had a few good years playing in me. My body was telling me I had had enough but my head was telling me to give it a go. My head ruled my body then and with hindsight it was a big mistake. I didn't offer Salford a great deal when I played for them, which turned out to be not very often. I only made 18 appearances for them after my debut at loose forward on the 21st of August at Wakefield Trinity when we lost 13-10. I made my home debut the following week and we edged home against Hull, 33-28. In my opinion, I only had one good game – at The Willows against Keighley, ironically the other club that had wanted to sign me.

Whilst I was at the club I went as an assistant coach to Wales in the 1995 World Cup. When I came back, I got a knee problem; there was a bit of cartilage damage that I had at Warrington and then I had played again only two weeks after having the arthroscopy. This time though it took me over six weeks to be anything like and I knew then that physically I wasn't the player I was before my knee and Achilles problems. All I can do is apologise to John Wilkinson who put faith in me and paid good money. I let him down through the sheer stubbornness of wanting to carry on playing. I really believed at the time that I did have a bit more in the tank but in reality I was spent. To my teammates at the club and the Salford supporters I can only apologise. Even though I tried, I didn't do the job for them that they wanted, needed and deserved. I realised then it was time to hang my boots up.

I played what ended up being my last game for Salford

and my last game ever of rugby league when I came off the bench on the 3rd of October 1995 at home to Hull and we won the game, 38-22.

I had to tell Andy Gregory, the new coach, of my decision but Greg knew; he had been in a similar situation himself. I just said to him that I couldn't play any more. I had to do the right thing for my own self-preservation later in life. I knew I had to accept that my time as a player was up.

I knew that St Helens had brought in a new coach, Shaun McRae, at the beginning of 1996 and we were playing them. I wasn't fit to play in the game but I went to watch it and after the game I met Shaun for the first time and began chatting with him. He said that he was looking for an assistant and following this initial conversation I met him in the Chalon Court Hotel in St Helens. I knew of his coaching background and his work as a conditioner. He had started as an assistant to Tim Sheens at Canberra Raiders, as a conditioner and coach with Australia under Bobby Fulton, so I had done my homework well.

We talked about life, the game and what he would want and expect from an assistant coach. We were talking on the same wavelength. Shaun was a bit older than me but he knew that the time was right for me to go into coaching and I think I knew that as well. I was coming up to 32 and over the last three years hadn't played many games, due to being injured a lot.

With the job at St Helens on offer the next thing was to see Salford and get released from my playing contract. Andy Gregory, although sympathetic to my circumstances, didn't want this and I understood that. John Wilkinson had paid good money for me – a lot of money for a crock. My life had to go on, the next stage was coaching and I was able to negotiate my release with Salford. I still consider John Wilkinson a good friend and I'll always be grateful to him for releasing me to begin my coaching career at Saints.

6

FIRST STEPS IN COACHING – WALES AND THE SAINTS

I began taking my coaching exams in 1989 because I already knew that I wanted to become a coach when I finished playing the game. I did all my exams at Loughborough in the summer off-seasons, on courses which were run by Phil Larder, the Great Britain assistant coach. I gained the old Level 3 coaching qualification in 1990, but it all changed when David Waite took it over and put fresh coaching systems in place. It's far better now, with coaches knowing the pathways they need to take if they want to become a head coach.

Before David changed the system I had worked with Clive Griffiths who was a type of mentor for me and took me on a number of coaching courses. Clive was also a teacher at Cowley High School and one of my coaching lessons was to take a team of his and do a coaching session on specific areas of the game. The players responded to me and it was a good session. Clive assessed me and we worked together for a number of years. This was good experience for me as I had my coaching badges and was learning how to work with players of all ages.

Out of the blue, Clive Griffiths phoned me up and asked me if I would like to be assistant coach to him with Wales in the 1995 World Cup, which was part of our Rugby League Centenary Celebrations. I was surprised but I jumped at the chance. In 1995, Wales had the likes of Jonathan Davies,

John Devereux, Scott Gibbs, Keiron Cunningham, Rowland Phillips, Allan Bateman, Kevin Ellis, David Young, Paul Moriarty, Mark Jones, Phil Ford, David Bishop, Richard Webster, Kelvin Skerrett, Martin Hall, Neil Cowie – the list goes on.

As I was still playing for Salford at the time I had to ask our coach, Andy Gregory, if I could take up the offer. Greg knew that I wanted to go into coaching; both he and the club were supportive and off I went.

We were based in Cardiff for a month and during that time I learnt a lot under Clive and from the players that I was coaching. The talent we had was second to none and a great bond developed between us. The game that stands out for me during that World Cup was when we beat Western Samoa at the Vetch Field in Swansea. The game was nothing but a physical confrontation between two enormous teams. The intensity of the game was inspiring and the crowd got behind us. The atmosphere was unreal and it showed how passionate the Welsh were about rugby league; we already knew of their passion for union. With the songs ringing out, the evening was so electric that we could almost touch it. It made me want to play. I was coming to the end of my playing career but I think I could have just made it into that Welsh team. I was proud to help Wales as my grandparents on my father's side lived there for 50 years, so I could have squeezed into the squad. Before our games, the Welsh National Anthem was sung but I didn't learn it, as I was never asked to.

The Western Samoa game was the crunch as we had both beaten France in our group games and the Samoans had a better points' difference than us. A draw was no good to us; this was the big one which we had to win to meet England in the semi-finals. The boys defended magnificently in an arm-wrestle and with that crowd behind us we won the game 22-10.

There was no sentiment about my roots as the semi-final against England at Old Trafford loomed. I had a job to do regardless of whom we were playing and I wanted Wales to win because I wanted to reach the World Cup Final against Australia or New Zealand at Wembley. The team gave 100 per cent in front of over 40,000 but on the day we just weren't good enough and we lost the game 25-10. We had been 80 minutes from the final and after the defeat I was absolutely gutted for Clive and the players, because they had put a lot of hard work into it. The nature of our game though is that there is always a winner and always a loser. We put it into perspective and dusted ourselves down and got on with life. Having said that, the whole squad and management and coaching staff did themselves and Wales proud.

During the World Cup campaign we had a lot of down time between matches; in fact Kelvin, Martin and Neil thought they had too much down time. They bought a PlayStation, but they couldn't get it to work with the televisions in their hotel rooms. So they bought a television between them, put it in one of the rooms and used that for the PlayStation. They got bored with that and bought remote-controlled cars and raced them up and down the hotel corridor. They then got bored with those and bought bikes and went biking around the streets of Cardiff. The Wigan lads had too much money as well as too much time on their hands.

For players like 'Jiffy,' Scott Gibbs, Allan Bateman and David Young who had played rugby union for Wales, it was different. In Cardiff they were treated as heroes of the other code – like Premiership footballers. We also had some good nights out together to improve the team bonding and that went from strength to strength throughout the competition. But it wasn't all relaxing; we did have a job to do and when we did it we did it well. At the end of the campaign I was happy with the way I had done my first coaching job.

There had been many false dawns with rugby league in Wales and this World Cup had been played between a truncated centenary season and the advent of Super League. I think that after this successful Welsh World Cup campaign a club should have been established. The game should have struck whilst the iron was hot and ripped into the Principality – not in North Wales but in South Wales, where there was the bedrock of rugby, whether it was league or union; the time was then.

I still believe that we should have a Cumbrian as well as a Welsh team in Super League. I know that we have now got a French side in Les Catalans, but I think we have got to make the game strong on our own soil, where we are always competing with a bigger game in rugby union. The fact is that rugby league is mainly played on the M62 corridor, although we do have amateur clubs all over the country playing in the summer Conference competitions. Rugby union is played all over the country and now all over the world. We have got to secure our game in rugby league's strongholds and that means Cumbria and now Wales, which has established amateur sides, junior development and now the Celtic Crusaders in National League Two.

I know that Workington Town was in Super League in its first season but Workington was relegated. I think that it needs to be a combination of all the professional Cumbrian sides playing together as one. It makes sense to me, although attempts to merge Whitehaven and Workington Town have always fallen through at the first hurdle due to the intense rivalry between the clubs and their fans. At the birth of Super League, clubs were up in arms when amalgamations were first mooted. Perhaps that boat was missed with Whitehaven, Workington, Barrow and Carlisle not joining forces. It would be great to get a Cumbrian Super League side, wherever it is based and for fans to get behind them. The players that have come through there in years gone by and the amateur set-up is second to none. It seems nonsensical to me that so much talent and ambition in Cumbria is not being fulfilled. I just hope it happens one day.

I returned to Salford after the World Cup, but a few months later following my retirement I was at St Helens as assistant coach to Shaun McRae. Also at the club was an old mate of mine, David Howes, who was chief executive. I had known David for years; he was the PR man when I played for Great Britain. He was the one who gave us our wages on the 1988 and 1990 British Lions Tours. He was a very good guy and I knew his door would always be open at Knowsley Road.

It was a great learning curve to be thrown in at the deep end with players that I had played against a few months earlier. Now I was telling them what to do and how to do it, which initially was a little strange but I knew it had to be done. I learned a lot from Shaun and saw that he was a great manager of players. He knew the buttons to push and he got the best from a well-organised team.

Not many people know this, but Shaun was a very good tennis player. Although I had never really played, he offered me a game of racketball, which is a cross between tennis and squash played on a squash court. Shaun was outstanding and to this day I have never won a game against him, although I'm sure he made his own rules up. I thought my fitness would overcome skill, but I was wrong. Shaun always positioned himself where I had to go around him, with all his bulk.

I had been at the club less than a month when St Helens were at Wembley against the re-named Bradford Bulls, formerly known as Bradford Northern, in the first Challenge Cup Final of the Super League era – how lucky was that? It was a game that we were losing 26-12 and a message came down from Shaun to me on the touch-line 'Get a better kicking game.' I passed this on to Brian Case who was the team's messenger and he told captain Bobbie Goulding, who within a short space of time put three bombs up and we scored three tries. On a red-hot day Bobbie put snow on the kicks and fortunately they were so good and put so much pressure on the Bulls' full-back Nathan Graham that we then led the game 30-24. We went further ahead and, although the Bulls pulled it back to two points, Apollo Perelini, who is now conditioner at the club, scored the decisive converted try and we won an amazing game 40-32. It was the highest-scoring final and the biggest comeback in the long history of the Challenge Cup – it was an amazing game.

It had been played in baking hot conditions and Brian Case came off the field after the game wet through after all the running on and off, passing on Shaun's instructions. He was as shattered as the players.

It was the final in which Robbie Paul scored a hat-trick, the first player to do so at Wembley; he scored the final one in a run from the halfway line. Robbie was a great player – he had electric pace, he could turn on a sixpence and had the uncanny ability to stop dead, spin out of a tackle and to go again. Robbie was awarded the Lance Todd Trophy as man of the match; I think any other year Bobbie Goulding would have won it after changing the course of the game, but it was a tremendous feat for Robbie to score a hat-trick in a defeated side.

Who would have believed it? A Wembley winner after only a month at Knowsley Road. At one stage during the game when we were behind, I thought my Wembley hoodoo was going to stay with me after my disappointments as an injured Wigan schoolboy missing the schools game and the 1990 final defeat by Wigan. The way Bradford had been playing, the deficit we had to overturn looked too much, but the boys came up with those special plays and two of the unlikeliest players got over the try line that day in Simon Booth and Ian Pickavance.

It was a funny feeling as we won the game and the hooter sounded because the win was mainly for the players. I think the old adage is that players win games and coaches lose them. I have nothing but praise for the way the side came back from the brink of defeat for an amazing win.

What I found out was that, as an assistant coach, I was mainly the link between the players and the head coach. The players don't necessarily want to go straight to him and I found at St Helens that they would come to me if they had any ideas or if there was something on their minds. I would then liaise with Shaun, discuss it and if needs be Shaun would speak to the player concerned. It was another aspect of learning the coaching ropes, when I was captain at Great Britain and Warrington I had been in discussions with players and the coaches all the time. Now I was being involved in it from a different angle and seeing it in a new perspective. This was now my working environment and I was absorbing all the information as I could, as I had done as a player.

One thing I recognised quickly with Shaun was that he was very meticulous. His preparation on the opposition left no stone unturned. We knew everything about who we were playing and the way we were going to play against them. That was one thing I really tried to emulate with teams that I coached; I think that attention to detail is the 'X' factor needed, especially in today's climate where teams are pretty close together. You can have Wakefield closely beating Leeds, Wigan and Widnes, but the nature of the game is that the best-prepared team generally wins. If St Helens was playing Leigh and Leigh has prepared well and Saints hasn't, I think it comes down to a bit more ability. But if your team is the better group of players and is prepared for the game, then your team will win the game nine times out of ten. A good player should always outplay an average player, but if the good player comes up short then the average player will turn him over. It happens, but not so often now with the way teams are prepared and put together.

As well as learning from Shaun's attention to detail, I learned how he dealt with players. I saw that coaching was about 30 per cent of the game and getting the best out of the players was 70 per cent. Coaches have to get to know their players inside and out, know how they tick and what makes them buzz. That's all down to man-management because there's only so much coaching possible for a game. There's only so many moves possible and the other coaches know as much as you. The difference is the players' talent, ability, attitude, mental approach and how to get the best out of those players and how players feed off others. What works at one time in a game may not work at another and a coach has to come up with different strategies for different games, different teams and different individuals. So my learning curve of watching, listening and asking questions continued; I learned a hell of a lot from Jack Gibson, Shaun McRae and David Waite – probably the three most influential coaches in the world.

I also picked up things from my coaches at Warrington – Kevin Ashcroft, Reg Bowden, Tony Barrow, and Brian Johnson. As I've said previously, a coach is a bit of a thief and takes ideas from everyone. I absorbed everything from every coach and every player I played with or against. I took what I needed as head coach and disregarded what I didn't believe in. I got rid of quite a few things because the nature of the game has changed and what worked well in the early 1980s wouldn't work well now. The game has evolved through players being full-time in Super League and coaches have to use the time a lot better if the players are to utilise their time to learn as much as possible.

Another big part of my duties at the club was video analysis. We had a computer system and I would put all the information into it, which would take about four hours. The computer would break down every play during the game. I went in the following morning and I had an individual tape of what, for example, Steve Prescott had done during the game, what Anthony Sullivan had done and so on for the rest of the players.

Once they had been put together, I would go though the game with the players Shaun wanted me to see and he would see the others. It was hard work but the players benefited from having the whole of their game taped throughout the season. Imagine the likes of Keiron Cunningham and Bobbie Goulding, for example, their game tapes would sometimes be between ten and 15 minutes long, whereas a winger may only have a two minute tape of his involvement.

At the end of my first season, St Helens won the Super League Championship to complete the League and Cup double and it was the first time the club had won the Championship for 20 years. I felt more affinity with them by then. I had done a lot more work for the club and I felt part of it, whereas in the Cup Final I had only had a bit part as I had only just arrived. I didn't think I had contributed anything to that win as I was just finding my feet in the new role. But with winning this inaugural Super League Championship of the summer era I felt that I had worked hard and contributed towards it.

We had Wigan breathing down our necks going into the final game a point behind us and we had to win the game to win the Championship. Our destiny was in our own hands against my old club, Warrington. We win, we win the Championship; we lose, we hand the title to our deadliest rivals, Wigan. There was no time for sentiment. I was now a Saint through and through, a big statement for a Wiganer who had played the majority of his career at Warrington. I knew where my bread was buttered.

We played the game at Knowsley Road in front of over 18,000 fans and we thrashed Warrington 66-14 to become Champions. The St Helens fans got behind the team and what a great feeling it was for me and everybody concerned with the club when the hooter sounded the end of the game. The celebrations began but I think the previous coach Eric Hughes deserves some credit. Before Shaun's arrival, Eric had got this squad of talented players together and it was he who brought Bobbie Goulding to the club. Maybe they became a bit hungrier when Shaun and then I arrived, but Eric's side had run Wigan close in the Regal Trophy final earlier that year at Huddersfield and I think he should be applauded for what he did in setting the foundations.

With the birth of Super League and playing in summer, the players went from part-time to full-time as they trained during the day. This was far better than my playing days which had just finished at Salford, when we trained at night for a couple of hours, normally in cold, wet weather. It gave us freedom in the amount of time we could have with the players. We could do weights in the morning, and then later in the day bring them back for the video analysis. What I found as a coach was that once the players had left, you had to prepare the daily, weekly and monthly training schedules and plan ahead what you were going to do.

During the switch of seasons, we did a lot of training at the front of the Knowsley Road ground but there was dog muck and broken glass all over the field. We thought that this wasn't professional so David Howes did a deal with Edge Hill College and we started training there. The facilities were good, the field was flat but we found in winter that it blew a gale. We found that a lot of pre-season work was affected. Our times for a 600-metre run were way out because the boys were being blown all over the place and we had to reassess our times in accordance with the weather conditions. We also got a machine for tackling technique, a big steel apparatus with spring-loaded pads – a bit like a scrummaging machine for two people who could hit it at the same time. I stood on the machine and took the forwards and Shaun would take the backs. On one particular occasion we had Ian Pickavance and Andy Northey working together – two good lads but daft as brushes. They had seen the exercise done so they went, hit the floor, got up, hit and drove the machine. They then had to change over and I think Andy got his left and right mixed up and both players hit the same hole. There was blood and snot all over the machine as they had collided with each other full whack. They didn't need stitching up but they were dazed and concussed.

I also coached the Under-21 side so life was pretty hectic. I had the Under-21 side and Brian Case coached the Under-18s' side, so the days were long but enjoyable. I had some good young players in my Under-21s' side – players of the calibre of Scott Barrow, Paul Wellens, Mike Bennett, Anthony Stewart and Mark Edmondson. Scott went on to play rugby union and was a great talent; he was my captain at one stage when I coached the England Academy side. There was some superb talent in that side and in my final season at

St Helens we won the Under-21s' Cup final.

In my second season with Shaun the club again reached the Challenge Cup Final at Wembley and it was a repeat of the previous year against the Bradford Bulls. The game wasn't as high scoring as the previous year. Tommy Martyn opened the scoring for us and scored a second to level the game after the Bulls had gone into the lead. We had been thoroughly outplayed but on the stroke of half-time Andy Northey somehow managed to drive over through a ruck of players to give us a lead. We stretched the lead further in the second half before the Bulls pulled some points back but we ran out 32-22 winners to retain the Challenge Cup.

The combination between Bobbie Goulding and Tommy Martyn was the difference between the two sides and Tommy's tries and overall contribution saw him awarded the Lance Todd Trophy. Tommy was a mercurial talent and character and he could do things with the ball that other payers wouldn't even attempt. He had a fantastic left foot and an elegant, long, kicking game. He also had a deft touch with his short kicking, which was phenomenal. All that Tommy lacked to go with his great ball skills was that blistering pace for a stand-off. He had been unlucky with injuries and had had a few knee operations which slowed him down. His ball distribution, his vision and reading of the game were superb; he could see things other players couldn't see and his combination with Bobbie was fantastic. They were poetry in motion at times and Tommy was a gifted player – one of the best never to play for Great Britain. That was largely because of his injuries, but he played a significant part in Ireland's adventure in the 2000 World Cup.

The camaraderie and the spirit that we had within the club was second to none and in that second Cup-winning season we finished third in the league and the following year fourth in the league. At the end of that season, it still upsets me that, after everything we had done so well at the club, we all got sacked. They didn't renew David Howes,' Shaun McRae's or my contract, which was a technical term for the sack. I believe it was because the board had lost a bit of power because of the bond that we had created between the players and ourselves. David Howes had worked tirelessly for the club but I think he could see the writing was on the wall and knew what was coming. To me, it seemed we were sacked by the board for being too successful and even now I find it hard to understand why.

All three of us moved down different pathways; David Howes went to the Leeds Rhinos, Shaun moved to the newly-formed club, Gateshead Thunder, who went straight into Super League, and me, I chose the glamour route and went as head coach to Swinton Lions.

7

THROWN TO THE LIONS

After St Helens I had nowhere to go, as the decision not to renew my contract had come out of the blue. I became aware that the head coach's job at Widnes Vikings had come up, even though Colin Whitfield was the caretaker coach there. Lee Crooks, Mike Ford, Dave Ellis and I applied for the job and all of us were interviewed.

I met big Jim Mills, Sammy Evans, the chairman Tony Chambers and the rest of the board. I gave a good interview and maybe I priced myself out of the job. I was asked what my expectations were but what I should have done was put it back to them and said that I wanted the going rate for a head coach, because to be quite honest I really didn't know what the going rate was at that time. It wasn't something that came up in conversation when I was a player; that part of the job was between the individual and the club.

Widnes were a better than average team and a massive club, so I wanted the job and I wanted it quite badly. I had served my apprenticeship under Shaun McRae and Clive Griffiths and with the Great Britain Academy side. I thought my natural progression was to head coach, but the Widnes board didn't give me the job and Colin Whitfield was appointed on a part-time basis; he was a postman away from rugby league.

The directors could appoint who they wanted, but I was absolutely gutted when I didn't get the job. When I came back home and knew I hadn't got the job, I thought to myself maybe coaching isn't for me. It was a drastic way of looking at it but there were no coach's jobs going. There were a lot of Australians in coaching positions over here, as well as a host playing, so I was a bit disillusioned. I really thought I had gone as far as I was going in rugby league and that I was better off out of it. So I thought about the Fire Brigade and the Police, going as far as enquiring for details, and I was ready to apply to both of them.

I was fortunate that Malcolm White, the chairman of Swinton Lions, telephoned me out of the blue and asked me if I would coach the club with Les Holliday. I had a meeting with Malcolm and Tony Barrow, who at that time was the chief executive at the club and who I knew from my Warrington days. This took place at Bury Football Club at Gigg Lane, where Swinton were based. I had a very productive meeting and Malcolm asked me to come on board there and then. I had a meeting with Les Holliday, who had coached the side for a number of years, but he was finding it difficult because he worked regular nights between 10 pm and 6 am. Les told me that it was hard work for him, although I knew from experience that joint coaches didn't work. There always has to be someone at the helm of the ship steering. The nature of the beast is that we all have different opinions on certain aspects of rugby league and this was no different. Les couldn't carry on the way he wanted, so I took over as part-time head coach of the club.

The players continued to train near Bury, where the football team trained. It was an area of fields and an all-weather pitch, but we also trained a few times at Bury RUFC. So we were nomads, as the club itself had been since the sale of the famous old Station Road ground, because of Swinton's financial problems. We did this for a while, but I wasn't happy with the standard of the training fields and at the time I was very friendly with the coach and chairman at Orrell RUFC, Sammy Southern. I wanted to change training from Bury to Orrell because it made a lot of sense. A lot of the Swinton players came from the Wigan, St Helens, Leigh, Warrington area and we only had a few from Salford. Orrell was a bit further afield for the players based in Salford to travel, but I considered that it was the best move for the club. I spoke to Malcolm and Tony and they agreed; the chairmen met and a deal was done. We used the training fields on Tuesday and Thursday evenings and Saturday mornings.

The job at Swinton was part-time, but I did get a car and a telephone. We had a squad of players, a physio in Norman Brown and a kit-man in Eric Skeetch, but we didn't have a conditioner. Maybe that was down to me as head coach, but I had enough on my plate coaching the team. Ideally, I wanted someone to come in and take conditioning sessions and speed work, so I could take smaller groups in situational coaching.

The first person I spoke to about this was Phil Chadwick who I had worked and trained with during my playing days at Warrington. He had moved on to London Welsh with Clive Griffiths, but he was missing his family. I spoke to him and he wanted to come back into rugby league, but I could only offer him a part-time position for next to no money, as our budget wasn't the biggest. Fair play to Malcolm White, he dipped into his own pockets as he had always done at the club and I completed my best-ever signing. Phil was invaluable to me, even during a period when he was travelling up and down between Orrell and London, serving his notice. That's the way he is and he didn't want to let anyone down. He also got his old job back at Warrington Council, so it was busy times for him incorporating that with his job at Swinton.

My first game in charge was against Steve Hampson's side, Chorley. I tried to change the way we played, although not too much as I didn't want to confuse the players. In a tough game we played okay and won the game, but not convincingly. I had players who could actually play a bit, but it was hard for me having come from a full-time role at St Helens. I had to change my own mentality and outlook on the game and not to expect too much from the players. Certainly there were heavy demands on their time. Some had physical jobs; some couldn't get away from work. I had all this to deal with as well as coaching and it seemed to me that I had been spoiled at St Helens. On reflection this was a massive learning curve for me. It was like being back in the early 1980s when I was playing at Warrington, but the job had to be done and I had to give it 100 per cent and more.

That first season in charge, Malcolm gave me a bit of money to spend. Players like Sean Casey, Paul and Tony Barrow, Ian Watson, Jimmy Evans, and Mark Bateman were all under contract. The money I got brought in the likes of Ian Pickavance, Jon Neil and Phil Veivers – older, wiser, more mature players. These were to complement a relatively young team, with players like Wayne English, Shaun Furey and Mick Nanyn. They were all good, young talent but very raw and I thought the best way forward was to get senior players in who could do the job. We did okay that season, we won 50 per cent of our games and I was looking forward to the following season and building on this.

The problem was that Malcolm was unable to offer any money, so during that following off-season I must have spoken to 50 players, offering them winning and losing pay. I spent hours and hours on the telephone with players and, come the first training and conditioning session, only six players turned up out of the 50. I couldn't blame them; some had been offered more money at other clubs, some had decided to retire from the game. It was hard work. Chaddy and I had prepared everything for that pre-season and to see only six players at that first session was disheartening.

But I learned more at Swinton than I could ever have imagined, dealing with all sorts of players, with a wide range of playing ability and a wide range of rugby league intelligence. I remember cleaning the changing rooms with my backroom staff before the players arrived for games on Sundays, following the footballers playing at Gigg Lane the previous afternoon. It was a necessary evil; nobody moaned, we all rolled up our sleeves and got on with it. We all did our own jobs and more if it was needed.

I also learned about the finances of the club, which was enlightening; what went where, how much had we got for players and the working and running of the club – the stuff which not even the loyal supporters of the club knew about. I had a good working relationship with Tony Barrow. He left me to do everything in relation to the coaching side of the club and would advise me on other matters.

I also had a very gifted person to fall back on in John Prince. He was the development officer for Swinton, so he went around schools, coaching and selling the game. He was excellent at that and put a lot of hard work into the town, even though we played our games at Bury, a few miles up the road. John was invaluable to me in relation to players I didn't know or had heard very little of. Whenever a name would crop up, he knew everything there was to know about them.

That first season with Chaddy and the rest of the backroom staff was great and during that time there is one game that stands out and that was when we were drawn at home to St Helens in the Challenge Cup. Cup competitions seem to do this sort of thing, pairing players and coaches against former clubs soon after they have gone their separate ways. This was no different for me, as I had left the club some months earlier after three enjoyable years cutting my teeth in coaching. I knew the players there very well, although there were some new faces, like Kevin Iro, for instance, and the new coach in charge was Ellery Hanley.

It was a daunting task to play against St Helens but we had a game plan to play football and hit them on the edges if we couldn't go through them or over them. Sean Casey took the game plan on board and scored a great individual try for us. He chipped over from the halfway line, and passed to Matt Bateman who went over for a superb try. Sean was the captain of the side and a good leader on the field. He was a very talented player who had begun his career at St Helens but had left the club prior to my arrival.

All our players had turned up to play and at half-time we led by 16-10, but Saints turned it around in the second half, showing the difference between part-time and full-time players, and won the game 36-22. It was Keiron Cunningham and a Kevin Iro hat-trick that did the damage. So it was not to be; there are not usually Challenge Cup upsets these days, especially from sides in the lower divisions against Super League opposition, although for a long time we did run Saints close. I was really proud of the way we played that afternoon and there was a great gesture by Ellery Hanley after the game. He asked me whether he could talk to my players and I said that he could. He was really emotional and said 'If you play like that and stick together the way you did you'll all be successful.' For a man of his stature to say that to some up-and-coming young players was a big boost to their confidence.

That side of Ellery is something that not a lot of people know about, because they have a different perception of him. I have played with and against him and have known him for many years and I think I know what he is like as a person. The gesture that he made showed the type of person that he really is.

On the field, he was always a very, very talented player who had received some bad press early in his career, rarely trusted reporters and didn't give interviews. So in their eyes he may have seemed bad news. But the Ellery I have known is not that type of person and other players within the game who played with him would echo my sentiments. He is a very knowledgeable and caring person, but most of all he is a friend to this day.

Last year he was inducted into the Rugby League Hall of Fame, which just shows the stature and the high regard he is held in, in this country and Australia, although he only had a couple of short spells down under. Not many English players have received the Golden Boot for being the best player in the world. Ellery has achieved that and every other honour in the game, apart from winning the Ashes – and many other greats have failed to do that since 1970. So I think it is right and fitting that he should have been inducted into the Hall of Fame, something that can never be taken away from him. All the players of his era would say what a great captain and leader he was in those Great Britain and Wigan sides.

If the game against St Helens was the one that stood out in my first season for the club and myself, a game the following season stood out as the low point for me – the Challenge Cup tie at home to the Leeds Rhinos who had been the beaten finalist the previous year. We had lost a lot of players and didn't have a wealth of experience but again I learned a lot from the game. Dean Lance was the coach and the likes of Brett Mullins, Bradley Clyde, Iestyn Harris, Keith Senior, Adrian Morley, Barrie McDermott and Kevin Sinfield were all playing.

We lost by a record 106-10 and everything that could go wrong did go wrong in that game. There was a big crowd at Gigg Lane that day and when Leeds hit the 100-point mark it was the lowest point of my coaching career. But they say you find out a lot about yourself, your staff and players when the shit hits the fan. I thought I would have a chat with Tony Barrow about resigning but he said 'No' and my staff said 'Don't' as did a few of the players. On reflection I think that it would have been a cheap and easy option to throw my hand in after that record defeat. I knew myself that I was a better coach than that and the players knew it too, but we caught a very good Leeds team on a very good day. I've never watched that game to this day. I didn't do a video review on it; I just put it to bed as a bad day at the office. It was a case of the cliché: 'Dust yourself off and start all over again.'

After the defeat, I went into the dressing room and the players looked devastated. It was like a mortuary and I went into the physio room to reflect. I was devastated as well and I just needed to be on my own, but I was being selfish to the players and the rest of my backroom staff. The players needed ice, the physio needed his room and we needed to do our normal post-match warm-down so we didn't change a thing.

I felt it as badly as the players and it would have been very easy to give them all a bollocking. It would have been hard to be constructive after that performance so I thought if I couldn't say anything helpful, don't say anything. All I said to the players was about the way that Leeds had played.

I had to go and meet the press and I had little choice but to be humble when I spoke to them. From there, after getting changed, I went to meet the fans, the sponsors and our chairman, Malcolm White, and speak with them about the defeat.

I'm the person I am today because of these kinds of situations, that's when I found out about myself and what's inside me. It's great when everything's running smoothly and the team is winning games, but when the team begins losing and things don't go according to plan that's when character shines through. I believe that, first and foremost, I'm a fighter. That's who I am. I think that showed in the demands I put on myself as a player, as a coach and going through this illness now.

That is what I demanded of my players and it didn't always happen. After the St Helens game the big call was to turn up with that same playing attitude for the next game, but we lost the week after. Following the defeat against Leeds, we turned up with the right attitude and won the next game. It was a case of when we won we were all in it together and when we lost we were all in it together and that's what made us a team. I believed emotionally and physically we had a tight unit, whether we won or lost. As a team, squad of players, coach, and backroom staff we were all going in the same direction and had the same goals.

At the end of that second season in charge of the club we finished fifth from bottom. Even taking into account our struggles prior to that campaign, I looked on it as a poor season. We wanted to improve and we showed in the first season that money could at times buy you that better-prepared player, whether you had £1, £1,000 or £1,000,000. I think it speaks volumes in football today when you look at Chelsea; money does make a difference.

The other highlight in my second season was when we went up to Whitehaven. I was told that we hadn't won up there for a long time. It was always tough going up to Whitehaven, especially at that time as my mate Paul Cullen had taken over coaching duties from Kevin Tamati. I knew that they would be well prepared for the game and I had also lost a good player in Howard Hill to them. He was from that area and he went back home because of the money that they offered him. I had no problems with that because rugby league is a short career; if anyone can make a few bob then good luck to them.

Whitehaven is not the friendliest of places and the players got changed in what only can be described as a shed; a few years earlier players changed in a railway carriage. When we went onto the field it was heavy and it was a damp, cold night. Whitehaven had a stubbornness about them, but we played very well and we just nicked a result. Mick Nanyn had a big game for us and it was the first time I had won at Whitehaven; it was a special day.

Paul was okay about the defeat because it had been a close run game and the result could have gone either way. I knew that Paul was a fighter as a player on the field and at Whitehaven and now at the Warrington Wolves his sides are going to have his same mindset, determination and physical toughness.

At the end of the season I took the England Academy side on the tour of New Zealand and Australia and on returning I had a meeting with Malcolm White. Basically, he came out with the old one 'We're not renewing your contract.' He said that he wanted a coach who had more understanding of the amateur game and had more contacts within that game; they wanted more ties with the amateur set-up. I had a few contacts, although not many, and I understood were he was coming from.

I could understand and accept not having my contract renewed a bit more easily than when the same situation happened at St Helens. I had been successful there and that was hard to take, especially when I didn't get the Widnes Vikings job. But I hadn't done well at Swinton. I believe I coached well and got the best from the players but I could only do so much. With the way the club were going down the amateur route I could accept it, although I didn't like being out of a job. Also out of a job at the club was Chaddy, whose contract wasn't renewed either but he had his full-time job to fall back on.

When I left I started thinking again about leaving the game and joining the Police or Fire Service. I was out of work, my wife Erica was heavily pregnant with Ben and our other son, Sam, was nearly four. It was a very emotional time, having a young family and being out of work. It was hard for me to take, as I wasn't expecting the decision when I met Malcolm. During my first year as part-time coach at Swinton, Erica was working during the day and I looked after Sam. I took him to the nursery, I would get the tea ready and when Erica arrived home I would go training with the team. But there was a change around the corner, because the following year Malcolm Reilly gave up the job with the England Academy and I took over the reins.

8

ACADEMIC EXCELLENCE

I first became involved in the England Academy set-up in 1997 through Joe Lydon, who was performance director with the Rugby Football League. I guess I was in the right place at the right time with a bit of nepotism thrown in as well. I had already got my coaching qualifications and was working as an assistant coach at St Helens. It was time for me to put my own individual stamp on the coaching system for kids and it was a job I really enjoyed doing. When I was at 6th Form College I had gone back to my old school at John Fisher to do some coaching with the kids, so I had always been interested in that side of the game. I also saw it as another stepping-stone to bigger and better things.

I knew I still had a lot to learn but from the coaches I had played under I had gained a lot of knowledge and with Shaun McRae at St Helens I had a good mentor. The kids I had at the start were very talented and many of them have gone on to represent the country in full internationals; players like Terry Newton, Lee Gilmour, Paul Johnson and many, many more.

In fact, I am probably the only person in the history of the game not to select Stuart Fielden. When I first saw him he was 17 and I could see what talent he had, but he had another year to go before he was eligible for selection for the Great Britain Academy side. I could see he had the makings of a monster and I was smart enough to pick him the following year.

In that first year, we played international games against France. If we had played them on a level playing field we would have murdered them at Under-18s so they came up with Under-19 and Under-21s' teams. We played the French side in a curtain raiser at Elland Road and Danny Orr captained my team. It was a good, entertaining game that we only just won and a great start for me.

We then went over to France to play them in their own back yard and I had Stuart Wilkinson, who is now involved at Wigan, as my assistant. The team played a blinder, putting in a sensational performance and leading something like 38-14 with time up on my watch. I came out of the stand, went down to the dugout and began thanking everybody as I awaited the final whistle. Time was up but the referee kept playing on and playing on and giving penalty after penalty until France scored. I thought it must be time now, but the referee restarted the game and I became irate with the French officials. Nothing had changed since I had first played against them all those years ago. We continued playing and they scored another try. We had played on for over eight minutes and I became angrier, having a go at the referee, something out of the Alex Ferguson and Sam Allardyce school of management. I wasn't happy with the way he was taking liberties with my team; all he was doing was making the score look respectable. I thought no way have they got time for another restart but how wrong was I? Off we went again and by now I had completely blown my gaskets and hurled even more abuse at the referee. All of a sudden, the referee held up play and I thought that was it, but he walked over to me and sent me off. I turned around and walked back into the stand and then he blew up for full-time. The players shook hands with everyone apart from the officials and they weren't to be denied victory by this man. I can't remember his name but I know that I would be able to pick him out in a line-up even now. I still bear a grudge and he is up there with another Frenchman who decided to reconstruct my facial features.

The manager of the Academy side was Jim Hartley, who had been a director at Wigan but was by then at St Helens. We go back a long way and Jim was with the Academy during the two stints I was involved in the set-up. I told him that we were not going to go to the reception after this shambles and that I wasn't happy with the way the referee had conducted himself throughout the game. Talk about spitting the dummy. I don't know how I would have been if we had lost the game. Jim, ever the diplomat convinced me to go, so the players, coaches and management went to the reception. In France there is never really a meal as such, just tit-bits and the players were starving. I said to Jim that we should go, but Jim had to do his bit and thank the local dignitaries, the French management, coaches, players and match officials. The referee, the smarmy little bastard had a smirk on his face all night and I went over to him smiling, shook his hand and in a low quiet voice said: 'Don't referee one of my games ever, ever again.' I think he got the message from that *tête-à-tête*, as it wiped the smirk off his face, I promise. We all left the reception for burger and chips and I let the boys have a victory glass of wine.

In my second year in charge, we again had a two Test series and this time I picked Stuart Fielden. Also in that squad were Kevin Sinfield, Scott Barrow, Paul Wellens, Chris Thorman and Chev Walker, now playing in rugby union with Bath. Once again we beat France at home and away and the previous season's referee wasn't in charge of either game.

After the second series' win I stood down as England Academy coach as a result of being appointed first team coach at Swinton. It was my first job in that capacity at a club and I wanted to put all my energies into it. The consensus of opinion was that Malcolm Reilly, my Great Britain coach as a player, would take over my job with the Academy side and everything fitted into place. It was a disappointment not to have an opportunity to work with Malcolm, knowing what I could have learned from him, but my priority was Swinton. The Great Britain coaching job became available and Malcolm and David Waite both applied for the position. David got the job as well as the job of coaching and technical director. Malcolm wanted the Great Britain job and when he wasn't chosen he decided to resign from his coaching role with the Academy side.

I've always felt that home-grown talent is needed to coach a country. I think that it's a passionate job and one that a coach should be proud to do. That's not to have a go at anyone coaching a national team who is not from that country, but I feel that it means more if the coach is from that country. In football, Sven-Goran Eriksson was the England coach, but surely the job he would want is to coach his own country, Sweden. Having said that, the best thing that happened to me as a coach was David Waite. He made me look at things differently, made me a far better thinker and had a major influence on my career.

Nick Halafihi, who had taken over from Joe Lydon at the Rugby Football League, contacted me. I knew Nick from St Helens when he was the academy manager, and I was asked if I wanted to return and take over from Malcolm. I jumped at the second chance to become involved with the England Academy side. My remit was the same as Malcolm's – to build a squad for the 2001 tour of New Zealand and Australia.

I had been to coaching seminars David Waite had run, but the first time I met him after I returned as the England Academy coach I had an argument with him about my squad for the tour. He said that no-one would be picked unless he had seen them as well. I took a bit of offence because I believed he was questioning my judgement and that of the rest of my staff. We had put a lot of time and effort in and I was still coaching at Swinton, so my home life was suffering.

I had an interesting discussion with David about this and he said that someone should have contacted him about the players so that he could have a look at them. I said: 'Well David, I've got off my arse and done exactly that. I had a look at them in depth before selecting them.' With hindsight, I know that Waitey had to be sure that we were all doing the job right. I worried that I might be out of a job, but I thought it needed saying and I think he respected the way I was.

Waitey was more than helpful and he went looking at the players as well and probably 95 per cent of the squad that I selected went on the tour.

Waitey made me understand selection criteria, where we were lacking and where we were quite abundant in talent. He was very knowledgeable on how you put a squad together and he set in place how future squads were selected. He really made me look at the game in a totally different way and made me think a lot harder than before about talent identification. He would expect me to know every facet of a player's game. How good a player was on a left-hand pass and a right-hand pass, if he could defend, his vision, his evasive technique, how he carried and protected the ball. Whether he could kick with both feet, how he was on contact and floor work. It really made me understand the player inside out. David Waite had the same effect on me as Jack Gibson had when I played at Cronulla.

Among that squad we had some great players like Rob Burrow, Danny McGuire, Sean O'Loughlin, Ade Gardner, Eorl Crabtree, Kirk Yeaman and Alex Wilkinson. What was beneficial was that we had players like Jamie Langley, Jon Wilkin, Dwayne Barker, Richard Mathers and Gareth Hock who all had another year to go. David went on the tour with us and I learned even more from him. It was a very rewarding experience to receive the kind of support I did from David and it ultimately made me the coach I am today.

Our first destination was Auckland where we played Northern Districts at Carlaw Park and I decided to keep a few of the players, like Rob Burrow, Sean O'Loughlin and Danny McGuire, out of the side because I didn't want to show my hand too early. I wanted to win the friendly but it was more important to win the first Test against New Zealand. We won the game, after a tough opening, by 40-18 but more importantly for the team we came through the game without injuries and the squad got an insight into how rugby league is played in New Zealand.

At the outset, I had told the squad that every player would

141

play in a Test in the two match series against New Zealand and that I wouldn't go against my word. Every one of them could force their way into the side for the Tests against Australia in the second half of the tour.

We travelled down to Wellington for the first Test and the conditions were awful. Continuous torrential rain was falling and it meant we would be playing in heavy and muddy conditions. We decided we would kick early in the tackle count and put pressure on them. We knew that New Zealand would be big and powerful but how much stamina would they have if we kept turning them around? Rob Burrow, our captain, kicked early on a number of occasions, got four 40/20s and we scored tries off nearly every one. We won the game 30-8 and the tactics worked a treat. Our overall fitness and the mobility in the pack were the deciding factor. It's difficult to single anybody out, but our half-back combination of Burrow and McGuire was outstanding and Yeaman, Gardner and Mathers weren't far behind. It was just a shame that because of the rain only a sparse crowd witnessed it.

I was a very proud man after that historic first Test win in New Zealand, because as a coach I realised how much work and sacrifice had gone into that one game. I had left Erica three weeks after Ben had been born and it had been a wrench to leave my young family. Sam was only four, so I knew that it would be hard for my wife at home without me. It would be worth it if we won the game and even more so if we could win the series.

For the second Test in Christchurch I changed the side as I had promised to do, although people thought I was a bit mad changing a winning side. I made it clear to everyone that the job wasn't done by winning just one Test, that we had to win the series. The players knew from the first game that they were a big, strong and dynamic side so I wanted us to play a fast open game and hit them on the edges.

Christchurch is a beautiful place and we had good, warm weather and were playing on a dry track, on which I knew the side could perform better, with the speed we had. They scored a try in the opening minute and I thought we were in for a hard time, but the lads upped their game. They never took their foot off the pedal and the players that came into the side did a good job. They did everything I asked of them and more and we won the game 72-16, clinching the series.

We left New Zealand happy in the knowledge we had won an historic Test series and won it in style and flew to Brisbane for the opening Test match. We trained at the Burleigh Bears and I knew our best 17 for the Test match. What I did was split the squad into three groups and my assistants, Stuart Wilkinson and Steve Crooks, told the players in their respective groups whether they were in the team or not. It was very hard from a coaching point of view, because I knew that the whole squad had given everything and more. It's the easiest thing in the world to tell a player that he is in but to explain why a player is out is hard and coaches have to stand by that decision. To be fair, the players that didn't make the first Test squad took it on the chin.

We played the first Test at Wynnum-Manly and lost 18-12. I know it might sound like sour grapes and being a 'whingeing Pom' but Australia's first try was definitely forward. We gave them a really good run for their money but overall they were the better team despite the phenomenal endeavour of our side.

We were leading 6-4 and Ade Gardner made a break down the right and passed inside to Alex Wilkinson. If the pass had gone to hand Alex was clear, but unfortunately he couldn't take it and the chance that could have made it 10-4 had gone. Teams have to take these chances against Australia whether it's rugby league, cricket, soccer or netball, because if they don't Australia punish them.

Sure enough, from their next set of six Australia went upfield and scored and went on to win the game.

We went into the second Test eight days later at the famous Sydney Football Stadium as a curtain raiser to the Sydney City Roosters versus Melbourne Storm game. I asked Adrian Morley to come into the dressing room and speak to the team and they were all thrilled about him coming in. What he said about the Aussies was dead right. 'They're only human, you push them close and they panic just like you. But they learn from their mistakes and that's where you went wrong.'

He's a great player, Mozz. He's played at the highest level in Australia and it's a great signing by Paul Cullen to have him at the Warrington Wolves for the next four years. I'm sure that he can take my old club to the next level. This time we came off second best as we lost 44-22 and were beaten by the better team on the night; not because of ability or determination but because we had scared them the week before. Players like Jason Netherton, Andrew Brocklehurst and Jon Wilkin were outstanding. Other players who have gone on from the tour and proved that our development programme is working are Kirk Yeaman, Gareth Hock, Richard Mathers, Shaun Briscoe, the list goes on. To see them now playing regular first team rugby shows that our England Academy system is working, although I still think we have too many overseas players.

It was a long tour but the players were great ambassadors for their country, although you might not have thought so if you'd seen our end-of-tour Kangaroo Court at our hotel in Manly. Jamie Langley found everyone on a charge guilty and ordered them to strip down to the buff, walk out through the busy foyer, across the road onto the beach and into the ocean. We had instilled such a team spirit within the squad that they all took it to that level and they all stripped off and went in for a dip. The ladies on reception in the hotel took it all in good spirit. In fact, they said that they had never had it so good. We all went out that night and really had a good time. The management and coaching staff left the players to their own devices at two in the morning. What I don't know won't hurt me, but everyone was back for breakfast.

I learnt a lot about the players and myself from the 2001 tour supported by the invaluable experience of Stuart and Steve.

Now it was time to plan for the visit of the Australian Schoolboys at the end of 2002. We had the nucleus of a team and a new crop of players coming through to replace the players who were too old for selection. I had David Lyon as my assistant coach and we were looking at players eligible for the Under-18s. Players like Luke Robinson and Tom Saxton had been playing with their first teams at Wigan and Castleford respectively. Mainly, though, we were looking at players in the Senior Academy set-up for Under-21s. Dave and I went everywhere watching games. Every player we were interested in selecting had to be watched, because David Waite would challenge us on our knowledge of him. Our analysis of the players came to the forefront of our selection process. If we hadn't watched a player and we were thinking of selecting him Waitey's system wouldn't allow that. He would ask questions about the player's strengths and weaknesses and reasons why we wanted to pick this player. It was a long process that had to be followed, but clubs benefited because we could give honest opinions on players. We got telephone calls – 'Why hasn't this player been selected, why has this player been selected?' – and we could then explain the why's and wherefores. It took away the suspicion that people were being selected because we remembered them from the past. Eventually we came with a squad that we felt was strong enough to take up the challenge ahead of us.

The Australian Schoolboys came over and Dave and I went to a few of their games, got videos of the ones we didn't and did our analysis through that. What we also did was take our squad to watch one of the Australian Schoolboys' matches against Great Britain BARLA which was being played at Widnes. We split the squad into groups and we gave them specifics to look for. Ten minutes from time we left. We had been watching the game from the main stand and walked out together down the tunnel to make a statement that we didn't need to see any more. We made it clear to the Australian coaches and management that we were leaving. We were making a statement to give us a psychological edge over them. Back at our hotel at Haydock we set a room up and talked about the strengths and weaknesses from a players' point of view and from the coaches' point of view. We asked the players how we counteracted their strength and all the answers came back from them. We didn't take the lead in this session and it created in the players a self-belief that had perhaps been missing before. I think they got a sniff of something special. I firmly believed that the Australian Schoolboys had an over-confidence about them, because they had battered BARLA. We were confident they could be beaten, especially with our back row which was outstanding. We had Gareth Hock, Jon Wilkin and captain Jamie Langley and they instilled in the team that mental toughness that we could beat them.

We played the first Test at St Helens and were full of confidence, but we couldn't plan for injuries. We lost Craig Barton, one of our props, early on and it could have been disastrous because we had already planned the rotation of the forwards. We hadn't pre-planned minute by minute but we had an idea in our heads when we were looking for our front-row rotation, so we knew we would have potential problems at the back end of the game.

In the front row we had Tom Gallagher and Bruce Johnson on the bench and Ryan Bailey who had started the game. It was a game when our young players became men. In adversity, the qualities of the side shone through and everyone stood up to be counted. We had in Bailey a player who took them on up front and he has proved his potential since then by playing for Great Britain and is sure to win more caps in the future. He just terrorised them and it was frightening the way he was ripping in. Luke Robinson had a great game as did Bob Beswick who played at number nine. The hooking spot had given us problems; we didn't have an outstanding one and they were all quite average. Bob played for Dave in the Wigan Under-21s and, even though he was a back-rower. Dave played him at hooker so that he could get to know the position. Even though he was playing out of position, he was outstanding. He could defend off both shoulders and could give a good pass right to left; not so good left to right but he worked hard on it. What we got with Bob was toughness around that area. He was an uncompromising, physical player and our only concern was his distribution and lack of concentration at times. We asked him to focus on every pass at that moment, nothing else. He came up with a great game for us, he was very physical up the middle and he hurt a lot of their big guys. He had an ability to hit people really hard and that was what we needed in that area to back up Bailey, Johnson and Gallagher. With the back three of Wilkin, Langley and Hock, who were all outstanding, we had physical strength all across the field. When we looked at the spine of the team, we had Bob at nine, Gaz Hock at 13, Luke at seven and Richard Mathers at six. They were all exceptionally talented players and, apart from Gaz, were all very vocal. Richard Mathers was also playing out of position because he had played his games at Leeds and Warrington Wolves at full-back, but we knew that he could do an exceptional job at stand-off.

We got off to a great start with two tries in the opening ten minutes when Dwayne Barker took a Richard Mathers pass to go over and then Gaz Hock powered over despite two Australians hanging onto him as he squeezed the ball down to make it 8-0. The Schoolboys came back with a Dimitri Pelo try but Chris Melling's penalty gave us a six-point buffer before Steven Ross intercepted on 25 minutes to go under the posts and the conversion levelled it up after 25 minutes.

We hit back following a penalty on the half hour 15 metres from our own line. Luke Robinson took a quick tap as the Schoolboys were trotting back into position and we caught them off guard. He ran down the middle into the heart of their defence before passing outside to Chris Melling who flicked the ball out to Dwayne Barker bursting down the right of the field, before he drew the cover and sent winger Matt Gardner in at the corner. Chris Melling converted from the touch-line and we were ahead again.

At the start of the second half, we increased the lead when

substitute Tommy Gallagher took the ball on the halfway line and he bulldozed through two Australian players and kept his balance for a 50 metre try despite an ankle tap and the conversion gave us a 22-10 lead. The Schoolboys cut the deficit to half through Pelo again before Matt Gardner scored his second try taking a pass from Richard Mathers and we led by 26-16. Our defence was superb but we had to up the concentration levels after Steven Ross scored with seven minutes left to bring it back to 26-20 with the conversion being missed.

They took the game to us as they searched for a converted try that would level the game but the pride and spirit saw heroic defence from us. The Schoolboys' indiscipline saw us drive upfield and in the last minute of the game we were awarded a penalty. We went for the kick 20 metres out playing the clock down and knowing if it went over we had an eight-point lead. Chris Melling coolly put the kick between the posts and the final whistle went for an historic first Test victory over the Australian Schoolboys.

In the last ten minutes our defensive play came to the fore and was the barometer of the performance. The commitment, desire and passion showed, especially in the last five minutes, when the Schoolboys were awarded a couple of back-to-back penalties near our line and they hit us hard as humanly possible. Our players had given every ounce and having to find a little bit more was absolutely magnificent. As the final whistle went, all that tiredness, the weight on the players' shoulders was lifted and we watched as they bolted like racehorses. They had beaten the mighty Australian Schoolboys 28-20. It was a special moment. We had been waiting a long time for that win.

It was a different kind of adrenalin for Dave and I as coaches; we couldn't get caught up in the euphoria of the win and it was important for us to stay focused. We watched the game again and completed the video analysis. We went to the boys and could see that they were chomping at the bit to go out but first we held an injury parade. We told them who could and couldn't go out for a drink, knowing that on Monday morning we would be preparing for the second Test five days later at Headingley.

It was important that we sent another message out that we wanted more and were capable of more. We'd won our first game but we wanted our players to taste that sweet taste of success again. We told them they had some improving to do on their weaknesses, but also some improvement in our good areas as well if we were going to win the series 2-0.

A big bonus here was Darren Robinson, a sports psychologist who had been with me on the 2001 tour. Before the first Test at Knowsley Road, he gave the boys a belief that they could win. It's very easy for a coach to say that we can win, but we also need the players to believe and have that desire. Darren was an integral part of our staff and he did an unbelievable job. We created an environment where the players had access to him if they wanted. Darren did some group work and individual work with some of the players as well. Players of that age are very impressionable, some of them will use sports psychologists and some won't. Some gained a lot of benefit from it and he played a big part in reinforcing the messages that we were sending out. Dave and I had a good relationship with Darren as did the players because he wasn't threatening to them. He was there as a shoulder to lean on.

With Craig Barton being fit, we named the same 17 that had won the first Test, a team which we knew would be very physical. It was Test match football and we knew everything would be thrown at us, with toughness every bit as important as the technical side of the game.

The Australian Schoolboys scored the opening try after six minutes to lead 6-0. From the restart, we were defending again when there was a full-on fracas and our players didn't take a backward step or flinch. Because of the team spirit which had been created in the camp, we could see the intensity in them. They were there for each other and it kick-started the boys. It's happened many times before that something like that ignites a game and our boys took the positives on this occasion. We had stood toe to toe, shoulder to shoulder during the fracas and I knew then there was no way that Australia were going to win the game.

They threw the kitchen sink at us in the opening 20 minutes and although we weren't firing on all cylinders our defence was superb again. We had more adversity when Matty Gardner had to come off after he collided with the advertising hoardings chasing a kick. We had to reshuffle the team as we had done in the first Test and moved Chris Melling onto the wing and brought Tom Saxton on to take over at full-back. We never lost our shape and the players once again came up trumps with three tries in an eight-minute spell.

On 25 minutes Gaz Hock broke from the base of a scrum 20 metres out and went on an angled drive for the line. As the cover was coming across, he passed outside to winger Matty Wray who scored in the corner. Four minutes later we attacked on the opposite wing and Dwayne Barker put a superb pass to Chris Melling who went in at the corner to give us an 8-6 lead. Chris scored his second try on 32 minutes after a brilliant move. Just inside our own half, Graeme Horne chipped over the Australian defensive line and Tom Gallagher went through the gap to collect the ball when it bounced kindly for him. He passed outside to Richard Mathers who moved the ball down the line to Dwayne Barker who gave the pass out for Chris Melling to again score in the corner. He converted the try and they came in at half-time leading 14-6.

Chris kicked a penalty after 45 minutes and two minutes later we scored our fourth try to lead 20-6. The Australian Schoolboys lost the ball 15 metres from their own line, Chris Bridge picked up and passed outside to Matty Wray who scored a classic winger's try hugging the touch-line. The Schoolboys showed their determination to get back into the game and Tom Learoyd went over after we had lost the ball and the conversion brought them back within eight points of us. With five minutes left the Schoolboys made a break downfield and as Tom Learoyd took a pass and broke through our defence he looked a certain scorer. But Tom

Saxton chased across from the opposite side of the field and put in a copybook tackle on the tall prop forward and his momentum forced him into touch. His superb execution of a great tackle visibly lifted the players again and from the scrum we went upfield and the visitors conceded a penalty 25 metres out. Chris Melling, as in the previous Test, stepped up to the mark and kicked the penalty. The hooter went and we had created history. We hadn't only won one Test, we had completed an historic 2-0 series win.

There had been some defining moments in the game. The fracas saw the boys' intensity rise after an indifferent opening and that was backed up by some special efforts, especially after we had to make changes following Matt Gardner's injury. The icing on the cake was the tackle by Tom Saxton which stopped them getting back to 20-16 with the kick to come. In a game played in continuous rain I didn't think it was the same level of performance as the boys gave in the first Test but it was good enough. We were better than the Australian Schoolboys on the night and we had been better than them over the two matches.

It was a special moment for Dave and me as the whistle went and the boys went into their victory celebrations. We had shared some special moments as players together for Warrington and Great Britain and Friday the 13th of December will live long in my memory. I jumped up and gave Dave a big hug. There was nothing that had to be said; it was just the emotion of it all. We were both drained after achieving the outcome that we had wanted so badly. We had worked hard to achieve it and it was very tiring, not physically but emotionally. The series, together with the 2001 tour, had made me a far better coach in knowing how to approach a Test series. I became more mature and my whole outlook and temperament changed.

We went into the changing rooms and all the players were ecstatic at what they had done that night. We gave every player in the squad a hug and said: 'You have made history.' In 100 years from now they will still be the first team to ever beat the Australian Schoolboys in a Test series. We wanted them to know that, but they probably won't appreciate it until they are a bit older. Looking back now, even I didn't realise what we had achieved. Looking at the history of the game, there are turning points and that series win gave the game the lift it needed.

Waitey has had a lot of input into the structure and development of players and coaches and Dave and I benefited from that. But the young players were the important element here and they benefited massively from him. We needed something to show the future internationals we were trying to produce that we were on the right track. Dave and I got a lot of praise on the back of the series win, but it wasn't just about us. There were a lot of other people behind the victory as well who had worked hard to put our game on the world map.

We got some great press after the win, but some weeks later I read that it wasn't the strongest Australian Schoolboys side which had come over here. And they call us 'Whingeing Poms.' If you look at the players who have made it from that side into first grade in the NRL, there's Justin Poore, Ashton Simms, Keith Galloway, Jacob Lilyman, Ryan Hoffman, Tom Learoyd, Michael Weyman and Tim Smith to name but a few. So they can whinge as much as they like. The Australians are the past masters of psychological warfare and they wage it through the media. The bottom line was that they had come to win and had failed.

Dave was given the opportunity to take over from me as head coach of the England Academy side and I have to congratulate him on his own piece of history. He took the boys on tour in 2004, defeated New Zealand in the series and beat the Australian Schoolboys for the first time ever on their home soil. So that's three Tests that the Australian Schoolboys have lost and long may that continue. The future is in safe hands and it's onwards and upwards. Every player I have been involved with has played first team football with a large number playing in Super League. Some of those players have gone on to play for England and others to bigger and better things with Great Britain, so it proves that the Academy system works and that we are going in the right direction. The sooner the younger players from the Academy set-up break into our Super League club sides the better. But the problem we have at the moment is that we have far too many overseas players coming in with British and European passports and exemptions under the Kolpak ruling. They are stopping our up-and-coming players breaking into Super League squads. I know all about the EU regulations but we need a limit, agreed by the clubs, that the clubs will stick to.

One thing I had wanted to do when I was coach at Wigan was to try and get a team of British players playing for the club, but I had to deal with Maurice Lindsay, who seems to prefer overseas players. I am amazed to this day why the likes of Stephen Wild, Martin Aspinwall, Luke Robinson, Shaun Briscoe, Paul Johnson and David Hodgson, who all came through the youth system at Wigan, were allowed to leave the club. All those players have proved they are good enough since they left the club, playing first team rugby at their various Super League clubs. Some have played for Great Britain and England.

I feel it's criminal to allow home talent to leave, because I know how hard they worked at Wigan with people like Brian Foley, Dean Bell and Mick Hannan and the former Wigan player, Martin McLoughlin. They put all that time and effort into developing and producing players. I knew the development programme at Wigan was a good one, because I had worked with it when I first arrived. The proof is in the talent coming through. During my time at the club the talent was there and the management let them go. All that time, effort, emotion and money invested in the programme just to let the players go to other Super League clubs who have reaped the benefit. That can't be right. What concerns me is who makes the decisions about who is and isn't good enough. It should come from the coach to the management, not the other way round.

9

COMING HOME

I have been very lucky that things have come up for me through being in the right place at the right time. After leaving Swinton I still had the England Academy job on a part-time basis. Later that same year Damian McGrath, who was at Leeds, and I went with the Great Britain Under-21s to South Africa as assistant coaches to John Kear. I had known John for a number of years and had even played against him, although he's a bit older than me. Sorry, I needed to get that in, John.

Damian and I worked closely with John in South Africa and I was constantly talking to him about the game. I think he was quite happy with what he saw and what I did on the tour.

When John got back to Wigan, where he was assistant coach, I think he mentioned me to the head coach, Stuart Raper, as they discussed the coaching structure at the club. They needed an Under-21s' and an Under-18s' Academy coach, although Billy McGinty and Dean Bell were involved at that level at the club. Billy had been very successful as the Under-21s' coach and they were unbeaten, but Stuart wanted to restructure the Academy system at the club. They got rid of quite a few players from the Under-21s' side, including the likes of Daryl Lacey, Wes Cotton and Phil Jones. They also let Billy McGinty leave and Dean was moved into a different position within the youth development set-up at the club. Stuart and John's outlook was to go for younger players and bring them through the system quicker instead of holding them back. So the players who had been in those teams were allowed to leave the club and play elsewhere.

A similar development took place after Ian Millward took over, with changes within the coaching structure under him and players being allowed to leave. The difference is that the infrastructure was already in place so that those players being released now are still relatively young. Those released in 2001 were all over 21 and it was the aim of the club to have very few over-age players in the future. That was what David Waite, the League's performance director and the Great Britain coach, wanted. His idea was for the youth to come through.

So I had a meeting with Stuart Raper at the club and one of the first things I said to him was that I would always be honest with him and would tell him what was on my mind if I needed to. I told him that he would never have to look over his shoulder and that what he saw was what he got. I had never stabbed anyone in the back and I wanted to get that out of the way straight away. I knew that it was a cut-throat industry. Frank Endacott had been sacked as the Warriors' coach the year before and I knew from talking to him how it worked at the club. With me saying what I said to Stuart at the outset I think he was quite pleased with my openness.

It was the first time I had ever spoken to Stuart, although I knew that he had played in this country and had previously coached successfully at Castleford. My first impression of him was that he was very abrupt, knew what he wanted and was very determined to get what he wanted from a team. He offered me the job as the coach of the Under-21s' side at the club. As I said, they were restructuring the Academy set-up and it was at the same time that they switched Denis Betts from a playing contract to coaching. Denis was to coach the Under-18s' side and we joked he was the highest paid Academy coach in the world. Even though he had retired from playing the club couldn't change the terms of his contract.

I had a meeting with Maurice Lindsay, the chairman of the club, about a contract which would be a full-time appointment. They wanted me to work with the first team as a skills coach and to work with Orrell RUFC as defensive coach but my main job was with the Under-21s. I signed a three-year full-time contract with the club, which was the longest deal I had ever had as a coach. It meant that, on the personal side, I could begin to plan ahead.

My first impression of Maurice was that he was very professional and articulate. Going into his office, which was his power base, was very daunting – something I had heard from previous people who had worked at the club. He didn't tell me what he wanted from me, but I believe he told Stuart that he wanted me on board and Stuart was quite happy with that.

I was really happy because I knew that I was going to be working with some world-class players in the first team and some great young players I had already worked with in the England Academy set-up. I had gone the full circle in my coaching career, from assistant coach at St Helens, head coach at Swinton, to the Wigan Warriors. It had been a very up-and-down rollercoaster ride, but here I was, although only the Under-21s' coach where I had been head coach previously. That was a bit hard for me to adjust to, but I decided to learn what I could from everyone connected with the club, which I had always done throughout my playing and coaching career. I still had ambitions to become a head coach, although I never really thought that I would coach the first team at Wigan; maybe somewhere else, by using my time there as a stepping-stone, but not at Wigan.

During that initial interview with Stuart, he had told me what he wanted and the way he wanted to play. I had my own playing philosophy, but Stuart was the boss and the bottom line is that the piper plays the tune. It has to be that way, because if he were to be sacked as a head coach, he would have to have done it on his own terms and in his own style. A head coach is under the spotlight and it's them who take the fall. I understood this well from working with Shaun McRae.

I had a great squad in the Under-21s, which included the likes of Sean O'Loughlin, who was in the first team squad but mainly playing for me, Stephen Wild, Martin Aspinwall, Bob

Beswick, Craig Barton, Luke Robinson, Desi Williams, Shaun Briscoe and Gareth Hock, who was a prodigious talent. At that time, we could have two over-age players, but we only played those a couple of times. Harvey Howard played once and Stephen Wild, who was establishing himself in the first team. Mainly it was 21 and under with the emphasis on under. The club had taken on board David Waite's vision and Brian Foley and Dean Bell had been involved in setting up that structure already at Wigan. We knew from the Under-14 level to the first team where each player was in their development, as they were all listed on a large board in their office.

The club had worked hard on the development programme and to this day has been very successful, when you look at the likes of Gareth Hock, Sean O'Loughlin, Luke Robinson, Shaun Briscoe, Bob Beswick, Andrew Crabtree and Jon Whittle. With players of this calibre, if they don't make it at Wigan they generally make it elsewhere. The players were getting a good grounding in the Academy, which would stand them in good stead. But what we said to all the players was that education was paramount to those who were not on full-time contracts at the club. Those who were at school had to do that anyway and rugby league was not the priority and a lot of our players were at university. Some players also worked, but there was a misconception among our fans that our Under-18s and Under-21s were on full-time contracts.

Under the salary cap the main concern was the money for the first team squad. They were full-time and I had a number of players who dropped back on a regular basis. The likes of Robinson, Hock and O'Loughlin were only kids and could still play for my side. The idea was to test them and push them as hard as we could and it proved to be very successful. Again the credit has got to go to Brian Foley and Dean Bell for their development plan – the way David Waite wanted all clubs to be run. It was working well for Wigan but we were still behind the Leeds Rhinos. The programme at Headingley is second to none and they are now reaping the benefits. Approximately 80 per cent of the players in their first team squad have come through this programme and part of my remit was to develop players and integrate them into the first team squad at Wigan. I believe that whilst I was in charge I did that.

In my first season in charge of the Under-21s we made the play-offs but were defeated in the elimination semi-final by Leeds. We had a very good side but they were the best team in the competition. They had the likes of Danny McGuire, Rob Burrow, Ryan Bailey, Richard Mathers – all excellent young players. During my first season, among the crop of our good players, two stood out – Sean O' Loughlin and Gareth Hock. I knew them from working previously with the England Academy side and I knew already how good they were. They were exceptional talents then and, even allowing for the injury problems they have both had, they will play for Great Britain for many years ahead.

Sean already has played for his country; I always believed that he would captain Wigan Warriors one day and that he will also captain Great Britain. He is a gifted and talented player who sees things that not many players can see and he can react on a move before others. I believe he is the next best thing to his brother-in-law Andy Farrell and he will keep it in the family.

Gareth Hock is similar but a bit more of a rough diamond and they both just need to be injury free. They were both out for most of the 2005 season and it affected the team dynamics. I thought then that if they could stay healthy and link in with a few of the new signings, they would have more success the next season.

Everything I did with the Under-21 squad was done during the evening, although some of the games were played at weekend. During the day I was working with the first team with Denis under Stuart and John at Christopher Park or at Orrell RUFC. It was a dream come true to be working with players like Rads, Faz, Terry Newton, Craig Smith, Terry

O'Connor – the list is endless. When I worked with them we had a laugh and they were great to work with. I'm not having a go at the Swinton players but these were great full-time professionals and it was a far easier job working at Wigan because of that.

As a coach I always tried to be prepared and very thorough and I knew what I was going to do with the players a few days in advance. But that wasn't how Stuart worked and from session to session I didn't know exactly what we would be doing. We had a meeting every morning with Stuart on what we were going to do with the players that day. Stuart liked to work that way and it worked for him. I'm sure that he knew what he was going to be doing in advance, but he never seemed to communicate it well. People felt his manner was very abrupt, but he knew what he wanted for the players and the side. The one thing I found with him was that he wouldn't take advice. That's not to say that John or I were right when we suggested things to him, but Stuart never really shared the workload and I think he put a lot more pressure on himself. Technically he was a very good coach, but I think his man-management let him down a bit because of his abruptness.

In that first season working with the first team we got to the Challenge Cup Final at Murrayfield against St Helens, which you could say at the time was mission impossible. No one gave us a chance, we weren't playing brilliantly at the time and had struggled to win our semi-final against Stuart's old club, Castleford Tigers. Saints were on fire, flying in Super League and thrashing Leeds in their semi-final with some brilliant tries at our JJB Stadium. They were odds-on favourites and rightly so, I suppose. In the week leading up to the final, we had a couple of injury worries with Gary Connolly and Rads. Gary was having a bit of a problem with his knees but was a very resilient and tough player and there was never a doubt that he would play in the final. Rads had got an infection in his toe and foot and it was so painful that he had been in a private hospital all week having antibiotics. It was touch-and-go whether he was going to play as he hadn't trained all week. On the day, Dr Zaman, the club doctor, packed the infection and Stuart selected him for the final. His decision proved to be the correct one as Rads had an outstanding game and was awarded the Lance Todd Trophy as man of the match.

Going into that final as underdogs would suit any coach and any team, but the way Saints were playing under Ian Millward was outstanding. We were playing okay but we had reached the final and in finals anything can happen.

Brett Dallas got the opening try for us after Gary Connolly had put him through. The old stager played tremendously at centre against his former club and he scored a try himself and won the game for us. The team were magnificent on the day, both in attack and especially in defence, and the occasion at Murrayfield was outstanding.

My role in the final was on the headset on the touch-line whilst Stuart and John were sitting up in the stand. My job was to relay the message to Denis and either he or Nigel Ashley-Jones, our conditioner, ran onto the field and passed on the instructions. I don't remember a lot about the game but Stuart's game-plan was that he thought we had a more mobile pack than Saints. What we did was try and beat them at their own game, run them about, be physical in the middle. It didn't all go to plan but a few individual pieces of brilliance got the game for us – Gary making that break for Brett Dallas to score, and Adrian Lam scoring in the first half.

There were quite a few faces still at St Helens from when I had been assistant coach there but that was far from my mind on the day. It was funny really, because as a player I had never won a great deal. I had won more as a coach or part of a coaching team. After the win it was a feeling of a job well done, but as part of the coaching team I didn't really feel in the fold because of the way that Stuart worked. That's not having a go at Stuart, it's just the way that he worked; to this day I have to thank him for the chance he gave me, although I never felt comfortable with him. I know that it may sound as though I'm bitter, but it was just his style. He was very focused and he didn't really let anyone get close.

Julian O' Neill also had a big game for us that day at stand-off and showed that he was a big-time player on the big stage. He and Jamie Ainscough had a bit of bad press prior to the game, saying that they weren't up to it. But they had both played State of Origin in Australia, so I would say that they were up to it all right. Big games bring out the big players and Julian, Jamie and skipper Andy Farrell were immense in that game.

Julian had not played particularly well prior to this game but what he does do well is pass and run. In the final he mixed his game up very well and the space he made caused quite a few problems in the Saints' defence.

Jamie Ainscough also proved his critics wrong in that game and he was a very laid-back person. In the modern game, I've never known players who smoke but Jamie smoked quite a bit and he might have been knackered doing a run during a game. He was sharp but his laid-back approach didn't make him one of the fans' favourites. He would give the impression that he wasn't bothered but I can tell you that he was. He never quite fulfilled what he wanted at Wigan but one thing about him was that he was very tough and durable. There was one occasion when a tooth got embedded in his arm and his wound was stitched up with the tooth still in it. His arm became badly infected and he was in some pain but he got it treated, got it right and got back on the field plying his trade.

The ultimate professional at the club was the captain, Andy Farrell, who would always be first at training, always doing extra training, always the first to look at his video review. He was always asking questions and he would be the last one to leave the club. Andy has won every domestic honour in the game, captained Great Britain a record number of times and was skipper when Sheffield Eagles created the biggest shock in Challenge Cup history when they defeated Wigan in 1998. So it was a long time between drinks for Wigan before they reached the final and defeated St Helens in 2002. Andy had completed his set of trophies and lifting the Cup as captain was a big honour for him in front of his family and the fanatical Wigan supporters. The only thing that he hadn't done was to win the Ashes, but there are quite a few of us who haven't done that.

He has now left rugby league and moved to Saracens to play rugby union and hopefully he can win some silverware and honours playing for England and I wish him luck and all the best in his career in the other code. The thing with Faz and other players is that they never take to the field fully fit but those Wigan players really toughed it out when they needed to. They all put their bodies on the line and Faz was the classic example when he came onto the field wearing a mask against the Leeds Rhinos in 2004 at the JJB.

Terry O'Connor, Craig Smith and Terry Newton were also fabulous to work with. Terry Newton got to training earlier and earlier. He would be in bed at nine in the evening and arrive at training at seven in the morning. So Nigel Ashley-Jones would get in early and he would give Terry and Faz a programme of work before the majority of players showed up. Nigel got there at half past six in the morning, and I normally got in at eight. The rest of the lads would be in for training at nine for the weights programme which they had in groups. By that time, Faz and Terry had done their extras before joining in with everyone else.

Apart from working with the Wigan Warriors, I was also very busy with Orrell who were also full-time. I did defensive work with them, mainly in the afternoons, but not every day. I remember one week I did 70 hours with the two codes. There were times when I was going to their games when I could, as well as being involved with the Wigan first team and Under-21s. So it was a very tough first year and I know that my family life suffered quite a bit.

Ross Reynolds was the head coach at Orrell – he is now involved with Australia, coaching the forwards. His assistant was Jim Mackay, who is head coach of the Cornish Pirates, formerly known as Penzance. What I did at Orrell was to put a lot of defensive technique into their game, which is a lot more specific than in rugby league. In union, body shape determines position; our game is a bit more uniform in shapes and sizes. In union players can be extreme sizes with 6ft 9in and 6ft 10in tall whereas in our game someone like Stuart Fielden is about as tall as they get.

A lot of union was about finding the floor and presenting the ball. I came up with a few techniques and strategies on how to perform defensively and that was really challenging. I really enjoyed my time with the players. They responded well and we improved the team defensively.

I had a good working relationship with Ross and Jim and they were really very friendly and encouraged me during the training sessions. I didn't really understand the game and still don't to an extent. It's more technical and skilful in the rucking, mauling, scrummaging and line-outs than I appreciated. I just thought it was organised chaos, but there was a lot more to it. The coaching staff were very organised and very thorough and I got on better with Ross and Jim than I ever did with Stuart as there was more dialogue between us about what they were doing and what I was trying to achieve. I was left to get on with it, whereas with Stuart he told you what to do a lot of the time, I think the word for it is 'dogmatic.'

It was Dave Whelan's ambition for Orrell to be promoted into the Zurich Premiership, as it was then. At the end of my first season with them the club had finished third in the First Division. The second year we finished second and then Dave Whelan withdrew his support. Since then they have struggled, losing Ross and Jim and a lot of their players. I'm still very good friends with those two and Ross sent a text when Australia were touring last year, wishing me all the best. Jim still keeps in touch and rings me up once a month to see how I am doing. I wish both of them every success in their game, apart from when Australia play England.

10

MOVING UP

At the end of the 2002 season, John Kear was approached by Hull FC where Shaun McRae was the head coach. I knew that Shaun rated John very highly and even though John had bought a house near Wigan his family still lived in Castleford. Hull was a bit closer and families come first. He also knew Shaun very well and they had coached against each other for years. John knew in his own mind that he was going to a club which was going places after years in the doldrums. Hull had moved into a new stadium and had some good, talented, local kids coming through, some of whom I had coached at Academy level.

John had begun his coaching career at Bramley, taken Sheffield Eagles to Challenge Cup glory, coached England in the 2000 World Cup and had been involved in the Great Britain coaching set-up with the Academy sides. He had been my line manager for the Academy in 2001 before he moved to Wigan as Stuart's assistant and I had been his assistant coach on the tour of South Africa. Kath Hetherington, the chairperson at Hull, also knew John from her days at Sheffield Eagles where he coached them to that shock victory over Wigan in 1998. It was a tough decision for him, but it proved to be the correct one, even though the Raper-Kear combination had been successful at the club.

John went on to take over as head coach at Hull when Shaun decided to return to Australia and take the head coach job at South Sydney. John coached the side to a Challenge Cup Final win in 2005 and into the play-offs, where they lost out to the eventual winners, Bradford. I was shocked when he was shown the door as he has proved that he is a great coach and his record of success speaks for itself, something that Wakefield realised when they put him in charge at Belle Vue.

Just before the approach for John Kear from Hull came, I was looking to further my career away from the club. Brian Noble had made it known that he was looking for an assistant and we met off the M62 at Prestwich. Brian offered me the job as his assistant and it was something I was really keen to do. I loved being involved with the Wigan first team and the job at the Bradford Bulls would give me more responsibility with their first team squad. Brian offered me a three-year deal which was the same deal that he had signed with the Bulls and would run in conjunction with his. I would be better off with the bonus scheme in the contract and would be concentrating on one job instead of the three I was doing at the JJB. They also had some world-class playing talent and it was a great and successful club. When I think of the great clubs in the modern Super League era, the number one pick would be the Bradford Bulls; maybe number two would be St Helens with what they have achieved in winning trophies. I came home and had a chat with my wife Erica, who has always been supportive of me throughout my career.

I then went to see Maurice Lindsay and was up-front with him and told him that I had an offer from the Bradford Bulls. Maurice was fine about it. He said that if I wanted to move to Bradford the club would not stop me. He didn't say that he wanted me to stay at the club but I got the feeling that he felt I would stay. I also told Stuart about the job, as I wanted to be totally up-front with him as well, like I had promised when I first met him.

So it was down to me and it was a big decision I had to make, but I decided to turn the offer from Brian down. The reason was the travelling time involved. That was maybe three hours on a good run there and back, five or six days a week, and that was time that I could spend with my wife and young family. At Wigan I was really spoilt because the travelling time to and from work was only five minutes each way. So even though I was doing 60 hours a week, getting to and from work was far easier and I could work my schedule around the kids.

It would have been a great move for me on a professional basis because I would have been working with a great coach who had been so successful. He was then the Great Britain assistant coach and was always going to be the Great Britain coach after David Waite.

After a few days mulling it over, I told Erica and then I phoned Brian with my decision. I apologised, thanked him for the offer but told him I was going to turn it down. Brian was disappointed but understood and said to me that I was the only person who had ever turned him down.

I was up-front with the club and told them that I had turned down the Bradford offer. Although the club could have been funny about it I was impressed with the way they were very good about it. I guess what Brian's offer did do was give me a bit more self-belief and confidence. I knew where I wanted to go and that I was on the right track to achieve this goal.

The Hull approach to John came in the November of 2002 and everyone at the club knew about it, as it's a small working unit; everyone knew that John was going to Hull. I think John and Stuart had a chat prior to him leaving and Stuart was happy with the way I worked and the way I'd been honest with him. I had told him about the Bradford approach and he was aware that I had turned it down. Stuart offered me the job as his assistant coach and I had no hesitation in saying yes.

I always said that as a coach I wanted to be challenged and this was a challenge. I got to know Stuart a lot better after I accepted the position, so turning down the Bradford job was a blessing in disguise. I would have hated going to the Bulls and then missing out at Wigan, being born and bred there. Luck and timing are everything in rugby league and that's how it turned out to be in my circumstances; again I was in the right place at the right time and I didn't need my arm putting up my back.

The only problem was that Maurice was in Australia when Stuart offered me the job, which meant more responsibility and a new contract. We couldn't get hold of Maurice but I had been selected to coach an England Sevens side in Australia at the beginning of 2003. Initially Stuart didn't want me to take the Sevens side, as it meant a week away from the club. At this time Maurice was on the International Board and he had been involved in organising the World Sevens competition. David Waite had asked me to do the job and I told Stuart, but he said I couldn't go. Because the competition was Maurice's baby, Waitey phoned him in Australia and Maurice okayed it with Stuart for me to take them. I still hadn't signed a contract as assistant at Wigan; all I had was a verbal agreement with Stuart and no increase in money.

It was agreed between the league and the Super League clubs that we would only take one player from each side, but that we couldn't take any from St Helens who were competing in the World Club Challenge. The squad I took was Andy Farrell from Wigan, Keith Senior from Leeds, Phil Cantillon from Widnes, Rob Smyth from Warrington, Richard Horne from Hull, Danny Orr from Castleford, Gareth Ellis from Wakefield, Marcus St Hilaire from Huddersfield, Andrew Brocklehurst from Halifax and Lee Gilmor from Bradford Bulls. I didn't have an assistant coach, but Phil Clarke was our manager. I think it was Phil's first time as manager in the international set-up, but he had been an exceptional player. Having played in Australia, his experience was vital and he did a great job. Part of the deal, because it was late January and the season was approaching, was that the clubs insisted that the squad flew out in first class. I had never flown in first class to Australia before and it was 100 per cent better than what I had been used to. In the first class area the chairs tilted as beds; the players were really impressed.

In Australia, I went to see Maurice about my new contract with Wigan. We talked about the job but we didn't come to any deal. He said that he didn't want to discuss it in Australia and that we would leave everything until he got back to Wigan. In fact, Maurice seemed miffed that I brought it up whilst I was over there coaching the Sevens side. Perhaps he thought that it wasn't the time or the place to talk about contracts. Maybe he was right, but I had a family to think about. I needed to know what I was doing, how long the deal was for and, the big one, how much I would get paid. Even though I loved the job I was doing, I needed paying for it.

Maurice stayed over there for a while longer whilst I came back with a successful England side which had reached the final before losing to Parramatta. Then it was off to Cyprus for our warm weather pre-season training. I was in a state of flux as I didn't know where I stood. I was doing the assistant's job for Stuart and still doing the Orrell job when I could. The training in Cyprus was awful. The pitch we were hoping to train on was waterlogged and when you go for warm weather training you expect it to be warm. It was wet and cold and what we did in Cyprus we could have done at home, but you live and learn. The work that we got done was good and being away for a week was like being on a mini tour and it brought the squad closer together. The squad was living together 24/7. We trained in the morning after breakfast on the weights, had a sandwich and then we would go on the field before lunch and do what needed to be done. This is where again I found Stuart to be very much his own man, even more so than when I first began at the club. I'd have ideas and some he would take on board but he had the first and final say. I was fine about that, but Stuart worked very hard to a point where he could appear insular. I think if he could have spread it out a bit more by using the knowledge of myself, Denis Betts and Nigel Ashley-Jones there wouldn't have been as much pressure on him, but each man to his own.

We trained on the field, almost needing flippers and snorkels and then we came back to the outdoor pool at the hotel which wasn't heated. We made the boys go into the pool after every session and used it as an ice bath. The boys had done it before and were used to it, but I don't think they expected it to be as icy as it was. It ensured that any swelling or lactic acid could be controlled and that they would be able to train the following day.

The pre-season in Cyprus was quite tough because of the weather conditions and Stuart also put an alcohol ban on the players. They were professionals and knew they had to turn up next day; they were grown men and that's the way Stuart did things. As assistant coach, the players came to me if they had anything to say or any problems and I relayed them to Stuart. A few of them asked why couldn't they have a drink. Stuart said that there would be a time and a place and that he had scheduled a night out with the boys in the town where we were staying. I'm sure though that the squad had a lot of common sense and if they wanted a drink they went out or didn't do it in the open. It would have been nice to have a bit of sun on our backs, but the week served its purpose and it got the players fit and made them into a team. The person who we had to blame for this 'warm weather training' was Nigel Ashley-Jones who organised it through the Olympic Association. We were the first to stay there to see whether they could use it for training camps.

By the time I had returned from Cyprus with the squad Maurice had got back from Australia and I went to see him about my contract as assistant coach to Stuart. I knew what the going rate was; I had been assistant at St Helens a few years previously, and I had had a good chat with John Kear who gave me a ball park figure. It had been good to talk to John and don't forget I knew what the Bradford Bulls had offered me. It was useful knowing those figures and it put me in a good position when I went to see Maurice. Wigan is always a good payer to players but that's not necessarily the same for the coaches. I was quite happy with the deal I negotiated with Maurice although I didn't get what I went in for at the beginning of the meeting. We met halfway but it was better than what I had been offered at the Bradford Bulls. Maurice is a very astute businessman and I think he had a good idea what I was worth and both parties were happy. The contract was for another two seasons and it was in conjunction with Stuart's, but Maurice did have a go at me for bringing it up in Australia. Maurice does things on Maurice's time scale so I had to adhere to it and we finally sorted out the contract. Denis moved up to Under-21s' coach and Shaun Wane coached the Under-18s.

Our season began with Denis's testimonial game and Denis played in his 369th and final game for Wigan against Widnes, our only pre-season game of the campaign. On a cold night it was a great turn out by the fans for a great professional who had retired from the game 15 months earlier and joined the coaching staff. Widnes didn't read the script for the night and we lost the game 20-16.

For our first defence of the Challenge Cup, we had a home tie against the Widnes amateur side, Halton Simms Cross, which we won by 82-3. We then had to wait for nearly two weeks before starting our Super League campaign at The Jungle against the Castleford Tigers. In a tough encounter we were leading 10-9 with five minutes to go when it all went wrong with Darren Rogers putting Castleford ahead and Waine Pryce clinching the win with a try in the closing seconds. We weren't helped by Paul Johnson being sent off and our cruel run of injuries began when Andy Farrell went off in the first half with a knee injury.

We travelled to Doncaster next for the Challenge Cup and ran out winners 50-10. We played well in a game which saw Gareth Hock make his debut and score two tries in three minutes after coming on for Mick Cassidy.

Our next Super League game saw us entertain newly promoted Huddersfield Giants at the JJB Stadium. A late try by Martin Aspinwall clinched our first win of the campaign after Huddersfield had made a comeback in the second half.

We added to our injury list prior to our next game, the

Challenge Cup tie against my old club Swinton Lions at the JJB, with Terry O'Connor joining Faz and Mick Cassidy. We won the game 70-10 and had reached the semi-final without really being tested.

We returned to Super League the following week at Wakefield, in what must have been a great game for the fans but put the coaches through a treadmill of highs and lows as we twice came from behind to win the match 34-29. We took on the London Broncos next at the JJB and after a superb start by us we lost 34-30 – the first time London had ever won at Wigan.

The following game saw a trip to Hull's brand new KC Stadium and we left there the same way we had done in our last visit to The Boulevard the previous year, with a defeat, this time by 20-4. The loss came at a cost as our injury list grew, with Brett Dallas suffering a torn hamstring, Mark Smith damaging a shoulder, Stephen Wild damaging his ankle ligament and Danny Sculthorpe picking up a sternum injury.

These were hardly the preparations we needed as we played the Bradford Bulls next in the Challenge Cup semi-final at Huddersfield. We had five regulars out but somehow got five others fit enough to play after they had painkilling injections.

Our injury ravaged side put up a brave performance against the Bulls' juggernaut; the boys recovered from being behind 12-2 to lead 16-12 at half-time thanks to tries from Terry Newton and Danny Sculthorpe and three goals by Danny Tickle, but the Bulls took the game by the horns in the second half and blitzed us in a 20-minute spell, scoring four tries and two goals to end the game as a contest. To make matters worse, we ended up with more injuries from the game. This included Kris Radlinski being carried off in a neck-brace. David Hodgson dislocated his shoulder, Craig Smith was suspected of having a broken finger and Gareth Hock had a leg injury. Luke Robinson also was injured during the game and we later found out that he had broken his hand. It was the club's first semi-final defeat in 35 years but Brian Carney epitomised the bravery of the side when he took on four would-be Bull's tacklers and fought his way over from the play-the-ball for Wigan's last try of the game.

So we were going into the 200th derby game against Saints on Good Friday without nine first team players. We were literally down to the bare bones and we brought four players in to make their debuts in this game – Jon Whittle from our Orrell club, David Allen, Mark Roberts and Kevin Brown. For Jon Whittle, who had been playing union, it was a big ask of him to change codes and play in the biggest game of the season. It wasn't fair but it had to be done; it was 'Mission Impossible' against a Saints side on top of their game. I could never predict the result of a Saints–Wigan derby, but hand on heart I didn't think we could do it. Emotionally, I knew that the boys would give everything as I had worked with a lot of these players the season before. I knew what they could do and I told Stuart that they wouldn't let the team or the club down. Besides that, there was no-one else. It was a case of having to blood them. Maybe blooding too many at once is liable to backfire but there was this outstanding team spirit that moulded them together.

I remember the week in training not going all that well, but when it came to the game the emotion and the adrenalin took over. The boys went into the second half trailing 22-12 following two tries from Darren Albert, one on the stroke of half-time, Micky Higham and Jason Hooper and three goals from Paul Sculthorpe. We had scored tries from Terry Newton and Danny Tickle with Danny kicking two goals but that late Albert try had set us back.

We had nothing to lose in the final 40 minutes and when Adrian Lam engineered the space for Mark Smith, who put Shaun Briscoe over for a converted try, there were only four points in it. Twelve minutes later we were amazingly in the lead as Terry Newton drove his way over and Danny Tickle added the extras. Terry had so many big games at the club before moving to the Bradford Bulls last year but I think this one was one of his finest hours. The final 22 minutes gave me some memories I'll treasure, the final one being Shaun Briscoe's tackle on Darren Albert to stop him scoring his hat-trick try, which I think would have won the game for the Saints. It was a desperation tackle and that summed the team up. The kids, plus the experience of Lammy, Terry Newton, Terry O'Connor and Craig Smith, had won the game for us.

It was pretty emotional after the hooter went to end a fantastic game and confirm a fantastic result. Stuart hugged every one of the players as the side left to a standing ovation and a deserved lap of honour. I remember Stuart talking at the press conference about the effect that the result would have on the history of the club, so it is a great shame to see that there are only three players remaining from the 17. The team that day was: Shaun Briscoe; Brian Carney, Martin Aspinwall, Paul Johnson, Jon Whittle; Sean O'Loughlin, Adrian Lam; Terry O'Connor, Terry Newton, Craig Smith, Ricky Bibey, Danny Tickle, Mark Smith. Subs were David Allen, Kevin Brown, Mark Roberts, Danny Sculthorpe.

We then had a couple of weeks' break before we faced Bradford, who had just won the Challenge Cup, and on an awful night for playing rugby league we let an 8-0 lead slip and lost the game 14-8 after Leon Pryce had scored his second try of the night with the game tied at 8-8. It was the first of three games over eight days. That was tough on us because of our injury problems, but four days later we visited Leeds, who had a 100 per cent record in Super League. We managed a 24-all draw with the beaten Challenge Cup finalists, with Danny Sculthorpe scoring his second try ten minutes from time to tie up the game.

Our run continued at Widnes and the following week we entertained Warrington, a game which saw the return of Andy Farrell for his first start since the opening round defeat at Castleford.

What a return he made for us and once again showed why he has the nickname Captain Fantastic. In a game that had ebbed and flowed throughout, two Lee Briers drop goals had given the Wolves a 20-18 lead and the points looked destined for them. But Faz kicked a crucial penalty to make it level and then with only seconds remaining he dropped the winning goal to break Warrington's hearts. The following week we had the second of three consecutive home games against bottom side Halifax and we had a comfortable win 58-12 in which Kevin Brown scored a hat-trick, to open his account in Super League and we moved up to fourth position in the table.

We lost the final home game to Leeds Rhinos 30-20, which spoiled Andy Farrell's 28th birthday after we had gone into an early 14-0 lead. Ex-Warrior Gary Connolly spoiled the party when he scored the match winning try for Leeds. It brought an end to our four match unbeaten run and next stop was a trip to Knowsley Road to meet the Saints.

The first thing that hit us when we got into the dressing room was that it was painted shocking pink. It certainly wasn't painted that colour when we had played there the previous season. Pink is supposed to make everything tranquil; it's supposed to affect the subconscious in a subliminal message and in theory it calms players down. We didn't want that before a derby game against Saints. Psychology at times is full of bullshit, but, whatever the paint was supposed to do, Saints started like a house on fire. It looked as if we had forgotten the extinguisher and were behind early on. Saints led 14-0 after the opening 20 minutes when we put Luke Robinson onto the field for the first time since breaking his hand in the Challenge Cup semi-final. We went further behind (20-0) but then came back to lead the game 36-20 before Saints fought back to within six points of us going into the final minutes. This was before Andy Farrell secured another victory for us with a penalty. Yet again the youngsters, in particular Luke Robinson and Kevin Brown, were exceptional and, with Browny being a St Helens lad, it must have been very special for him when he scored his two tries. In fact earlier in the season, Stevo from Sky had bought Kevin a watch following the Good Friday Saints victory, even though he wasn't voted Man of the Match. Luke was outstanding coming off the bench in the first half and he went on to record a hat-trick of tries, the first tries of his career. They were both only 18 and had the world at their feet but sadly Luke moved on to the Salford City Reds and is having a fantastic season as I write and Kevin Brown has moved over the Pennines to join Huddersfield Giants.

We continued our winning run for the rest of June with wins over Hull, Bradford and Castleford. The 28-14 home victory over Hull saw David Hodgson's second try minutes from time clinch the win and move us into third place. We maintained that position with a 35-22 win at Odsal – the first time we had beaten them this year. Andy Farrell was again instrumental in the win scoring his 100th try for Wigan and kicking eight goals. Against Cas, we were trailing 10-8 but late tries by David Hodgson and Paul Johnson gave us a 24-10 victory.

We had had a great June with these victories considering our injury situation and Stuart was deservedly named Coach of the Month. The irony of ironies was that in our first game in July we went to the McAlpine Stadium and lost to Huddersfield for the first time in 22 years. We had recovered from 14-6 down at half-time and Brett Dallas who had come back after a hamstring injury scored a hat-trick which put us ahead in the game. But two tries and a penalty gave Huddersfield the win and that didn't seem to go down well with Maurice.

We then played Wakefield at the JJB and won the game 38-12 although at one stage the Wildcats cut the deficit to 16-12 after we had been leading 16-0. Stuart and I found out after the game that Dave Whelan had spoken to the players during the warm-up and Stuart was unaware that it had happened. Apparently he hadn't been told by either Maurice or Dave that it was going to be done and he wasn't happy about it.

In the lead-up to the game in London there was speculation in the media that Stuart was going to be leaving the club and it continued after the 28-12 win over the Broncos which was sweet revenge for our home defeat by them earlier in the season. On the way back, though, on the coach from London, Stuart informed us all that he was leaving at the end of the season, because of his children and their education back in Australia. Although there had been all the media talk, I was taken unawares when he made the decision, but Stuart was his own man and did things his own way. The club then announced Stuart's decision to the media but as far as I was concerned it was business as usual and we began preparation for our home game against Widnes. Everything had gone well in the build-up, even though we had to make changes to the team after Shaun Briscoe had turned an ankle in training. We lost the game 22-18 the first time that Widnes had beaten us for 13 years. The game itself was lost in the first half when Widnes led 22-0, although we had a Lammy try disallowed in the opening minutes of the game. We scored a try at the beginning of the second half and the boys tried their best, but Widnes defended superbly. We finally scored two tries late in the game but couldn't complete a comeback win.

The highlight and biggest cheer was when a female streaker made an appearance for the start of the second half but I didn't see her, I promise, as I was taking up my position for the final 40, honest.

The fans weren't happy about us losing at home to Widnes and it turned out to be the final nail in the coffin. It was unlucky for Stuart on the night, the boys had played well in the second half but although it was our seventh defeat of the season we had had further injuries during this game. We had first-half injuries to Craig Smith and Mick Cassidy and although Craig was able to return in the second half Mick had problems with a leg injury and we only had three fit substitutes left with over an hour of the game remaining. Even though we had lost, we were still third in the table, seven points behind Bradford and Leeds but two points ahead of St Helens and Hull.

An emergency meeting was called on Monday following the defeat. The meeting was between Stuart, Maurice and the players but Denis and I weren't invited. It seemed a bit strange and unusual to me but Stuart said he didn't want us there. So be it, it was Stuart's decision and he was head coach so I abided by that. As I said before, it's a small tight family at Wigan and a whisper was coming out before the meeting that Stuart and Maurice had met before it and that Maurice had sacked him. I didn't know whether that was right or not but I just got on with my job as normal taking all the stats from the game tape against Widnes whilst the meeting was going on.

Stuart came out of the meeting and hadn't been sacked, but it seemed Maurice had a change of heart later on in the day. I spoke to Stuart about what had happened in the meeting and he said everything was as normal. The players trained and did a swim and then went home for the rest of the day. I was still at the club that afternoon when I got a telephone call from one of the players. He told me that Stuart was going to be sacked that afternoon and that I was going to take over. I was shocked when I was told this as I thought everything had been sorted out that morning so I arranged to meet Denis later that day. Neither Maurice nor Stuart had said anything to me about what I had just been told on the telephone. Stuart worked in a separate office from me, so I went to see him but he wasn't there. I thought he must have gone for another meeting with Maurice to be told he was being sacked. I didn't see either of them for the rest of the day and didn't get any further telephone calls.

I told Denis what had happened and that I had arranged for us to go to Andy's to find out the full story. He told us what Maurice had said to him about sacking Stuart and I was taking over in his place. After the meeting with Faz and Denis I went home and phoned Stuart and asked him what was happening. He told me Maurice had sacked him. Maurice rang me at home later that evening and I arranged to have a meeting with him on the Tuesday. It had been a hectic day and I telephoned Erica, whom with her sister

Lynne had taken the children on holiday.

Denis and I arrived at the club at eight o'clock the following morning and from what had happened the previous afternoon and evening, we knew what was going to happen. It was a bit awkward because by that time Stuart had usually arrived but obviously this morning he hadn't. Some of the players were already there doing their weights' session and I think they knew what had happened to Stuart. I wasn't happy with the way that things had turned out and the way it was done but I knew that I'd take the job if it were offered to me.

It was a frantic day that Tuesday and the club finally announced that Stuart had been sacked. I had a meeting with Maurice and it was arranged that I would be caretaker coach in charge of the side and that Denis would be my assistant and we were introduced to the press later that afternoon.

Stuart came into the club later that week to clear his desk out and I met him in his office. I wanted to tell him how I found out about his dismissal. I wanted him to know that I had done everything above board whilst I had been working under him, that I hadn't gone behind his back and that it had nothing to do with me, even though I didn't agree with all his training methods. I had a lot of respect for him as the head coach and I looked him in the eye when I told him and he believed me, which was pleasing. One thing I am if nothing else, I'm straight and honest. He said that he was pissed off with the way it had been done, but he was fine with me. After the Monday fiasco he said that he had calmed down, although still very irate, and accepted what the club was doing. To be honest, he took it quite well, all things considered.

During my time as Stuart's assistant I saw that he was very professional in every way. He did it his own way but we were fine working together and sitting together during the games. Previously at the games I had been on the end of a two-way radio in the dugout, but now with John Kear leaving I was promoted upstairs into the stands to be with him. One thing

I noticed from this was that Stuart was a very emotional person when the game was flowing and he was very abrupt and emotive on the radio headset; that's the way he was. I said to him that rather than him on the headset, maybe it was better that I go on it, and he should relay it. So I took over and I found that it worked better. Stuart may not agree but I feel he calmed himself down during the game and I learned a lot from him, how to do things and how not to do things. We were two different characters; I'm a bit more easy-going, more like Shaun McRae, the first coach I worked under. It takes all types in the coaching world. I've been under some fearful bollockings and also been given some constructive advice in the past. What I tried to do was marry the two together, but Stuart was a bit more emotional than me. That's not a bad thing or a good thing; it's just the way that we are and I can get carried away with the best of them.

I remember Shaun McRae advised me when I first started at Saints 'Remember you're hired to be fired and the first day in the job is your best.' I took that on board, but I was shocked by the way Stuart had gone. I think we were playing well. He had won the Challenge Cup a year earlier and we were still in third place after the defeat at home to the Vikings. I didn't agree with everything and I chatted with Stuart and gave him the benefit of my experience and a bit of advice. That was my job, to assist him. It was up to him whether he took the advice or not; usually he didn't.

With the success that he had, I don't think Stuart was expecting the sack, even though there is always pressure at Wigan and high expectations. I think his downfall came after he declared that he wanted to leave at the end of the season. The players might not be playing for him after that and then the defeat came against Widnes. Everything came together and just sealed his fate. I have to repeat that he was a good coach, even though he had his own way of doing things. I'm sorry it hasn't worked out for him as head coach at my old Australian club, Cronulla.

11

THE DREAM JOB

It is the irony of ironies, it always seems to happen in any sport and the story couldn't have been written any better. Warrington at Wilderspool was my opening game in charge as caretaker-coach, against my old mate, Paul Cullen. In the build-up to the game, I wanted to make changes to the way we played but not wholesale changes. What I did was focus on two areas of our game, which I believed needed improving. They were our marker defence and our kick-and-chase and on the back of that we worked on our go-forward and our attacking options. These were the two main areas where we had lost a number of games. I knew we could play football and I gave the players a bit of freedom, but my main concern was marker work and getting the kick-and-chase working.

What I did on the Wednesday was bring a number of the senior players into my office, players like Andy Farrell, Terry O'Connor, Craig Smith and Kris Radlinski. I told them my ideas to improve the team and asked them to go away and think about what I'd said and come back tomorrow with some feedback. All the feedback was positive as the players were professional and they knew that we needed improvement. So the week's preparation was all about kick-and-chase, marker defence and our go-forward; it was quite simple. I used this every day to prepare for the Warrington game, which was being played on Sunday, and I brought the players in on the Saturday as well.

Stuart Raper generally gave the players Friday off if there

was a Sunday game, but I believed that players should have the day off before the game, so normally I would give them the Saturday off, to give them a full 36 hour recovery. But going into this game they came in the day before because of the importance of it; I knew the game at Wilderspool was always going to be tough. Knowing Paul the way I do, I knew his team would be prepared physically and mentally for the game so we worked a lot on belief, spirit and team bonding. It was something I'd always had as a player and I knew that the team had to be strong and tight before they got any success. The old cliché 'a chain is only as strong as its weakest link' is very apt and I wanted the team to be strong in every facet of the game.

Going into the match, I remember that Maurice and David Whelan were sitting behind me in the stand and Denis was in the dugout with the headset on. A bit more pressure, which I didn't need, but the boys had trained well; in fact our first few training sessions together were probably the best we had trained all season. Maybe the players had had the weight lifted off them and put onto me. My thought was to make it enjoyable but to win. It's easier coaching a winning team than a losing one and in the game at Wilderspool I wanted to start off with a win.

We were trailing 14-6 with 13 minutes left and we hadn't made many breaks in a game which I knew would be physical and proved to be, but we had two pieces of brilliance in the game. Kevin Brown came 'in and out' and fed Brett Dallas for him to go over in the corner and Andy Farrell converted from the touch-line. The Wolves increased their lead with a penalty, but then near the death Terry Newton made a burst up the middle and none other than Craig Smith was supporting on the inside and scored under the sticks. Andy Farrell's kick gave us an 18-16 win, and the winning two points.

I remember going to the boys at the end of the game and I was very emotional. I didn't realise until then how much it meant to me and how much effort the players had put in. I was close to tears; emotionally, I hadn't realised how much the game had taken out of me. I'll never forget it because as I was speaking to the players I nearly lost it completely but just about kept myself together. Quentin Pongia came over to me after I had finished speaking to them and said 'The boys all understand where you are coming from and showing that emotion means a lot to us as a team.' That meant a lot coming from a senior player who had done everything in the game, who was probably closer to my age than to the others; it was what I wanted to hear. I didn't know that I was going to be close to tears, but a wave came over me, connected with the way that first game as caretaker-coach had been at Warrington. I was on automatic pilot, but I knew throughout the game that what we were doing was right and that the players would respond. They just went out and played and I probably put a bit too much pressure on myself and it all came out at the end in the dressing room with the boys. It showed that I was human, that I did wear my heart on my sleeve and how important it was to get that initial win. I didn't break down again.

From that win we went on an unbeaten eight-match run which took us into the play-offs in third position at the end of the season. Included in the run was another 24-all draw at Leeds and a 28-4 win against St Helens at Knowsley Road which gave us three out of three against them. During the run I was aware through the media – our weekly press conferences, national and local rugby league press – that the fans wanted me appointed as the head coach, but that wasn't my main concern. My main job was preparing the team, both through the game plan and the physical aspect, with a bit of enjoyment involved. I mean there was no-one worse than me for enjoying training, having a laugh. It was part of our plan not to make things too intense, to let the players enjoy training and the game.

I remember going up to Headingley when we drew 24-all again and Danny McGuire scored in the final minute. Kevin Sinfield had the kick to win it but he missed and we deserved a bit of good luck on the night. A couple of other games stand out in that unbeaten league run. We played Bradford at the JJB and they came on the end of an unbeaten eight-match run. Kris Radlinski was back in the side after being out for 14 weeks for wrist surgery. What a return he made for us and he scored one of the team's five tries. We had been working on a reverse kick and Luke Robinson used the ploy from the scrum at the end of the first half, Kris read it and plunged over for a try which gave us a 20-0 lead. It was another good win against a very good side.

The other game was against my mentor Shaun McRae, head coach at Hull with John Kear as his assistant. We won the game 28-6 and we played really well in a victory in which Luke Robinson had another superb game at scrum-half. To be quite honest, in fact, in that run we didn't under-perform in any of the games and the boys take all the credit for that. Whatever we threw at them, they came up with it and each week we picked an area of improvement. Initially it was kick chase and marker defence. Then there was our go-forward, our attacking options, our tap penalties; everything was methodical and planned out. It went from the ruck outwards, from the back field to the front field.

The results were going well, Denis and I were working well together on the coaching front, with Denis having been appointed as caretaker assistant coach. I had known Denis from years back and had played with him when I captained the Great Britain side that had toured Papua New Guinea and New Zealand when Maurice had been our tour manager. But I felt that Maurice didn't want Denis to assist me and that he thought I should have a more experienced assistant. Denis and I discussed this. I am sure Maurice would have had someone in line for the job – a John Kear-type coach – but I knew from talking to Denis that he understood the game and he was a very knowledgeable coach. In the build-up to the games, Denis and I spoke candidly about the way the changes needed to happen and Denis was in agreement and had an understanding of what I wanted to do. I also needed our conditioner, Nigel Ashley Jones, there as well for what we were trying to achieve. I gave Denis areas we needed to work on and let him get on with it and didn't interfere because I didn't believe that was right. We had already spoken about what we needed to achieve, so Denis did his job and I did mine and we finished the season in third position – a remarkable effort given the horrendous injuries we had throughout the season and the change in the coaching structures at the club.

As the run gathered momentum there was a groundswell coming through to give me the job. The fans had taken to Denis and me. Speaking to them, I guess they wanted a Wiganer to coach Wigan and the overwhelming feeling was to give me the job. I believe that it was first the players and then the fans that ultimately got me the job. The way the supporters reacted during the run was unbelievable and I think the pressure that they put on the club really got me the dream job. Even to this day, I don't think Maurice saw me as a big enough name and didn't really want me as head coach.

I didn't pester Maurice during the run and concentrated on the team, as that was all I could actually control, but the boys were fantastic in their approach to games and in the way they responded to me. I have got to thank them for their application, because as a coach you are really governed by the performance of the team.

At the time, I was doing the caretaker head coach's job on an assistant coach's money. I had a meeting with Maurice about it and he said it would be okay and that he would sort things out. That would be done at the end of the play-offs and there is one thing about Maurice, if he says it, he does it.

Our opening play-off game was at the JJB Stadium and like my first game in charge it was against Warrington and Paul Cullen. We had the home advantage but they really tested us and the atmosphere generated by the Warrington fans on the night was fantastic. Games for Wigan against Warrington were always special and, after playing in so many games for

Warrington, I knew that they always raised their game against Wigan and that night it would be no exception.

To be quite honest, the 25-12 score line flattered us; although we were the better team, Warrington ran us all the way. They led 12-6 at half-time with tries from Darren Burns and Nathan Wood's intercept from Adrian Lam to go 80 metres. Graham Appo had kicked a penalty and a conversion; all we had to show was a Lammy try and Faz goal. But in the second half we nilled them and defensively we were very strong. It was one of the areas we had put right, especially around the rucks. We had been a bit lax before and we had done a lot of work on that. Danny Tickle forced his way over at the beginning of the second half and converted his try as Faz was off injured. Then we took a two-point lead when Luke Robinson kicked a goal. A Robinson drop goal and tries from Brett Dallas and Craig Smith saw us home and we had survived our first task.

Our second task was against the current Super League Champions and our deadly rivals from over the hill, St Helens. Faz was passed fit to play in the game just before kick-off and although he wasn't our goal kicker that night his presence on the field meant everything and again showed the bravery, desire and character of the man. That was the best game we had played up to then. We were outstanding, especially in the first half when we led 34-6, as everything we touched came off. The only setback of the first 40 was when Adrian Lam, who had already scored two of our tries, snapped his cruciate. Lammy had been instrumental in the way we performed in the game until his injury. Brett Dallas had scored an early try and Danny Tickle also crossed the whitewash. We regrouped and Mick Cassidy got on the score sheet and, although Jason Hooper crossed for the Saints, we finished the stronger when Sean O'Loughlin tricked his way over and then Brian Carney brought the Warriors' supporters to their feet with an 80-metre effort. Darren Smith pulled a try back for Saints but Kris Radlinski scored our final try and Tickle kicked the goal to give us a 40-10 advantage. Although the Saints came back it was too little, too late and it was the Warriors who marched on.

Lammy's injury turned out to be a tragedy for us, because he had been instrumental in our unbeaten run; a very knowledgeable and gifted player, Denis and I were spoiled to have his talent in the dressing room. He has since moved on to be assistant coach to Stuart Raper at Cronulla, but during his time at Wigan he was outstanding. He would challenge you, because he knew the game inside out and was a typical, cheeky scrum-half. He always tried things and I let him lead the side around the field. After a game he would sit down in the dressing room, think about what had happened during the 80 minutes and analyse it. He would always ask the questions: 'Should we have done this or that, or how did that work?' He was a good and dedicated professional and a good fellow to boot. He was always last out of the dressing room because he couldn't switch off and it would take a while for him to come down. I think in the long term that Adrian will be a great coach; he couldn't be too bad if he could captain Queensland. Wigan has had some great scrum-halves at the club over the years and I rate Adrian as one of the best; comparable to the likes of Andy Gregory though he didn't have that bulk. What he did have was speed and guile, but what was similar about both of them was that they were always a step ahead of the rest. Lammy was so very intelligent and made my job a lot easier.

After the victory over St Helens, Maurice and I spoke about the job and what I had done as caretaker-coach. I honestly don't think that if we hadn't had the run we had, I would have been offered the job. It was only during that meeting that I realised that I was now number one for the job in Maurice's eyes. There was speculation about other coaches but I never focused on that. I was smart enough to know that it was results that would open the door.

The next game saw us travel to Headingley to face the Leeds Rhinos for the fourth time that season. We hadn't beaten them in the previous three games, although we had drawn 24-all twice at Headingley. The game will be remembered as the Brian Carney show. Brian scored two long-range tries which were a bit special when we were under pressure on our own line. Leeds had finished second in the league and had played well throughout the season, finishing three points behind the Bradford Bulls. Although they were coming off a play-off loss to the Bulls, I don't think many people apart from our loyal supporters gave us a chance, especially with losing Lammy. I had Luke Robinson coming into the side as his replacement and it was a big ask for him and the rest of the players. There was a belief within the team, though, that after the way we had beaten St Helens we could do it.

It takes a special player to come up with special plays and Brian came up with them. For the second try, he had to beat four men to score. He beat Dave Furner and Keith Senior from dummy-half as his upper body strength pushed them off and he outpaced the cover defence of Wayne McDonald and Richard Mathers, who had had a magnificent season, to go 80 metres to score in front of the jubilant Wigan supporters and take us into a 22-20 lead. That was the second time that we had come back from behind in the game, although Brian's first try had given us a 4-0 lead. Andrew Duneman had punted the ball downfield and Brian had collected the bobbling ball and set off on a jinking run and combined with Kris Radlinski to score. The Rhinos hit back with two tries from Danny McGuire and Rob Burrow, and three Kevin Sinfield goals gave them a 14-4 lead. But we got back into the game just before the interval as Sean O'Loughlin drove over and Andy Farrell added the extras to make it 14-10. In the second half, Burrow scored his second try to make it 18-10 before Sean O'Loughlin's second converted try brought us within two points of the Rhinos. On the hour, Sinfield kicked a penalty before Brian's fantastic try restored our lead two minutes later. We were defending desperately to stop the Rhinos but Sinfield levelled the game up with a penalty five minutes from time. As our troops were tiring, I had visions of extra time but Danny Tickle was in the right place at the right time and stepped up to the mark with a coolly dropped goal. Danny was still a youngster – he was playing for Halifax when he was 17 – but during that season he matured as a player and he took on more responsibility. During the second half, Faz came off and Danny stepped up to the plate and did his thing and gave us a decisive one point going into the last three minutes. It was a great team performance especially in those closing minutes when the Rhinos threw everything at us and once again our defence won us the game. When the hooter went, the players and the fans celebrated as we had created history in being the first team to reach the Grand Final at Old Trafford from third position.

During the game, Maurice and Dave were sitting behind me in the stand and, as the hooter went to finish the game, I was ecstatic. I turned around to Maurice and said 'I'll sign the contract now.' Maurice had spoken to me about the head coach's job before the Leeds game, but we had kept it quiet because I wanted the team to be focused on the game not on me signing a deal. Maurice had been as good as his word about my pay as caretaker head coach and then he offered me the job as full-time coach of the side. After a bit of to-ing and fro-ing we agreed on certain parts of the deal but I didn't want to sign it then. It was important that everybody stayed focused on the Leeds game. Everything had been agreed before the game; it was just a case of when it was announced. I always thought, after the way we had played and the response I got from the players, that I deserved a shot at the job. During the negotiations, I knew roughly what Stuart had been on, so my plan was to up it a bit as I had done in the previous contracts at the club. So when the negotiating phase had finished, we met in the middle. I made sure that I didn't sell myself short at the biggest club in the world. It was a dream come true for a Wiganer coaching Wigan, but a lot of work and a lot of pressure. I put pen to paper on a two-year deal which I was more than happy with.

I also wanted Denis to carry on as my assistant, even though Maurice seemed to want to have someone with more experience. After working with him, I knew he was a thoughtful coach. We were similar in our outlook and we created a good system. I was happy with Denis and he sorted a deal out with the club a few weeks later. My deal was a two-year contract and we planned the announcement for a few days after the media day for the Grand Final which was held at Old Trafford on the Monday before the final the following Saturday evening. We thought that it was better not to distract the players or the staff from the job in hand. We would hold everything back until after the media day.

I remember that at all the weekly press conferences at the club I was continually asked whether I was going to get the job. All I could say was 'Ask Maurice,' because the decision was his. As our momentum gathered and the players responded, it was a case of waiting for Maurice to decide. If someone else had been brought in, I would have left the club. I know that it's easy to say after the event, but I believe I am a man of principle. If I didn't think that I could have done the job I would have stepped aside for someone else, but I knew I could do it. I was an honest coach with the players and they would respect that whether it was good news or bad. I knew I could do it, so if I hadn't been given the job I would definitely have moved. I thought when I first came to the club that I would gain as much experience as I could and I never expected the first team coach's job. Maybe I am selling myself short, but I didn't see myself as a big enough name for such a club as the Wigan Warriors. I was lost for words when Maurice said I was first choice and offered me the job.

To be appointed head coach of the Wigan Warriors was the proudest day I've had, apart from my sons being born and my wedding day. It's the pinnacle of anyone's career to coach your home team. Being born and bred in Wigan, I had that passion, mentality and understanding of the speccies. They eat, drink and breathe Wigan rugby league. It was that old cliché, 'A dream come true,' something I still thank the club for.

During the lead-up to the Grand Final, Lammy was hopeful of getting himself fit for the game, although the physio and doctor realistically knew he wouldn't be. It was a million to one chance but Lammy trained hard all week giving his all and doing really well. He had a lot of strapping on and was maybe a risk I could have taken. But the crunch came late on in the week when we were training on the first team pitch at Orrell. He was okay running in straight lines but when we were playing a bit of opposed stuff in a game situation he went down injured. He had to come off as his foot and knee gave during the session and he was down on the ground for a while. Lammy was distraught and in tears as he realised that he couldn't play in the final. I felt for him, as a player who had come all that way in the season we had been through, only to fall at the last hurdle. I knew a bit about that myself during my own playing career and it's a bitter pill to swallow. Everyone felt for him, no-one more than me, but it did make my job easier. I'm not callous or unsympathetic, but, as a coach, I like things black and white. I knew that Lammy wouldn't be fit for the final and Luke would keep the shirt.

So we came to the Grand Final at Old Trafford against the Bradford Bulls. We lost 25-12 and to come that far, play the way we did and not win was hard to take. I remember Terry Newton in tears after the game. It meant so much to the players who had come through adversity, as well as to our faithful supporters. We had come into the final on an unbeaten run in 11 games, finished third and fell at this final hurdle. It was one step too far and I really believed at the time that you could not win from that position in the table. So great credit to Brian Noble's Bradford side that they did it in 2005. That was very special.

We had played and beaten Warrington, St Helens and Leeds in the play-offs in hard-fought games. Those matches took their toll and in the second half of the Grand Final we looked a bit tired. We had led 6-4 at half-time thanks to a try from Danny Tickle. In the second half the game was tied at 6-all when Brian Carney went off injured, after a double tackle by Danny Gartner and Leon Pryce. It was one of those decisions that can go for you or against you. I think it was a bit close, a 50-50 maybe, too close to call, but I thought the tackle was a bit high. When he hit the ground Brian had a bit of concussion and to lose him was a big blow, especially considering the way he had been playing in the lead-up to the game, when he was on fire. You have to take these things in your stride, but it turned the game. Bradford got possession and Stuart Reardon scored from the next set to make it 12-6.

Things go for you or they don't and in this one we were unfortunate to be on the receiving end, although we showed our spirit when we scored ten minutes from time. We were 19-6 down after Shontayne Hape had scored another Bradford try which Paul Deacon had converted as well as putting a drop goal over. From a scrum 15 metres from our own line Luke Robinson passed out to Martin Aspinwall who broke away through some Bulls tacklers and passed to Rads, who scored the try which Faz converted with eight minutes left to make it 19-12. It was a consolation try as it turned out, as James Lowes scored in his last ever appearance for Bradford. We had a few battered and bruised bodies out there, but take nothing away from Bradford; they were the better team on the day. I was very proud of what the players had achieved in a relatively short time.

I also felt proud of our supporters, who were magnificent on the day and had supported us all the way to the final. Finals are all about the fans and the atmosphere they created was nothing short of superb.

I had tasted defeat in big games as a player before but now as a coach I felt a bit more for the players and the rest of my coaching staff, for all the hard work we had put in together. It's harder as a coach to accept that. I guess on the flip side, if the team wins the rewards are even greater than when playing and as a coach you realise that all the hard work and time has been worthwhile. Alas, I've never experienced a win in a major final yet as a head coach.

It was an interesting close season at the club because a couple of weeks before the Grand Final Maurice was telling me that because of the salary cap we needed to lose players and he told me the players who had to go. The players I was to lose were Shaun Briscoe, Paul Johnson and Stephen Wild. I didn't agree with this, because I needed all the players I could get. They were all local Wigan lads and they all had a year left on their contracts, but as a coach I had to make tough decisions. But following that conversation, things were complicated when Adrian Lam, who had been waiting to sign a new contract, snapped his cruciate. I spoke to him on 'Mad Monday' following the Grand Final defeat. I explained the conversation that I had two weeks earlier with Maurice and that I couldn't afford to lose three players when he was out of contract and injured. I explained that, although not yet of the same calibre as him, we had Luke Robinson. Adrian was as good as gold and understood the situation. He was a seasoned player, he had been there before and he went and spoke to Maurice.

I didn't know the exact details of what Adrian's new contract was to be but I was aware that he hadn't signed it and it would mean that, if he left the club, we could keep the three players. It made sense to me. Even though Adrian was so valuable to us I couldn't afford to lose three players. I could lose one and I told Maurice this. Maurice though was adamant that these three players would go and that Adrian would stay. Maurice told me to have a meeting with Shaun Briscoe, Paul Johnson and Stephen Wild and tell them that they were going to be released. I told him on a number of occasions that I didn't want this but Maurice appeared to have his own agenda which was significantly different from mine. Maybe I should have been a bit more forceful as a

Scoring a try at Wembley in 1990.

Wembley 1990, Warrington v Wigan. The tackle that nearly was – on Shaun Edwards. Even with a broken cheekbone he still managed to offload to Mark Preston!

Schoey, Bettsy, Foxy, Jiffy and me after the test win at Port Moresby in 1990. It was warm!

The innocuous tackle in the 1990 Lancashire Cup against Runcorn Highfield at Wilderspool which ruptured my anterior cruciate. I was never the same player after that.

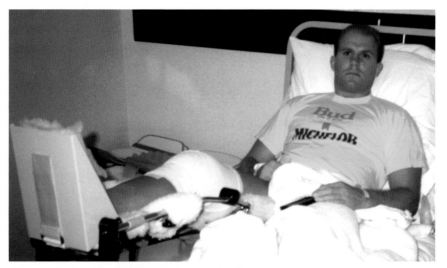

Down and out in March 1992. The face says it all.

Joe and Nicola's wedding day. Who would have thought that four years on the roles would have been reversed? My wife, Erica, is in the pink.

Doing the double with Saints in 1996.

The GB Academy squad in Christchurch, New Zealand in 2001. History in the making with our 2-0 series win.

The coach deep in thought and sunshine, with GB and Wigan captain, Andy Farrell.
© RLphotos.com

What talent. The 2002 England Academy squad that beat Australia in a Test series for the first time ever – history had been made!
© Andrew Varley Picture Agency

A family photo taken in December 2002. My best achievements yet, my devoted wife Erica and our two sons, Sam and Ben. A blissfully happy family not realising the devastation awaiting us around the corner.

What a great club with superb players and backroom staff – I was proud to coach Wigan.
© Wigan Observer

The Book Club. We started meeting over a year ago – here we are at 'Butty's' wedding. My lifelong mates Nick, John and Butty, with Butty's best man Mac.

Two gym owners – two legends. Walter O'Malley a body builder, Royce Banks a wrestler and rower – both great friends and my training partners in days gone by.

A very special day by a very special club – Warrington. Surrounded by friends Phil Clarke, Royce Banks, Fred Ralphs, Glen Sweeney, and Charles Hantom.

coach, but ultimately Maurice was the boss. So I spoke to the boys and it was the hardest thing that I had ever had to do as a player or coach, to tell them they were no longer needed at the club. I told them this was the club's perspective but I told them straight what I had done to try to keep them and my opinion.

Shaun Briscoe had been sensational in the 21s and had been great when he had played in the first team. He knew that he would be relying on Kris Radlinski being injured to force his way into the side, so I think to further his career maybe it was a good move. He moved to Hull FC where he has gone on from strength to strength.

Stephen Wild said, 'No, I'm not going anywhere' and I was glad when he said that. Paul Johnson wasn't happy about it but eventually moved to the Bradford Bulls and he's said to me since that he's got to thank Maurice for the best move of his career. Don't forget all the three players had a year left on their contracts and they didn't have to go. Shaun Briscoe had played for England, Johnno was in the Great Britain team and Stephen Wild was in the Great Britain squad. All three were thoroughly pissed off with the way it was done. Maurice liked to sign players, but it was up to me to break the bad news. Don't get me wrong; I'd have gone about it the right way if I believed it had to be done, as I had done with Adrian, but not with these three who were very good young local players. To lose players of that calibre was unbelievable. I don't know to this day why Maurice came to the decision and talking to him about the club's point of view regarding players was difficult. It didn't make sense in my book; Adrian Lam got another 12-month contract and he would have made sure that he got a good deal from Maurice and quite right too. What was ironic about the situation was that I couldn't allocate the number seven jersey to Luke Robinson; it had to be left open. If you have seen the 2004 team shot, Lammy isn't on it because he hadn't been registered.

It seemed to me that Maurice thought he knew better than anyone about the ins and outs of players, but it's the coach who should be able to choose his team and squad, who should stay or go. Ultimately you are hired and fired on how that squad performs. If Maurice picks the players, surely he should have been the one fired and not the coach. Speaking to a number of previous coaches at Wigan – Graeme West, Frank Endacott and Stuart Raper – I know that the club signed players they didn't want. Apparently, Maurice had signed the players without really discussing it with the coaches and that had gone on for years. He may have said 'What do you think of him?' but it was all down to Maurice.

I had spoken to Martin Gleeson, Gareth Ellis, Rob Parker and Andy Coley for the forthcoming season; all were Great Britain players and internationals of the future. If we had kept the three players already at the club, I think that these four would have complemented the team very well. I told Maurice this, but it seemed he didn't rate Andy Coley or Rob Parker and he didn't offer any explanation. Saints wouldn't sell Martin, and Gareth, I think, was quite happy in Yorkshire and later signed for Leeds. I thought it was naïve of him but I don't think Maurice thought he had to explain himself to me. Once a week Maurice and myself would meet to discuss players and games. My interpretation of one such meeting was that he felt that Sean O'Loughlin wasn't good enough or quick enough. I told him that Sean was one of the most talented players that we had at the club. After that I took his opinions with a pinch of salt. He seemed to have little insight into a game which I believe has now passed him by.

He ran the club as its chairman and was only answerable to Dave Whelan. I thought to myself that if I'm going to be sacked I need to get sacked because of the players I've brought into the club and picked, not the signings that Maurice made. In his early years at the club, Maurice certainly made some sensational signings, but I could have told you at the time that Brett Kenny was a good player and a great signing. It wouldn't take hindsight to work that one out.

As the season approached, my mate Terry O'Connor had arranged for his testimonial game to be played at the JJB

Stadium against the London Broncos and the game was to be our only friendly. But it seemed that the politics of Wigan Athletic and Wigan Warriors came into play and on the weekend before Terry's game there had been quite a bit of bad weather. Before I went into the weekly press conference, at which Terry was to promote his game, I had a meeting with Maurice. He told me that Terry's game in five days time had been moved to Orrell. I was taken aback because I was aware of the financial implications for Terry. There was the sponsorship, corporate hospitality and the difference in ground capacity. It meant that I had a very irate and upset player in Terry O'Connor when I informed him and he knew that it would cost him a substantial amount of money. I have to say that Terry was very professional throughout the press conference when we made the announcement. I didn't agree with what had happened and I telephoned Paul Jewell and had a meeting with him at Christopher Park the day after the press conference. It really confirmed what I had first thought – that Paul had nothing to do with the decision and he understood that it would cost Terry a lot of money. Paul said that he had no problem with Terry using the pitch for his testimonial and he is a very genuine guy who told me straight. Allegedly the decision had been made by the main man at the JJB, David Whelan. To be fair, there was quite a bit of rain on the top of the field on the Monday leading up to the testimonial but the game wasn't taking place until the following Sunday. There wasn't much wrong with the field and I felt for Terry after he had done ten years at the club. The least he could ask for is a game at his home ground. I think the decision showed a lack of respect for what Terry had done in his time for the club.

Although we won 26-16 the game was a real downer. We didn't have a big crowd, the build-up to the game was awful and it was difficult to motivate the players even though it was our last serious friendly before the start of the season. I'm not a believer in friendlies personally, but I have no problem with testimonials, especially having played in the annual

Locker Cup for Warrington against Wigan. I know that players can get injured any time and I have seen quite a few injuries in nothing games. If teams are going to play a friendly they have to play at least three or none, in my opinion. Three will give the team a chance to get a bit of match fitness; none will mean there are no injuries.

We were going into the season without Andy Farrell, Adrian Lam and Mick Cassidy. I didn't have the biggest squad and could ill-afford a few more injuries. In fact, Dave Hodgson damaged his Achilles and was out for a while. Danny Orr made his debut in that game for us and looked a good signing for the club. He had played very well against us for Castleford Tigers in the previous season's last game. He was outstanding for them that day but there is a bit more pressure playing for a bigger club. Expectations are higher and maybe that's why Danny has taken time to settle. That and the fact that he's had a stop-start career at Wigan with injuries.

12

THE FINAL CHALLENGE

I knew that we had to revise our play book for the 2004 campaign, so Denis and I spent a lot of time coming up with new calls, new moves and principles of how we were going to play. I had to stamp my own personality and character onto the team and how I wanted them to play, so a lot of work went into it. It was a new start, so I could go hell for leather for the changes I wanted to make. We got together with our conditioner, Nigel Ashley-Jones, to put together a new training schedule. I wanted us to be bigger, better, stronger and faster.

With Denis moving up to assistant, it left a space for a coaching appointment for the Under-21 side; Shaun Wane was coaching the Under-18s. I knew that the best junior coach in the country was David Lyon, a close personal friend. He had left St Helens as they wanted him to go full-time. Dave worked for the Council and had a good job and the coaching role I offered him was part-time. I found it amazing that Wigan didn't keep him on at the end of his contract but were able to offer Adrian Lam a role. I am glad to see Dave is now involved in the Great Britain set-up with Brian Noble and has done a lot of work in preparation for the 2006 Tri Nations Series.

Denis and I started issuing filofaxes, not because we fancied ourselves as yuppies, but as a means to making players responsible for their time at the club. The most important item in the filofax was our mission statement, which I wanted the boys to focus on. I must confess I was guilty of a little plagiarism here, taking ideas from New York Nicks' coach Pat Riley's book *'The Winner Within.'* It was all about being controlled, hard working and aggressive in everything we did, whether we were training, on the field, in the gym or on game day. The covenant was to bind the side together, treat them on an equal footing, shouldering responsibility, supporting each other to create a foundation for teamwork. Most of the time, the side achieved this.

The mission statement read as it did because our main area was our defensive structure. I knew that we could play football and the talent in the team was outstanding. What I questioned at times was whether we were physically aggressive enough.

There was a weekly schedule inside the filofax, so they knew from day one until the end of November what they were doing and it made sure that there were no excuses. For example, it told you where you had to be, at what time, what kit and footwear to bring. These were grown men and they were aware of everything in front of them.

The players were also aware of turning up on time for the training sessions and I took on board a quote from the great American Football coach, Vince Lombardi: 'If you train at seven be there at half past six,' which John Kear had come up with when he was assistant to Stuart Raper. I didn't expect the players to be that early but at least 15 minutes before we were due to start the sessions, usually at eight o'clock. I didn't want early arrivals waiting for latecomers. If they needed to see the physio before training or after, they would have to go and book it and no more than three were allowed in the room at one time. To be quite honest, the boys were very good time-keepers.

It was a pleasure to coach this squad. It didn't feel like a job, really, and as my wife Erica said, I was paid for a hobby. You can't class coaching rugby league players as work. It was a pleasure to come into work every day.

I came up with a code of conduct for the players. I wanted to create a culture and a working environment which was enjoyable but which would challenge us individually and as a squad. We were what the Wigan motto on the badge represents: 'Ancient & Loyal.' This is what we stood for, with no compromise. Be part of that or you wouldn't be at the club. I had been around the block enough to know that it would be good for the players. Everything had the purpose of making them better players on and off the field and I believe we achieved that. I wanted us to portray ourselves as proud to wear the Wigan badge and carry the responsibilities of playing for Wigan, including being role models for the club, the town and its children – to live up to what the badge represented. We were a world-famous club and still number one in the eyes of many people. With the eyes of the world looking at us, I didn't want stories coming back regarding the behaviour of players away from the club. I wasn't re-inventing the wheel; it was just common sense and good values.

During pre-season, I didn't mind if we were training on Saturday and they had a few beers on Friday, as long as they trained hard the next day. I had been a lad myself, so I knew what they might get up to and my aim was for the boys to enjoy training but work bloody hard when we were at the club; nine times out of ten they were very, very good. This is what I wanted us to be about and I can't emphasise enough that our standards were high. To achieve what we wanted to achieve that season in the Cup and Super League meant we had to make a lot of sacrifices.

I wanted to create that 'rip and tear' culture at the club and I wanted us to do a lot of body-to-body contact in training, more than ever before and so I brought Royce Banks in. Royce was a wrestler and he did a session every week on the mats with the boys and it was all about body position, being stronger in certain areas when your body is unbalanced. Ellery Hanley was one of the best players to illustrate this. He could be off balance on one leg and he was still dynamically stronger than his opponent. Our aim with Royce was not so much to use wrestling techniques in the game, which would be quite hard, but to use the techniques and training to strengthen the players' bodies. The idea was to out-muscle the opposition and use it for conditioning.

The players were given a game sheet on the respective opposition about how we were going to play and the players would come up with their own goals for that game and what they wanted to achieve. From a coach's point of view it was an insight to see what a player's goals were and what he wanted out of a particular game.

The 2004 season was always going to be tough, especially with an opening game at Bradford. Even though I hoped we could win every game I knew that the odds were against me. The way we broke the season down was to win every game but not get carried away or upset with the results early on. Even though I didn't give my goals to the media, I wanted to finish in the top two to have a chance of winning the Grand Final after the previous season's disappointment of finishing third.

The Bradford Bulls had just become the World Club Champions after defeating Penrith Panthers 22-4 seven days earlier at the McAlpine Stadium. It was a cold evening in Bradford and got even colder from a Wigan point of view as we lost 34-6 and Lesley Vainikolo scored five tries against us. Although the score doesn't reflect it, we played well in the first half and we really had Bradford on the back foot. We were losing 12-0 at half-time and it didn't reflect the effort we had put in, which wasn't helped by Luke Robinson getting sin-binned.

We were up against it in the second half as Vainikolo came up with four more tries. For his final try in the closing minutes he got the ball in the corner on his own line, knocked four of our players out of the way and went through the gap he had created to score a magnificent try in the corner. Unfortunately for me, I was in the new stand on the right hand side behind the posts where he scored those four tries. Lesley is a mountain of a man and he was up against

Brian Carney, who is no slouch himself, but Lesley took the spoils. Bradford were better than us on the night although the boys gave their all.

The following week we played the Widnes Vikings in the Powergen Challenge Cup, live on *Grandstand*. We won the game 38-12 and it was literally the old cliché – a game of two halves. It was marred for us as our injury jinx came back to haunt us when Brian Carney broke his leg. Brian is incredibly strong but on this occasion he was a fool to himself. What he did was, instead of taking the tackle, he carried four Widnes players on his back and something had to give. Unfortunately it was Brian's leg. I guess his strength and unwillingness to go down cost him. I love Brian as a player, character and friend but this was a case of taking the tackle, not fighting it and getting a quick play the ball. His bravery and stubbornness showed his commitment to the cause at a time when we were struggling to get into the game and we were 12-0 down.

The Widnes side deserved to be leading at the time and during the break I had to raise my voice give the players a few home truths. I was normally constructive and analytical and didn't work that way, but on this occasion it had to be said and a rap on the knuckles and a bollocking worked. Credit to the boys, they came out in the second half and showed what a class act they were by scoring 38 points. Mark Smith, who had come on for Brian, scored two quick tries made by Sean O'Loughlin, following a Martin Aspinwall try to give us an 18-12 lead. We then moved up a gear and Sean went over followed by Terry Newton and Kevin Brown. To put the icing on the cake, Danny Orr scored just before the hooter and Danny Tickle kicked five goals with Faz being out injured.

With Brian having broken his leg, the club management made a business decision to de-register Brian so that they could register Lammy. We couldn't have more than 20 players on £20,000 and if Brian had been left on and Lammy added we would have had 21. Unbeknown to me, the club put out a press release, apparently in my name – though I knew nothing about it – to the effect that Brian would be out for a while. Brian came to see me and asked me about the press release and when I asked him what press release, he read and showed it me. I didn't know anything about it and couldn't believe it when I read it and I told Brian that. He was very upset because at that time we didn't know the severity of his injury and he could have been back in a couple of weeks.

Apparently the club had already put out the press release saying it was for a couple of months. They had put it out in my name and hadn't even spoken to me about it. It was about this time that Adrian signed his new contract but I didn't know the finer points of it, as I was only the head coach. I confronted Maurice about it but I felt he just fobbed me off, saying that it was in the best interests of the club. But the damage had been done and I think Brian lost a bit of faith in me, although I had nothing to do with it. There was a bit of a strain in the relationship I had with Brian, but now we are very good friends again and it's great to see him doing so well in Australia playing for Newcastle Knights with the great Andrew Johns.

In my opinion Maurice is a law unto himself and he doesn't seem answerable to anyone apart from Dave Whelan, who lets Maurice get on with the rugby side. I think Graeme West summed it up when he said 'A coach should sign players not the chairman.' I believe Maurice did the same with John Monie, Andy Goodway, Frank Endacott, and Stuart Raper. Maybe if I had been allowed back to work and survived to the end of the season, I might have been told who I was going to have playing for me, just as Maurice had told me that Lammy was staying and three were going before the 2004 season.

The following week we entertained newly promoted Salford City Reds and we won the game 20-10 for our opening Super League win, which was far from easy. We were 4-0 down through an Anthony Stewart try, before

Martin Aspinwall and Sean O'Loughlin gave us a 10-4 half-time lead. Salford came back to level the game with a Stuart Littler try before Terry Newton gave us the lead again and we clinched the victory with Sean's second try in the closing minutes.

Our next game was in the Cup, where we had been drawn to play Limoux in France and I was aware of the short turnaround as we faced the Leeds Rhinos five days later. I realised that the Leeds game was the priority, as I knew we would beat Limoux and that the score was irrelevant. I wanted a performance and we got it as we crushed them 80-20. Bearing in mind the Leeds game, I wanted to get in and out on the day and get the job done. Maurice wasn't happy with this and he was planning for the weekend as he likes the South of France. Denis and I spoke about chartering a plane and, fair play to Maurice, he was good about it. He realised it was probably the best way to do it for the players and in that respect he couldn't do enough for them. He knew the main priority was the welfare of the players, so we got our way and flew out on a charter plane with a lot of fans travelling with us.

We travelled to Headingley following the short turnaround and lost the game 36-24. Things went from bad to worse in the opening 12 minutes, when we lost Chris Melling with a bad knee injury following one of the first tackles of the game. We then went 12-0 down after the Rhinos scored converted tries from Jamie Jones-Buchanan and Danny McGuire. Danny Tickle kicked three penalties to bring us back into the game and Kevin Brown scored a try in between Jamie Jones-Buchanan and Danny McGuire scoring their second tries and we went in trailing 24-12 at half-time. Following a Kevin Sinfield penalty we had a Sean O'Loughlin try disallowed and then Leeds scored through Chev Walker to make it 30-12. The boys showed their spirit when Stephen Wild went in for two tries to make it 30-20 but Matt Diskin's converted try gave them a lead from which we couldn't recover, although Martin Aspinwall scored the last try of the game.

We then had a week's respite before we played the Wakefield Trinity Wildcats at the JJB in the Challenge Cup for a place in the semi-finals. We knew it would be a hard game and that no quarter would be given or taken, especially with the way they played under Shane McNally. They were a very aggressive side with a good offloading game and a strong physical pack with David Solomona, Michael Korkidas and Olivier Elima. Those three players were all gifted with good offloading skills and the half-back combination of Jamie Rooney and Ben Jeffries was superb. We knew it was going to be tough and it proved to be, but we had Faz and Mick Cassidy back from injuries and we won 20-4. The way we kept them try-less was a credit to our defence.

It could have been anybody's game going into the final quarter as we only led 6-4 after Kris Radlinski scored a converted try following up a Terry Newton grubber in between two Rooney penalties in the first half. But we scored three quick tries through Kevin Brown and two from Martin Aspinwall and we clinched the game with 12 minutes left. The scoreline didn't reflect the effort put in by the Wildcats on the night.

We were in the semi-final and one of our goals at the beginning of the season was to reach the final and win every game, but the season is about peaks and troughs and we hoped that the troughs would come when everybody else was in a dip. To play Bradford and Leeds Rhinos early on was unfortunate but in the cold light of day they weren't games that I had scheduled for a win, so I wasn't too disheartened.

Our next game was at the Huddersfield Giants and we lost 26-10, which was a bit of a jolt to the system and a defeat that I hadn't accounted for. I noticed later from this game that I had put a lot of pressure on Luke Robinson, a young up-and-coming player, to boss the team. On hindsight it was probably one game too many, but Lammy was still injured and I blamed myself for putting too much on young shoulders. Luke learned from the experience and he is a far better player today because of it and doing a great job at the Salford City Reds. I found it amazing that the club decided to let a potential Great Britain scrum-half leave the club. I think in the long run they will regret that decision, as could be seen when he was instrumental in knocking them out of this year's Challenge Cup. He did really well for me and he was great in the Grand Final but maybe I needed a slightly more experienced half-back.

I was expecting us to win at Huddersfield, but without doubt they were the better team. For some reason we lacked aggression, enthusiasm and we were poor for the whole 80 minutes. Although Danny Tickle's try gave us a 4-0 lead we went in at half-time trailing 14-4. A Brett Dallas try brought us back to 20-10 with 14 minutes remaining but we couldn't come back and an injury-time converted Giants try gave them victory. It turned out to be a memorable win for Huddersfield as Wigan hadn't lost to them for 40 years.

I went into the away dressing room and I was speaking to the players when Maurice came in and gave all the squad his two-penn'orth of what he thought. It was unexpected and something he had never done whilst I had been in charge of the team. He had been in previously after games to have a chat with individual players, which was fine, but not to address players like that. I thought it was inappropriate, as it was my side and he had no right to give his opinion. He had no idea about our pattern of play or how we could have played in certain situations. What he said wasn't rocket science but I was very annoyed at him undermining me. The bottom line was that we didn't perform on the day, I knew that and the players knew that. They didn't need Maurice coming in and telling them. The players never responded to him; they knew what he was like, they were smart enough to know that he was our chairman and not the coach. Alas, he pays the wages and, being the boss, it would appear he can do what he wants!

I was furious when he went out and I struck out with my hand at a metal kit container. It didn't half hurt, but I couldn't react and show the boys I was in pain. I told them that it wasn't about Maurice, it was about us in there, sticking together and sorting this out. I didn't go and say anything to Maurice about what he had just done, because I knew that he was, for a want of a better word, my line manager. I had to tolerate it. I didn't like it, but I don't think I was ever going to change Maurice.

We had only played a handful of Super League games and it was a stop-start situation with Cup games on alternate weeks, but now we had two Easter games before the semi-final. We were in a déjà vu situation as the previous season we had only two points from eight and a Good Friday trip to St Helens at Knowsley Road. So we went into the game as underdogs and, but for Sean Long's drop goal with seconds remaining to make it 21-21, we would have won the game. It was a typical Saints–Wigan derby – full on, full of fireworks and incidents. They raced into a 14-point lead in as many minutes. Jon Wilkin was outstanding for them and he pounced on a loose ball to score, but Kevin Brown's converted try before the interval and an Andy Farrell penalty kept us in it at 14-8 and it was a big lift for us. The players were very confident about the second half and everything had been very constructive at the break. They had the attitude that 'We'll get this game,' were very positive and went out and played some superb stuff.

We scored at the beginning of the half through Danny Orr to level the game and did the same again to make it 20-all when Terry Newton scored after Willie Talau had scored for Saints.

Then a game that was always going to be ferocious got rather heated and there was a bit of a fracas between Terry Newton and Jon Wilkin. It spilled over into a bit of a brawl and Dom Feaunati hit Stephen Wild. Faz took exception to this and went in on him and it kicked off again with Paul Sculthorpe getting involved. They were really giving it to each other and I know myself after doing Joe Lydon what can happen when it's win at all costs. Players might be good friends but that is how the game should be when the passion is aroused. Every now and again, it builds up and this was one of those occasions. I knew there would be repercussions after the game but everyone dusted themselves down and got on with it and Terry and Jon got ten minutes in the bin to cool down.

Then Faz, an exceptional athlete both physically and mentally, kicked a 40-metre drop goal with nine minutes left for a 21-20 lead. I didn't think at the time he was going for the goal. It looked a bit hurried and a bit of a snap shot, but he hit it sweetly and we were in front. I knew, though, that that's when Saints are most dangerous – going into the final minutes with their backs against the wall and behind on the score sheet. They made a break from their own 20 and Kris Radlinski made a desperate tackle to save a try. All the boys showed in that phase of the game exactly how much they wanted to win it. They all got behind the ball and defended the next six, but unfortunately for us Longy came into play for them. He went in at dummy half and it looked as if he was going to pass the ball, but I couldn't see who he was going to get it out to. With a touch of genius he spun around and kicked the drop goal to draw the game. It was probably a fair reflection of the game but to draw in the dying seconds was a tough pill to swallow. I think the way that we had played we deserved something out of the game, so it was a point gained on the day.

On Easter Monday we played Warrington, who we had also been drawn to play in the semi-finals of the Challenge Cup six days later, and I had Adrian Lam on the bench following his injury lay-off. It was a superb game, which we won in the closing minutes, and a great appetiser for the fans for the next clash, as we won 26-24 after twice coming from behind.

Martin Aspinwall's try gave us a 4-0 lead before Warrington's Gary Hulse and Dean Gaskell scored to give them a 12-4 half-time lead. Two Brett Dallas tries and three penalties and a conversion from Andy Farrell gave us a 20-14 lead and that looked to be it until Richard Varkulis and Jon Clarke's converted tries edged Warrington back in front at 24-20. Then in the closing minutes it looked all over as Warrington got a penalty, but they didn't find touch and in the next set Danny Tickle went over and Faz kept his cool to kick a winning conversion. So we came away with a win and, after all the bad luck we had had, this was some overdue good luck. We were fortunate to win as Warrington were the better team. I spoke to Paul Cullen after the game and apologised to him. He is a good mate, having played with him for all those years, and I was being honest with him that we didn't deserve that win, but that's rugby league.

I started the build-up to the semi-final with a trip to the Rugby Football League that week with Andy Farrell after the incidents against St Helens. They had Scully and Feaunati attending as well over the same incident and, with both sides in the semis, they wanted their captains available. I looked at the incident on video and together with Faz we put a case together for the disciplinary hearing. So we put our case forward in front of the panel and Faz was fined but not suspended. Scully was given the same verdict, but Feaunati was suspended as well as fined.

The fine had to be paid before Faz could play in the semi-final and it's the player and not the club who have to pay the fine. It was a massive boost for the club to have Faz available for the semi and I began to prepare the side for the game, which was being played at the Halton Stadium, where the atmosphere was bound to be electric with the close proximity of the fans to the pitch.

We knew the clash against Warrington was going to be tough and that they were a resilient side, having just played them. I had Adrian Lam on the bench again and Brett Dallas was making his 100th appearance for the club. As it turned out, it was one appearance that he will remember for a long time. We knew we would have to be on top of our game to reach the final. We led the game 12-2 at half-time and we scored two tries off Warrington mistakes. The first try came from Mike Forshaw's pass going to the ground on the right hand side of the field on the halfway line. Brett was first to react to the ball going onto the floor. If the ball had gone to hand for the Wolves they would have had an overlap but Brett's vision and devastating speed off the mark saw him race 50 metres under the sticks. Players make their own luck in the game and defensively we put the Wolves under a lot of pressure and reaped the benefits. On the second occasion, Kris Radlinski scored after he collected Lee Briers' kick through and he found a gap and went 70 metres. Again we created the try because of the pressure we applied with our defence. Lee Briers kicked a penalty, but the interval lead was a slight exaggeration in our favour.

In the second half, Warrington were on the score-sheet first following a mistake by Kevin Brown, who lost the ball for Ben Westwood to score in the corner, but a Farrell penalty saw us maintain the lead as the Wolves threatened a comeback. Brett then collected the ball, this time from a mistake between Daryl Cardiss and Dean Gaskell, to extend the lead to 14 points. Warrington hit back with a converted try of their own through Darren Burns and were pulling out all the stops, but Brett did the job for us after another Warrington mistake and he went 80 metres for a glorious hat-trick and a 26-12 lead with eight minutes remaining. It was all over and Stephen Wild made sure as he crossed the line three minutes later, but to the Warrington side's credit they had the last word as Mike Forshaw scored a consolation try. It didn't matter; we had reached the Challenge Cup Final and we were waiting to see whether it would be against St Helens or Huddersfield.

The lesson of the game was that you can't beat pace, in our sport or any other, and one thing Brett had was pace and plenty of it. He was very sharp off the mark as he showed, very dynamic and added more than anyone in the defensive line. When he came in for a defensive tackle he never missed and the opposition knew they had been tackled, because he threw everything into the hit. He used his body as a weapon very much in the style of Des Drummond and in fact they were very similar players.

Following the win over Warrington, we had a month before the final and had three Super League games to get us moving in the right direction up the league table. At the beginning of the week, I made an announcement in a press release about an illness I had been suffering since the start of this season, which is documented elsewhere in this book.

We began with a 64-8 win over the London Broncos at the JJB and led 40-4 at the break. We finished off the job and Terry Newton, who was making his 100th appearance for us, followed suit with Brett Dallas the previous week and celebrated it with a hat-trick. It was a bit of an emotional game for me given my announcement and I got a great ovation from the fans.

We then travelled to Castleford and came away with a 42-28 win that saw us go into the top six for the first time that season and we were on course for where we wanted to be at the end of the season. I know that earlier in the book I have given my thoughts on Shaun McRae but when he heard about my circumstances he rang me up and also came to see me at this game. It just shows the measure of the man and it was good to know that people like Shaun were behind me.

We then entertained the Widnes Vikings on the eve of the build-up for the Challenge Cup Final and we won the game 26-8, so we had done what I wanted the side to do and gone into the final with three wins under our belts. It was very rewarding, especially under the circumstances, and the boys reacted magnificently to my situation with the way they trained and performed on game day.

By this time we knew that we would be playing St Helens at the Millennium Stadium and we approached the week leading up to the final as a normal week, travelling down to Cardiff on Thursday. I was very conscious of it needing to be as normal as possible. We had our Cup Final suits and all the palaver that goes with that and the press conference to build up the game. My main priority was to make sure our training was sorted out, so I phoned David Young, who had played at Salford with me and was now head coach at Cardiff, as I wanted a nice, easy run-out on the Friday and he arranged that for me.

I wanted to name the team to the players on Wednesday and I had an injury dilemma leading up to that announcement. This related to Martin Aspinwall, who had got a hamstring injury in the semi-final. Up to that game, he had given everything for me whilst I had been in charge and hadn't missed a game. Martin had done everything asked of him and he had trained really well, but I could see that he was carrying the injury. When we went into an opposed training routine I instructed our physio, Alan Tomlinson, to work him hard and make him sprint flat out. He pulled up and could only get up to 90 per cent and wasn't quite fit enough. I realised this and I had to make one of the hardest decisions in my coaching career. It was a tough call, but that's what the job is all about and those are the decisions I had to make. I pulled Martin to one side and told him that I didn't think he was quite fit enough. Like a good pro, he said that he would be okay and that he wanted to play. To be fair, Martin knew he wasn't quite fit enough and although upset he handled and accepted it very well. He travelled down with us to Cardiff as I thought it essential that we kept the squad together. The bonus was that David Hodgson was back in the frame after he had returned to the side following an injury in the pre-season game against London Broncos. He had made a comeback the previous week in the victory over Widnes and had scored a try. I knew I had a ready-made replacement and I decided to play him on the wing in the final.

In the build-up games, I had rotated my four props and second row forwards to see how they responded to healthy competition. I wanted to keep everyone on their toes and the aim was to make them compete for a starting jersey for the final. The four props were Quentin Pongia, Craig Smith, Terry O' Connor and Danny Sculthorpe; the second rowers were Mick Cassidy, Danny Tickle and Gareth Hock. In the Widnes game, Sculthorpe, O'Connor, Hock and Tickle started with Pongia, Smith and Cassidy on the bench. Terry and Scully had been my interchange props and I wanted to see how they would perform from the start of a game.

I was very lucky at prop with Craig Smith and Quentin Pongia, two senior pros who had done everything I had asked of them all season. With Terry another veteran, I knew he would battle for the team and me. In Scully, I had probably the most gifted prop in rugby league in terms of skill. I mean there were times when he offloaded the ball and I thought how on earth did he do that. The trouble with Scully was his fitness, he was a big fellow but with his injuries he was sometimes struggling to do the sessions. For a diabetic, what he has done is a marvellous achievement and Scully is a great role model for others with a similar problem.

Tickle had started in the second row in all the games leading up to the final and I swapped between Hock and Cassidy for the starting shirt in those games to decide who would wear it in the final. It was another difficult decision to make but I opted to have O'Connor, Sculthorpe and Cassidy on the bench for the final.

We had a final training session at the club on the Thursday and then a meal with Wigan's sponsors and former players like Henderson Gill, Bill Ashurst and Graeme West. It turned out to be a very emotional occasion for me. I didn't know at the time, but Bill Ashurst is a born-again Christian and he got hold of me in a big bear hug in the middle of the room and said 'Can I say a prayer for you.' Bill's a larger-than-life personality; he gave me another bear hug, kissed me and we said a prayer together. I think quite a few people were gob-smacked.

After the meal, we got on the coach and travelled down to Cardiff which was a fair old journey from Wigan. Maurice invited Denis and me for dinner, which was nice of him, and we gave the players some free time. On the Friday, I wanted them to see the Millennium Stadium and whilst we were there they were putting the turf down for the game, which I thought was a bit late. The roof of the stadium was open at the time and it was an eerie atmosphere going into an empty ground. We then went into the changing rooms to familiarise ourselves with what we were going to do on the day. All the staff came with us as well as the players, because they needed to know where to do the rubbing down and where the strapping was going to be done. I wanted to ensure that we had dotted all the i's and crossed the t's and were thoroughly prepared for the game. We took them for a light run-out I had arranged earlier in the week, next door at Cardiff Arms Park, and it blew away the cobwebs from the players.

A lot of preparation went into the game-plan for the Challenge Cup Final against St Helens, in relation to their strengths and weaknesses and how they played. For example, in the case of the Bradford Bulls, we knew how they were going to go for a route one, power approach and all the other sides have different ways of playing.

St Helens were very gifted with speed at the play-the-ball and they did a lot of work from dummy-half. We knew that there was no way that they were going to change their style of play, so it was up to Denis and me to make sure we had everything covered. For a normal Super League game we would give the players just enough information on the opposition, but we covered every base over and over with St Helens.

We made sure that everyone knew everything about their players and did a pen picture of all of them who were going to play. For instance, Paul Wellens – how he is under a high ball, a low ball, what hand he prefers to carry the ball in, what foot he steps off, how he links up, how he is defensively, how to get him out of position.

Another example was the strengths of Paul Sculthorpe, a predominantly right-sided player. Scully came very tight off the ruck, right hand carry with a very good left arm fend and he stepped off his right foot. He made inroads behind the ruck, which was one of his big strengths. It was all really a game of chess and we did this with every player. We made sure that the details we had were very thorough and correct and we did this by watching games, videos and DVDs of every player that played for St Helens. We showed our players clips and examples of what we were talking about in the pen pictures and what we were looking for.

Our first priority was that we knew our own strengths and weaknesses and our own game plan; the way we were going to play and certain principles that would come out during the game. But the first thing we had to do was nullify the way that St Helens played. We knew we had to number up defensively and make it physical against their ball players. People like Cunningham, Sculthorpe, Long, Higham – hit them hard in the tackle, spot them when they had the ball and make them tire. Work them over or find them, find them again and again. The more times we could find them and tackle them the better. Slow them down with our physical presence, because they were quality players with good feet and they were able to get in good positions, hit the floor and get a quick play-the-ball. It was up to us as a team not to make it easy for them and our own body positions in defence had to be spot on. It was nothing new; we were targeting the better players and planning to out-muscle them because we knew that they were a very fast team, very explosive and very sharp from dummy-half. They also played with a lot of width with decoy runners going through and they always had a lot of men in motion and lots of options. Under Ian Millward, St Helens was a very quick and skilful team.

In the week leading up to the final we made the players focus on the game as individuals and on what they were going to do for the team to win the game. A belief, desire and commitment binding us together, training together, winning or losing together; whatever it took, we were all in it together, all for one and one for all. Belief is the psychological side of the game of rugby league; if players believe it works, it will work. Teams have to have that ethos, that belief inside them. I'm not a sports psychologist, but I knew what I believed and the way I wanted to go about achieving those beliefs. Ultimately belief comes from within; people have to have goals and aspirations in life as well as in sport.

I'm a believer in Pat Riley's book *'The Winner Within'* which is very poignant for me now and probably the most inspirational book I've come across. I have always been a fighter and I have never liked losing whatever I am doing. That competitive edge has never left me and if I didn't fight this illness I would be letting down myself, my wife, my two boys and the support I have received from the rest of my family, colleagues and friends. I feel the only two people who didn't support or believe in me were Dave Whelan and Maurice Lindsay and I don't give a stuff about them.

I didn't want any finger-pointing at the end of the game. I wanted the players to be able to look in the mirror and know they'd done their best. The players would know whether they had or not and it didn't need me to jump on them. What we as coaches would do after the game is dissect the way they had played and give them feedback on their performance.

So everything was focused on the day; we had done everything right and the squad and media knew the team. I wanted to keep the day as normal as possible. We left the hotel for the Millennium Stadium about half past 12 but before that we had a meeting. I asked all the players what it meant to win a Challenge Cup Final. I had seasoned professionals like Andy Farrell and newcomers like Gareth Hock and Kevin Brown. From one extreme to another, I wanted their thoughts. The biggest shock I got was from Craig Smith, who was in tears as he told the players what it meant to him. I thought for someone as experienced as him to show that kind of emotion was outstanding.

The boys knew the battle plan and it was time to go. They looked immaculate in their new suits for the occasion, but the players weren't happy about the ties. They were a hideous luminous red, a shocking colour and all I can do is put the blame on Denis for that one. On the ten-minute journey to the stadium, I noticed what's unique about rugby league is that, apart from supporters from St Helens and Wigan wearing their shirts, scarves and hats there were fans from all the other clubs, cheering and singing as we drove past them. All ages mingling together, creating a great family atmosphere – the rugby league family.

I was looking to see if I recognized anyone and as we were arriving outside the stadium I saw a mate of mine nicknamed 'Strawb' – Ian Winterbottom. I had played with him at Wigan St Patricks before I signed for Warrington. He had a pint in his hand and mouthed to me 'Good luck.'

I felt fine, had no butterflies and was quite cool about the whole affair. I was happy with the players, their demeanour and approach to the game. In the changing rooms, I got a message from George Unsworth, our kit man, that Ellery Hanley was outside and wanted a word. I assumed he had heard about my illness and had come to wish the team and me luck. I knew Ellery well, having played against him many times and with him for Great Britain and we always had a mutual respect for each other on and off the field. I went over to him and he handed me his Challenge Cup winners' medal, against my team, Warrington in 1990. 'It's brought me good luck,' he said. 'Hopefully it will bring you luck.'

I said: 'I can't accept that.'

'If you don't I'll break your arm,' he said, smiling.

So I took the medal – a symbol of the support I had and the measure of Ellery himself, one of the most talented players ever to grace our game. I was very touched. It had been an emotional moment and I knew that this was my last game in charge of the club before I went on to America for treatment, but my main concern was the final.

I returned to the dressing room and it was a case of having to reinforce certain messages about our game-plan before they entered the fray. The boys also went out for the warm-up and I watched that for a bit. We then went into the tunnel and were given the signal to walk onto the field. As we did so I was hit by a wall of noise in the Cardiff sunshine. I knew where my whole family were sitting and when I saw them in the stand there was a lump in my throat. That's when it really hit me and I began thinking for the first time about my boys, Ben and Sam, and how I would be leaving them when I set off for America on the Monday. But I had to get my thoughts together about the next 80 minutes. Leading the Wigan side out in front of me was Billy Boston, which I thought was a nice gesture. It was very apt that Billy, the Wigan, Great Britain and Rugby League Hall of Fame legend, had the honour of leading the side out at Cardiff as he was born and bred in Tiger Bay.

We knew what St Helens was going to do. They hadn't changed their game for years and we needed to match them for speed, tempo and control, not worry about them but concentrate on our own game and match their quick play-the-ball. I feel that we achieved that, especially in the first half. It may seem that I'm wearing cherry and white glasses, as we were losing at half-time 20-10.

The first St Helens try after three minutes came from a charge-down and we should have coped with it better. Kris Radlinski made a mistake with his clearance kick and Willie Talau reacted quickest and put Lee Gilmour in. Right on half-time, as we were only trailing by four points, Paul Wellens went in under the sticks for a typical St Helens try, when the ball went through seven different pairs of hands. It was against the run of play and I know we were the better team in the first half but the points on the board are what determine the outcome of the game.

We bounced back from that start but had tries from Terry Newton and Kevin Brown disallowed by the video referee. In between those decisions, Terry Newton was first to an Adrian Lam grubber following a break from Kris Radlinski who was trying to redeem himself for his earlier error. Sean Long kicked a penalty awarded against Quentin Pongia and then Willie Talau finished off one of Long's kicks after 26 minutes and we were 14-6 down.

Andy Farrell then led by example and put a fierce hit on Martin Gleeson inside his 20 as he was clearing his line. Lammy picked up the loose ball and got it out to Brett Dallas who went in at the corner. Even after Wellens' try, I said to the boys at half-time: 'Don't worry, it will happen. Carry on playing the way you are.' I was happy with the way that we had played, apart from the score.

St Helens took the game to us and Kris brought off a superb try-saving tackle on Darren Albert, but Kevin Brown then made a mistake and Sean Long picked up the crumbs to send Paul Sculthorpe over for a try 11 minutes into the half. Sean kicked the goal as well as another penalty and we were trailing by 18 points. Kevin showed great maturity to get over his mistake to make a superb break from his own half for Brett Dallas to score his second to cheer our fans up with 14 minutes left. But Sean Long knocked on the head any chance of us coming back when he began a move which was continued by Lee Gilmour and finished by Willie Talau for his second try.

In that second half, a couple of key decisions went against us. St Helens were the better team in the second half, but the final score doesn't reflect how close the game was. I thought Terry Newton played particularly well for us and Kevin Brown, who had played strongly all year for me, did well. For such a young player to perform like that in a final was fantastic. Mark my words, Kevin Brown will one day play for Great Britain. In what position, I don't know, because Trent Barrett has been recruited at Wigan and Kevin has moved on to Huddersfield.

All in all, it was a great team effort. Sean Long deservedly won the Lance Todd Trophy for his performance. He is one of the best scrum-halves in the world and it was Shaun McRae who signed him for the club when I was his assistant. He had gone from Wigan to Widnes when the club signed him in 1997 and I knew he was a class player. The thing about great players is that whatever other players try and do, legal or illegal, they rise above it. It shows the measure of the man, that when he is pin-pointed – make him work, make him defend, put pressure on him – he still comes up with a man of the match performance like that. For his side's last try he chipped over and kicked on again. It isn't possible to take away the vision involved in that and it can't be taught. A player can be coached but when under pressure, it's a player's own individual brilliance that will shine through. Longy proved to be the difference between the teams.

The hot, sunny weather suited two teams who wanted to play a fast, direct, open game and I believe that's what a crowd of 73,000 got. There was one moment in the game which I will remember forever, even though at that time in the second half we were getting beaten and playing catch-up. My face came up on the big screen in the stadium and they did a close up of me. I was engrossed in the game and I didn't notice it, but all of a sudden the crowd in the stadium erupted and it was so loud that it grabbed my attention. I instinctively looked up at the screen, saw my face and felt quite emotional. It wasn't just Wiganers, it was St Helens supporters and rugby league fans from all over the country. That meant a lot to me and I felt I had the support of the rugby league world. It was very touching, but I didn't cry.

When the hooter sounded, I was more disappointed for the players and the rest of the staff, after the hard work we had put in. It was an experience I'll never forget, in what turned out to be my final game in charge of the club. It's an awful occasion for the losers in a final, whatever the sport, and for the fans who come to watch. We had to watch the winners collect the trophy and, although it's part and parcel of sport, it's not a nice feeling. I had done it twice with Wigan, but when I get better and move on from this, it won't happen a third time.

I went onto the podium after the players had collected their medals, shook the hands of the dignitaries and then applauded and thanked our fans who had been magnificent in defeat. In the dressing room, I thanked all the players and staff for their efforts. I knew I would be leaving on Monday for America, so I went round and thanked them all individually and finally collectively as a team, because we had all been in this together.

I then went to meet all my family, but by that time my parents had taken Sam home. So Erica and I quietly left the Millennium Stadium and walked to our team hotel. Once again, all the fans we passed on our way were superb in their encouragement, even though they couldn't have known the gravity of my medical situation.

When a side loses a final, the players still try to have a good time and enjoy themselves that evening. We all had a meal at the hotel with family and friends, but it was quite subdued. I think for quite a few players it was a big night and we gave them a little bit of leeway to let their hair down and decided that they could have a drink on the way back. I was on the coach with them and I think that even Maurice was with us. What I wanted was for all the squad to be together, not just the team but everyone in the first team squad. It was a good atmosphere, because life goes on even when you lose a big game. You've just got to dust yourself off and get on with it. There was some good singing and good drinking, although it was a lot more civilised than when I had come back to Warrington after our defeat to Wigan in 1990.

Unlike 2002, when we won the Challenge Cup and had an open-top bus back into Wigan and a civic reception, this time we went to the JJB Stadium. A few of the players were a bit worse for wear, but they were good as gold. There were thousands of supporters and I felt like I did in 1990.

I began to get emotional and tearful again when I saw all the people who had turned out after a loss to come and cheer us, knowing that the following day I was going to America. We all went into the ground where the supporters were waiting to greet the players. To me this was for them and not the coaches, but I could hear the supporters outside chanting my name and I went outside at the top of the stand to greet and acknowledge them. I was in tears again. I could only thank them all for the support they had given me. They were the only reason, I still feel to this day, that I was appointed as first team coach. They had given me their support on this emotional roller-coaster ride and I went down to the pitch, thanking and waving to them as I broke down again.

After some time, I returned upstairs and asked our chief executive, Carol Banks, to arrange a lift home for me. When I got in, I just collapsed, not physically but emotionally. I was completely whacked after the weekend, with the emotion of what I thought was the temporary interruption to my coaching career whilst I turned my attention to the trip to America. I will never lose my sense of gratitude to everyone who supported me during that time at Wigan.

13

THE FIGHT OF MY LIFE

Now, for the first time, I'm going to tell the full story of my illness, my and my family's battle against it, my fight to get back to work and for the truth to be heard. It is the biggest challenge of my life – to beat this illness and prove the doubters wrong.

I didn't know when this all started, what was happening inside my body and it's only in retrospect that I can figure out what happened. In January 2003, shortly after being made assistant coach at Wigan, I went to Australia with the Great Britain Sevens' side which was taking part in a tournament in Sydney.

We were there for ten days and during that time I believe I was bitten by a tick, or some sort of insect. I didn't feel the bite and there was no immediate sign of it, but the insect in question is almost microscopic. What this tick does is to hook onto the skin and feed off the blood. It gets engorged and so fat that the weight of the blood makes it drop off. So most people don't actually see it or, if they do, they just think it's a black spot and scratch it off.

This tick feeds on any warm-blooded animal, but it prefers sheep, deer, cats and dogs. It has the borrelia bacteria in its own gut and when it bites its digestive juices go into the bloodstream; that's how borrelia enters the body.

When I got home from Australia and got over the jet-lag I still felt very tired, although at the time I put it down to several factors. Our 18-month-old son Ben hadn't been very well, I was involved with the Great Britain Academy squad and I had just been made assistant at Wigan, although I hadn't signed a contract at the time. I was also still involved at Orrell, so I was a busy, busy man with a young family including a baby who had been ill. So I didn't feel anything was abnormal at the time. I'm not the sort of person who suffers from flu, even in winter, but in February I developed a bout of it.

Now I have to give an insight into my family life and admit that I used to sleep with nothing on. Our five-year-old son Sam was becoming inquisitive, so I thought it was prudent to start wearing boxers in bed. One beautiful sunny morning in March, I had gone to the bathroom and when I came back into the bedroom Erica was awake and having a cup of tea. The boxers were off and I was going to begin dressing when Erica said: 'What the hell have you been doing, how long have you been on that toilet seat?'

I said: 'I don't know. Why?'

'You've got a large red ring on the centre of your bum, it looks as if someone has put a dinner plate around the cheeks of your bum and drawn round it with a red marker pen.'

I turned my head around but my neck wasn't that flexible and I couldn't see what Erica was talking about. As I struggled in the vain attempt to see it we both started laughing. I was just about ready to put a clean pair of boxers on and I asked Erica if it was still there. She was still laughing and she asked if some of the lads had been messing about in training. She said that it was still there and that it was like a circular florid rash one inch in width – very distinctive – and that there was clear and normal skin colour inside it.

Erica said: 'Maybe you have been sat on a toilet seat that's been cleaned with bleach. You might have some dermatitis or have you been on a sun bed?'

I said, 'No, have I heck' and finished dressing. Erica asked if I would go to the doctor's about it but I certainly wasn't going to show my bum to a doctor. It's a man thing. If it had been a rash anywhere else I would have probably gone, but I just thought that it was a bit of dermatitis and would clear up.

So I got on with life and everything was fine, I had got over the bout of tiredness and flu, life was rosy. I was busy at Wigan and Erica was busy with the family and as time went on I thought nothing of the rash, although it was still there. It wasn't bothering me, although Erica kept mentioning it and I kept telling her I hadn't time to go to the doctor's.

At the end of July, Erica and her sister Lynne had taken the boys on holiday so I was at home myself and I had difficulty with my key for the front door. When she came home I told her that the front door was crap and that I couldn't get my key to turn in the lock. Erica said that it was an old door and perhaps a problem key for the door so she gave me hers. I tried the door with that key and it was okay and carried on using it, thinking everything was all right.

One beautiful day in August I was sitting in the garden when my attention was drawn to a twitching sensation in the bicep of my right arm. It felt like the type of twitch you get in your eye if your eyes are tired; the twitch looked almost like a wiggly worm under my skin. I called Erica over and showed her what was happening and she went: 'Oh I don't know about that, Mike. Maybe we need to see a doctor.'

I told Erica that there was no need, that I was fine. Even though the twitching continued, it wasn't bothering me. It was just something that I hadn't felt before and I thought it was nothing it would go away whatever it was. Shortly after that, I came back from the club and went for a lie down in the conservatory and got a headache which got worse and felt like I had a golf ball at the back of my head on the left hand side. I told Erica, who was also at home, about it. I never got headaches but I thought it must be the stress of the job at Wigan. Time went on and it eased, although I still had the twitch in my arm. I just didn't think about it.

I know some people might think this makes me pretty thick, but I had played rugby league all those years and now gone into coaching. I had put my body through a grilling for over 20 years, suffered the nightmare of serious injuries and battled through them until time caught up with me. There is always going to be some payback as a result and that's what I thought this was.

In October, I had a stiff neck, the headache had come back with the feeling of a golf ball again at the back of my head, the twitch was still there in my arm and I had the sensation of stiffness in my wrists which had given me problems opening the front door. So I decided to go and see my doctor although I still blamed the symptoms on rugby injuries. He examined me and he thought the twitch was a bit odd, I had a neck problem and a little bit of arthritis in my wrist, old injuries in a body that was approaching 40. He thought the neck problem was maybe a trapped nerve, causing the twitch and a problem with the wrist.

I went to see an orthopaedic surgeon, as it was thought it could be a bulging disc or something structurally wrong with my neck. I also had an MRI scan which showed some degenerative wear typical of a rugby player. There was some bulging disc but nothing serious, so I thought it was okay. The twitch was erratic, but the orthopaedic surgeon said that he thought I needed to go for nerve conduction studies and I went to see a neuropathologist. There was some sort of abnormality but they couldn't say it was categorically this or categorically that.

On Monday the 13th of October I was on the Wigan coach on the way to the press conference at Old Trafford for the forthcoming Grand Final against the Bradford Bulls. It was hot on the coach, I hadn't had anything to eat, my eyes rolled back, I went into a cold sweat and collapsed. I was brought round a short time later and I thought at the time I had collapsed because of the pressure that I had been under at Wigan. I was the acting coach and the pressure was extremely intense at times. The public were saying 'Give Mike the job,' the players were saying 'Give Mike the job,' the media were clamouring for me to get the job, there were polls in the papers with me, Andrew Farrar and Chris

Anderson supposedly in the frame for it. Wigan seemed to keep moving the goalposts, but prior to me collapsing on the coach I had unofficially been given the job permanently, although it had to be given the final okay.

It had been a very stressful situation to be in. I thought all that build-up, rushing around and burning the candle at both ends had caused me to collapse on the coach. I did the press conference, came back to the club and felt fine and I thought it was just a blip.

I came home and told Erica what had happened. She was anxious about it and wanted me to go and see my doctor straight away. I told her that I wanted to relax and chill out. So I had some steak which I knew would do me good and I felt fine afterwards. The following day Erica was still worried and anxious about me, so I went and saw my doctor. I told him what had happened and he gave me a full examination and also decided to run some blood tests. The doctor said it would take five days for the results of the blood test to come back, but with me having a temperature 24 hours after I had collapsed, this was indicative of an infection. The doctor put me on antibiotics which I began taking.

During that week, it was officially announced that I was the new coach of the Wigan Warriors. We played in the Grand Final and lost and I didn't think any more about the collapse, although I continued to take the antibiotics.

At five one morning at the back end of October, unbeknown to me at the time, Erica woke up and the red rash that she had seen on my bum in January had suddenly come back to her. She began to make sense of my situation. I had been given an MRI scan which was clear, I had got some nerve abnormality connected with the ongoing twitching in my arm, I had collapsed, had flu, headaches, stiffness and the lump at the back of my head. All these symptoms and ailments I had never had before, because I was a healthy person. At that time of the morning Erica wouldn't normally get out of bed, but with all this going on in her mind she went downstairs and turned on the computer.

She went on the Internet and did a search on 'red ring rash.' The search came up with ringworm but she didn't think it was that, then something called 'Lyme Disease Borreliosis' came up and Erica clicked onto that site. Our computer at the time was an old knackered one and couldn't call up pictures of the condition.

At half past six the same morning Erica rang my dad who had a more high powered computer and asked him to go onto a particular website and get a picture up on his screen. From what she had read on our computer, this condition required 'immediate intervention' and Erica was in a blind panic when she read those words. So much so that at eight that morning she woke me up and said: 'Stand up, turn around, I'm taking a picture of your bottom.'

Erica looked in a state and said that she needed to get the photograph developed quickly and that she was off to Tesco to sort it out. Luckily her sister Helen worked in that department and she developed the picture immediately. Erica went straight to my mum and dad's. My dad picked up the picture off his computer and showed it to Erica. It was a picture of a man's pectoral where he had been bitten. Erica said to them: 'That's it, that's what Mike had on his backside.'

It confirmed to my wife what the magnitude of my problem might be and the need to do something about it immediately.

Erica came home, upset and in a state of panic, and explained what she had been doing and showed me the photograph she had taken earlier that morning and the one my dad had taken off the internet. It was coincidence that Erica at the time was at Edge Hill College doing her second year of her Masters. She had access to all the scientific journals like *The Lancet*, *The Journal of Immunology* and other publications. Erica hit those journals and became worried about what they were saying about testing. The testing in the United Kingdom could be 90 per cent inefficient and the only way to actually diagnose someone having borrelia was the red ring rash.

Erica printed copies of all this information and research and within 48 hours we went to see my doctor. Together we explained what had happened and Erica asked me to drop my pants and show the doctor the red ring rash or what was left of it and he examined me. I showed him the photograph that had been developed a few days earlier and Erica gave him all the research that she had gathered. He was aware of the condition and said there was a test that could be done to determine it. At the same time, we were still awaiting results relating to the neural problem. It was a hive of activity, my doctor had done the borrelia test he had spoken of and we decided to go away for a two week family holiday. We ended up at the windiest place on earth – Fuertaventura. It certainly blew the cobwebs away and the whole family had a wonderful time. We came back in mid-November and our doctor contacted us with the results of the borrelia test. He told us that the result came back negative and that didn't surprise us. When he went back to the national testing laboratory in Southampton, however, they described the results as 'equivocal,' meaning that they were so ambiguous that they couldn't be sure one way or the other.

That told us something about the difficulty of what we were we dealing with. It's like telling somebody that you sort of have HIV, but then again you don't. My doctor said that there was a doctor in Bolton who, if anybody knew anything about this type of thing, then he would. I told him to send me to see him urgently. Although we were still pursuing the headaches and the lump at the back of my head, we didn't know if the two were connected.

I was just concerned that, if they were connected, all of this had started in January and we were now nine months down the line. All I could remember was Erica and I laughing about it all those months ago, but now we were on a mission. Erica's brother-in-law Neil, who is a pharmacist, also got involved, going through reams of research between them.

We had gone into December when we got an appointment with a consultant neurologist at Hope Hospital and also with the doctor in Bolton. Erica, Neil, my dad and I went to Hope Hospital first and the consultant looked through the MRI scan and the nerve conduction study that I had had a couple of months earlier. I had this nausea, I could hardly breathe and had a knotted feeling in my stomach. I suppose some people would call it a sixth sense. He then told us what in his opinion was wrong with me. He said: 'You've got progressive muscular atrophy.'

In layman's terms, the consultant was saying that it was a form of motor neurone disease, although he couldn't be sure because there were other things that can cause these sorts of symptoms. He continued that motor neurone disease was a whole group of symptoms and not just one thing that causes it. So I would have to come back in a week to have a series of tests done. I left there in a state of shock. All I could think about was that my body was going to get progressively weaker and weaker unless the following week's tests came up with something. There were still lots of things which could cause me to have the condition that I had, rather than motor neurone disease.

About the same time, Erica and I went to see the doctor in Bolton and in his office he had a very sophisticated microscope, linked to a video unit. He took a sample of blood and put it on a slide and videoed what was happening.

Borrelia is a spiral-shaped bacteria and it lives in different places. It can live in your organs, in the blood stream, and within the blood cells. When a blood sample is on a microscope slide with a glass cover on top of it, the oxygen levels drop and under these conditions it is possible to see the borrelia – a test that has been proven by another doctor in Hungary.

Erica had worked in bio-chemistry, so she knew that red blood cells when examined under a microscope are supposed to look doughnut-shaped. When my blood went on the screen via the video link she shouted 'jeez.' My blood cells weren't doughnut-shaped; they were star-shaped and my blood didn't look like blood at all. Erica explained it simply to me and I understood what she meant.

The doctor turned round to us both and said 'I believe you're chronically infected.' Then I saw something move quickly from one of my blood cells. It looked like a water flea and the doctor said 'That's one. I think you do have borrelia, but I want to cultivate your cell for another 24 hours and then I'll know.'

We felt very positive after what we'd seen and heard and about six hours later he phoned us to confirm that I had borrelia. That was great news to me after what I had been told at Hope Hospital, although the doctor at Bolton was just a general practitioner. He had got involved with people who were suffering from ME, or chronic fatigue, and had become aware of borrelia through that link. Pieces of the jigsaw were coming together.

Erica and I went back to Hope Hospital and I had a variety of tests, including the lumbar puncture, which was awful as I went into some sort of a fit. The results of the tests were that there was something abnormal but nothing else. It was just like the result my own doctor had got when he sent off a blood test and confirmed what I had read from our own research. The doctor in Bolton wanted to send the blood samples off to a laboratory in America. The consultant at Hope was supportive of us going down that route, although he thought there was only a very small chance that it was borrelia which was causing my illness.

Around this time we found out that that there is some scepticism by some medics in the UK regarding the validity of borrelia tests in America. But our view was that they have researched more into borrelia in America than we have in this country. It was first diagnosed in America in the 1960s and like everything else in America they have put money into it. Erica and I agreed with the doctor in Bolton and a sample was sent off to the lab.

Amid all this, I was also involved with pre-season training

at Wigan so it was a very busy time. I was very conscious of not letting my focus slip and my arm felt fine, although I had that lack of rotation in my wrist. The headaches had gone and the sensation of the bulge wasn't there. During warm weather training I was sound and I trained with the players and got involved when I could.

The result came back from America in February and it was highly positive that I had borrelia and another infection called babesia, which you only get through a tick bite. As I try to explain things as they stood at this time, people will be thinking was it motor neurone disease or not? To be honest, I don't really care what people call it. Progressive muscular atrophy is a more useful term, because people know what that is. That meant that my muscles were going to get progressively weaker, but it is what underlies it that is so ambiguous. Has borrelia caused the motor neurone illness or has it mimicked it? I don't know. But instead of putting someone like me in a box and saying you've got motor neurone disease – a terminal illness – and you are going to die, there is another group of patients that medicine and science don't fully quite understand. They know of people with borrelia, the infection presenting itself as having a motor neurone illness. By treating the borrelia or treating the abnormality it is possible to change what happens and that's all I needed to hear. That's why I believe the neurologist gave me his blessing to go out and seek the information because he had done everything within his confines. Go out and fight for your life, he was saying in effect, and that's what I did.

When I got back from warm weather training with Wigan the results from America had come through and whilst still going down this path I also continued to see other consultants within the NHS. We went to see an infectious disease consultant, who said that it could be argued that the borrelia was causing my illness, but that he wanted to do more tests.

I was aware that my speech was becoming slightly slurred

and some comments were going about that had I been drinking. A girl radio reporter had asked the club: 'Does your coach always speak like that then? He sounds drunk.' I didn't want the club thinking I was under stress and had been drinking. Apparently some people thought that I had had a stroke. We both knew by then that we were going to go over to America for treatment, so I talked it over with Erica and we both felt that I should speak to the club about it. Up to that point I had decided that this was a personal thing. The consultant at Hope had said that I should just carry on working and let them try and figure things out first and that's what I wanted to do.

There were so many unanswered questions but we decided to go to Wigan and present them with all the facts regarding my condition and our plans, which were to see the consultant in America as soon as possible. So on the Monday following the Challenge Cup semi-final win over Warrington, Erica and I had a meeting at the club with Maurice and Carol Banks, the Wigan Warriors' chief executive. It was an informal meeting to inform the club about my situation and no notes were taken. I told them that my symptoms were neurological and I also informed them about the tick bite and all the research we had done about the underlying problem, and that I had seen my own doctor in Wigan and a doctor in Bolton, who had diagnosed that I was suffering from borrelia. I made them aware that some of the clinicians in my case believed that my symptoms were caused by the infection and I told them that I intended to go to America for treatment as soon as possible.

The meeting appeared to go very well. Maurice said that he could put our minds at rest, that the club would look after my needs. If I was having a bad voice day, Andy Farrell, Denis Betts or Maurice himself could cover the media. If I needed time to rest I could do that and Maurice was emphatic that he wanted me to take the club to Cardiff. I thought to myself that it was fantastic that the club was going to support and look after me. Maurice had checked with

Carol Banks in relation to medical insurance and I was surprised that I didn't have any with the club. Although it was made clear that there was no offer of any help to pay for my treatment, Maurice had said that they would look after me.

I knew before this meeting that dates were available to go to America earlier, but after what Maurice had said about the support they would give me I didn't want to go straight away. I wanted to carry on and go after the Challenge Cup and Maurice and I agreed on that. Erica was going to book for us to go out on the Monday after the final. Everyone was happy with the outcome of the meeting although at the outset Erica had wanted me to go for the treatment as soon as possible as we were making up for lost time.

Then I had a meeting with the coaching staff, physio and players to inform them of my situation. First of all I spoke personally to the coaching staff, the physio and some of the senior players in the squad – Andy Farrell, Terry O'Connor, Craig Smith and Kris Radlinski – and I managed to control my emotions when I told them. I think they realised that something was wrong but not exactly what and they appreciated me telling them first. They were upset for me, but I said that my illness wouldn't affect our preparations and that this was a minor setback for me, not for them. They said they would give me any help they could and I told them it was business as usual. I was conscious of not letting my illness affect what the club was trying to achieve that season.

Maurice was present when I then met the whole first team squad and made the announcement, which was quite emotional for me. I was tearful when I was telling them all and it wasn't as easy as when I had announced it earlier. It made me cry, for the first time in my playing and coaching career, especially in front of men. It was hard for me to tell them how I felt. It was upsetting for all of us and a few of the players were in tears. It was a very humbling experience when they said that they were 100 per cent behind me.

During that afternoon Erica and I had a further meeting

with Dr Zaman the Club's medical advisor, and physio Alan Tomlinson. I told Dr Zaman I had been diagnosed as having progressive muscular atrophy by a consultant neurologist and that I also had borrelia. I also explained again that some of the clinicians involved in my case believed that the infection was at the root of the problem and that I needed to travel to America for treatment.

There was a final meeting that day, again involving Maurice, Dr Zaman, Alan Tomlinson and myself where we discussed producing a press release about my illness. When it was sent out, although I knew what the club had told me in relation to paying for the treatment, I think some people may have thought that the club was going to pay for everything, including the treatment and the trip to America. Not one single penny has come from the Wigan Warriors, apart from paying my salary, which they had to do. The club has never paid for anything directly, as a goodwill gesture or anything like that. It's purely been the money raised by the fans, absolutely nothing to do with the Wigan management. The long and short of it is that they've never contributed to my treatment and healthcare and any idea that they have is a misconception.

At least I could now concentrate on team matters up to and including the Challenge Cup Final – an unforgettable experience I've described in an earlier chapter. On the Monday following the final, Erica, my mum and I flew out to Houston via Philadelphia and on the Tuesday afternoon I had an appointment with Dr Harvey. Even though he had received a lot of information from my doctor at Bolton, I had no idea at the time of seeing him whether he was going to say that he could do anything for me. He noticed the way that my hands were and the way my balance had been affected and he said: 'classic signs of borrelia. A very rare manifestation, but classic borrelia and I want you to start the treatment.'

Everything was geared up and I went into hospital and saw Dr Harvey every day in a jam-packed week. I had the infusion line fitted and the medication on my 40th birthday and returned to the room at the hospital I was sharing with Erica and my mum to keep costs down. The next day, Erica and my mum had to start learning how to do the intravenous infusion, as everything else was being put into place and would be managed by our link doctor in Bolton, which was great news for us all. Being an auxiliary nurse, my mum was competent but Erica was a bit shaky the first time she tried it. She looked absolutely terrified as she had never done anything like this before, but Erica was determined and conquered the medical procedure.

Dr Harvey has one of the finest minds I have ever come across and his whole attitude towards illnesses wasn't about putting people in boxes. He saw it as looking for and attacking the root cause and he was talking my language. He said that he had had positive results and that the initial treatment was 12 weeks but in the meantime I could still work. After the 12 weeks it would be reviewed. They had people who had responded very, very slowly over the years, so it was a spectrum and I would fall into it somewhere. We didn't care how long it took as long as it happened and we felt that Dr Harvey had given us that assurance. The three of us came back from Houston thinking we knew what we had to do and determined to do it.

We couldn't travel back straight away because we needed to make sure that I wouldn't have an allergic reaction to the antibiotic. Everything was all right but we had an arduous flight home back from Houston to Philadelphia and then to Manchester. It took all day and when we got back I was exhausted.

When we flew to America we knew that we would have to pay for the flights, the accommodation and all the treatment. The way it worked was we paid for everyone we saw and every department we went in; it was very compartmentalised. It's not like Wigan Infirmary where patients go to see the haematologist and then go and see someone else and have some tests done all within the same area. When we went to Houston we went to see Dr Harvey at his clinic which was next to the hospital, but I went somewhere completely different in the hospital when I had the intravenous line fitted. With every different step, someone else got involved. So we payed for all that, the anaesthetist, the surgeon, the equipment, the room, the surgery. Everything is a separate bill and this is why people are knackered in America if they don't have medical insurance. When we went there for the treatment we didn't know what we were going to be hit with, but it was thousands and thousands in the end and Dr Harvey's bill was the least of it. We had to have someone to train Erica and my mum and we had to buy the infusion packs and antibiotics. Going over for the treatment was money going into a black hole. My salary was being spent on the usual bills at home and any extra money was consumed by these medical bills. Over £50,000 has gone on a variety of treatments. I have been over to America twice, Rotterdam and I have had consultations, tests and therapies. Each test costs hundreds of pounds, not like £5 for a pregnancy test or whatever in this country.

After a couple of days I was feeling fine and ready to go back to work. Whilst Erica was busy on the computer continuing her research I contacted Maurice. I outlined to him what had happened in America and that Dr Harvey favoured me returning to work, so I told Maurice that I wanted to return to the club and resume coaching the side. He said that I should take a month off work. I wasn't enamoured with it but I thought I'd still go to matches. I was feeling restless at home and was definitely ready to return to work. On the 1st of June Maurice wrote to me asking for a medical update, so I went to see my own doctor who had received all the correspondence from America and was privy to all my medical information. I told him I was ready for work and my doctor agreed and on the 4th of June he wrote to Dr Zaman at the club giving an update and confirming that I was fit enough to resume work.

On the 9th of June Dr Zaman wrote back to my doctor

and said that the club would not support my return to work. He went on to say that 'as head coach of a world famous club, his authority and opinions are vital and it would not help if he was afflicted in any way and his speech in particular. Management of the dressing room and match day operation in particular call for massive concentration and clear speech was important. The club have expressly stated that they only want Mike to resume his duties if he is fully fit to do so.'

This letter was when I first began to suspect that Wigan Warriors may have been discriminating against me. They had been aware from April that I had progressive muscular atrophy and borrelia, that I was having problems with some day-to-day activities and that I fitted within the Disability Discrimination legislation. I felt that saying to someone who was disabled that he had to be 100 per cent fit was an unfair benchmark, because if someone were 100 per cent fit he wouldn't be classed as disabled.

Naturally, I thought back to what Maurice had said to me when I first told him of my illness – that they would do everything they could. My doctor wrote back to Dr Zaman saying that he understood the club's point of view, but the club should be doing everything to support my return to work, that it would be good for the club and that it would be good for me.

On the 29th of June I attended a meeting at the club and was aware that David Whelan and Dr Zaman would be there but Maurice wouldn't, as he was in Australia. We went into this meeting feeling very positive because we would be talking about the medical side of my condition and where we were up to. Erica had continued dealing with the medical side and we went into this meeting with all the information and positive things from Houston, so I was in an optimistic frame of mind. I knew what we needed to do was to get the message across to David Whelan and Dr Zaman,

Erica began by confirming that my condition was neurological, known as progressive muscular atrophy. She then talked about the involvement of the infection in my condition and that others, just like me, had received the treatment and returned to good health. But David Whelan appeared to dismiss it as not relevant which as a result left me feeling that he did not wish to understand, something I could not comprehend as we had provided him with information from specialist doctors who have published their work in the internationally renowned journal Acta Neurologica Scandinavica. David Whelan said he would not normally get involved but that Maurice was in Australia. He went on to say that his sister's son had suffered with MND and that is what he believed I had and that there would be a rapid deterioration from which I would be unlikely to recover. He added that if I was not fully fit then I could not do the job. I was shocked and deeply hurt by what he said.

Dr Zaman barely said a word in the meeting. It was just David Whelan, entrepreneur, multimillionaire giving his opinion on sensitive and complex medical issues by referring to what had happened to a family member. It appeared he was making stereotypical assumptions and his mind closed.

We were talking about my life, not a business proposition, and he was saying I was going to die. I was left with the impression that whilst he was sorry, that it was all, terribly unfortunate, he needed to move on with the business. It appeared that he knew what was going to happen and no-one could tell him any different. I was naïve and I was beating myself up trying to explain things to them and they just seemed not to want to know. That's what we were up against in the meeting. Whatever Erica and I said to them did not appear to change their minds.

He wanted to send me off to an independent medical advisor and I couldn't understand why. They were welcome to the reports from all the doctors I had seen. I thought they should accept the opinions of these highly knowledgeable people. And this is a club that said they would support me through hell or high water. We had come back with all this cutting-edge information from America and it seemed to me they didn't want to know.

Erica and I left the meeting in a state of shock as a result of what David Whelan had said. He wrote to me, though, saying: 'Thank you for bringing your wife to the meeting, what a fighter on your behalf.' That's what the meeting with David Whelan and Dr Zaman had been, a downright battle of battles. It seemed to me that there was a hidden agenda and I was concerned that the club might be planning to sideline me.

Dr Zaman met with my own doctor and the link doctor in Bolton. Then three to four weeks later Erica and I had another meeting at the club with David Whelan. During the time up to the meeting all I wanted to do was go back to work as the coach of Wigan. David Whelan had a report which was addressed to him. We were handed that report. To us there appeared substantial errors in the report, with information not in the right context, saying that all the doctors we had seen were saying that I had got motor neurone disease, without proper reference to the relevance of borrelia. Erica said to David Whelan: 'I'm really disappointed with that' and to be honest so was I. Clinicians had said that I had a motor neurone problem, but that it could be linked to the infection. Deal with the infection and we would resolve the motor neurone problem.

I was disgusted with the report It did not appear to give the true picture. It read as if 'Look, there's nothing we can do. It's just like I said in that first meeting in June.'

Erica asked David Whelan if we could have a photocopy of the report and he said, 'You'll have to ask Dr Zaman for a copy, because this is not my report to give you.' Erica said that it was a report about my health and that we were entitled to a copy but he wouldn't budge.

David Whelan said: 'Look, you've got motor neurone disease. Dr Zaman's report says it.'

I said: 'Hang on, you went to press saying you'd support my 12-week treatment programme and I'm only halfway through it. I should be entitled to complete the 12 weeks.'

'Well, if you can't demonstrate you are going to be 100 per

cent fit in four weeks you will really have to consider your position. I will recommend that you resign and leave the club with honour. You must not force me to make the decision for you.'

At my meetings with David Whelan there were times I felt threatened and I couldn't help but keep thinking back to the time Maurice said they would help me when I first told them about my illness. By this time it was obvious we needed to get some legal advice of our own.

We went to see my own doctor and asked him if he had received a copy of the medical report from Dr Zaman and he said that he had and he let us look at it. This one was addressed to Maurice and it appeared different from the one that had been written for Dave Whelan that he had shown us when we met him. When I asked to see a copy of the original report I was informed 'No, this is the only report.'

14

BITING BACK

It was becoming clear to us that the whole stance that the Wigan Warriors were taking was wrong and that we needed some legal representation and intervention. Fortunately I was in the Coaches Association, which was part of the GMB Union. It was in early August when I met Neil Derrick, the Coaches Association rep, with Erica. During that first meeting we explained the medical journey up to my present circumstances, the meetings I had had with the club and what was said at them. The discussion was about how the club had positioned themselves to be supportive of me going to America and how everything suddenly changed after I had taken the club to Cardiff.

As a result of this meeting Neil wrote a letter to David Whelan on the 11th of August and in the letter he said:

'I refer to Mike Gregory's letter of 3rd August to Dave Whelan in which Mike Gregory has said on medical advice he was ready and willing to resume work. Mike Gregory expressed concerns about the club's position in relation to his future at Wigan. He also referred to a meeting that took place with David Whelan on the 29th of June. Mike Gregory and his wife believe that David Whelan was planning to replace him and at that meeting it had been made clear that he did not feature in the club's plans. I ask for a meeting as soon as possible to discuss the current and ongoing position.'

Erica and I brought Neil up to speed with the medical advice, but his opinion was that I had been signed off to go back to work. The contentious point was that Dr Zaman was not entirely in agreement with my doctor's opinion, arguing that I should only return to work if I was fully fit.

That was the issue, because I felt setting a benchmark at being 100 per cent fit was unfair and unreasonable when they knew I was ill. They knew what my illness was, they knew what I was trying to achieve as far as the treatment was concerned. Erica and I began to suspect that they were setting this benchmark so high in order to exclude me from returning to work. The reasonable employer ought to say: 'Look, someone who is classed as disabled is never going to be 100 per cent fit and we need to make reasonable adjustments.' But it was very clear to us that they weren't looking at making any adjustments. If I wasn't 100 per cent fit I had to stay away and Neil, Erica and I felt that employment law doesn't endorse that view. The law says that if someone is disabled you need to look at making reasonable adjustments and it doesn't matter what my illness was.

From that first meeting, Neil Derrick registered his interest in representing me. The club was saying that it wanted me to go and see an independent specialist. Neil Derrick said that until they talked to the GMB we should not do anything and we heeded that advice as they were now representing me.

On the 23rd of July, David Whelan wrote me what I considered to be a hurtful letter and from it I felt a change in his stance.

After getting over the letter I wrote back to David Whelan on the 3rd of August and I said 'Look, you were told about everything right back in April, about the muscular atrophy, about the infection and why I wanted to go and get the treatment.'

Another letter came on the 6th of August, this time from Maurice Lindsey. He was apparently taking the same stance as Dave Whelan. I wrote back to Maurice on the 10th of August saying that I had told him and Dr Zaman everything that had happened to me. I also stated: 'I believe your support is no longer available. Therefore I have little alternative but to seek advice on my future.' I believe they now saw me as a liability. Now it was the GMB and me versus the Wigan Warriors management.

On the 20th of August Erica was at home with the children when David Whelan rang to speak to me. Erica told him that I was out. He said that the four week deadline was coming up and, if I couldn't demonstrate that I was going to be 100 per cent fit, I should 'resign from the club with dignity.'

Erica said: 'Hang on, there are people who are saying you should be facilitating Mike's return to work. Mike loves this job, it's his dream. His own GP, his own consultants are saying he can return to work, so why are you blocking him?'

David Whelan said that if we persisted with this attitude that he would equally persist in demonstrating that I was incapable of doing the job. The reality facing me were the alternatives of continuing to fight to prove my capability or resign and walk away with £32,000.

When I got home Erica was very upset about the telephone call and we emailed the GMB and informed them about it. I wrote to Dr Zaman to inform him that the GMB were involved and they had recommended that I took no medicals until after a meeting with the club on the 2nd of September.

I was really angry that David Whelan had upset Erica. The £32,000 offer was a lot less than my contract but that wasn't the point. My contract was anyway probably one of the briefest contracts on earth; there was no medical provision or sickness clause in it. David Whelan had talked about a staff handbook, I hadn't got one, hadn't had one sent to me and didn't know one existed. On the 21st of August, lo and behold, the staff handbook arrived through the post. It was a little reminder, because I wouldn't go for the medical.

A couple of days later I was up at Orrell, where the side were training. I had continued going despite being told to stay away, when Maurice Lindsay, who had just come back from Australia, came over to me. I thought it was a bit rich after what he had said in his letter of the 6th of August.

He said he'd come up with a solution that would solve the stalemate. They would stage a testimonial game at Wigan against Warrington. 'We'll send you off in style, you just focus on getting well, Mike.'

This testimonial was to be instead of the £32,000 lump sum which David Whelan had offered me. So both Maurice and David Whelan were coming at me; it was like the good cop, bad cop routine. I didn't respond to Maurice's offer and I didn't contact David Whelan in relation to the lump sum offer. However, on the 27th of August, David Whelan wrote retracting the offer of £32,000 and suggesting a meeting to discuss my medical capability to continue in my role.

On the 2nd of September Neil Derrick, Erica and I met David Whelan and Maurice Lindsay. What surprised me was that there was no secretary to make notes for something as serious as this. Initially, everything was quite amicable because David Whelan wanted us to take the offer, which was back on the table, and disappear. Dave and Maurice went out and we discussed the matter. I decided that I didn't want the £32,000. I wanted to go back to work and that stance was never going to change.

On being informed of that, Dave's demeanour changed; he just flipped. He jumped out of his seat and began banging his fist on the table, pointing his finger close to my face and shouting at the top of his voice 'I'll take you down the capability route, I'll take you down the hard way, I'll take you all the way.' I was shocked but I said 'Dave, I feel well enough to come back to work, I want to come back to work.'

David Whelan was shouting louder and trying to stop me speaking. It was an absolute tirade and all I wanted to do was jump over the table and hit him because of the way he was behaving. He was absolutely disgraceful and Neil Derrick stood up and told him so. That seemed to stop him in his tracks, as if no-one had ever stood up to him before. I doubt he would have shouted at me in that way had I not been ill.

He left the meeting and it was time for 'good cop'

Maurice Lindsay. He said that he still wanted to explore the testimonial.

I wasn't completely enamoured with that, but the GMB were saying it was probably a good compromise. I was still of a mindset that I wanted to return to work, but at the end it was agreed that I would go for a medical and that Wigan would look into the testimonial.

Arrangements for the testimonial fell apart. It appeared to me that Warrington had gone to great lengths, but there wasn't going to be a game between them and Wigan. Maurice suggested a game against Leigh at Leigh. I felt Wigan was trying to put all the financial responsibility onto Leigh and I thought that it should lie with Wigan. The original concept was that I should have the chance to say my farewells to Warrington fans as well as Wigan and go out on a high.

Maurice Lindsay then sent me a very emotive letter saying that Leigh felt demeaned that I didn't want to play there. It was nothing to do with Leigh, and I wrote to them saying that. So the testimonial just fizzled out, which I was quite glad about because really I wanted to go back to work.

Maurice then wrote a letter saying: 'There is no alternative other than to proceed in a more formal way by going down the capability route'.

Because I wanted to go back to work I agreed to go and see a consultant so the club arranged for me to go and see a neurologist at Hope Hospital. It was the same one I had seen in December the previous year. The appointment lasted for about an hour and a half and he examined me and I did some tests regarding balancing, co-ordination and all of that. He spent quite a length of time discussing the type of job that I did and I began explaining how a head coach worked, as the consultant didn't know. He was a very intelligent man who figured out what a coach would do strategically and tactically and that you would have to deal verbally with management, media and players. I told him how I would plan my training sessions and work through a black book I had with all the other teams' plays, all the strengths and weaknesses of the opposition. I talked to him about Denis Betts, my assistant coach, Nigel Ashley-Jones, my strength and conditioning coach, and my other coaches and backroom staff. I went on to tell him about using people like skipper Andy Farrell, who were not on the coaching staff but who had supreme talent for teaching other players. I was talking for ages and when the examination finished I had no idea whether he was going to be positive or negative towards me.

The report was sent to me on the 30th of September and I read it nervously. The consultant discussed his clinical findings, said that he had spoken to me at length about the job and concluded that I was fit enough to return to work with some adjustments. I could fulfil the core duties of my job. He wrote:

'In terms of his ability to do the job as head coach of Wigan rugby league team, this depends on the nature of his duties. His problems are largely confined to the upper limbs. I presume that his work is mainly strategic – advising players on tactics rather than hands-on demonstrations. If so his current condition will permit him to undertake the duties expected of him. Equally there is no reason why he should not report to the management and the media since his higher cerebral functions are intact.'

The consultant was supportive of me going back to work and I was over the moon as that was what I wanted to do. So the Wigan Warriors got a copy of the report which was favourable to my returning to work and I thought 'champion.' This was a consultant that Wigan wanted to use otherwise they wouldn't have contacted him.

On the 11th of October Maurice wrote to the Consultant at Hope Hospital. The letter read:

'I do note ... you have passed considerable comment on his ability to do his job as head coach for the Wigan rugby league team. With all due respect, I am not sure that you are fully qualified to make such a decision unless you are fully aware of the duties involved. It is impossible for you to form a judgement. In truth being head coach of the world's most famous rugby league team is a physically and psychologically demanding post. It is a job for a fully fit person and I make the judgement having been the most senior administrator in this game for thirty years.'

This was a consultant neurologist who had been doing his job for 40 years, the consultant that Wigan had wanted me to see, so really they should have been happy with his findings. As one of Britain's leading neurologists, he was high as you can get.

On the 21st of October I attended a meeting at the JJB Stadium with Erica, Neil Derrick, Joe Lydon, Maurice Lindsay, Dr Zaman, Carol Banks and Christine Embleton who took notes.

I asked Joe to attend because we knew that this meeting was going to be about capability; he had played the game for a number of years, he was a qualified coach, and had worked in administration at the Rugby Football League. He was also phenomenally knowledgeable about sport, the Wigan management, the Wigan coaching structure and how I worked.

It all boiled down to a dictaphone; that's all I needed. I had identified that my writing had slowed down, so in a match I would use a dictaphone to record my thoughts if things were going wrong on the field. In theory, I wasn't the person who should have been coming up with reasonable adjustments, Wigan Warriors should have come in and said 'How can we adjust your job Mike?'

Expert agencies should have come in and said: 'Right Mike, you're going to do your job. What do you find difficult about it? Can you operate that telephone or do we need to get you something else?' I knew from my own break-down what I needed and was ready to help the club and tell them. That didn't happen because Wigan decided that the consultant's report was invalid because he hadn't been provided with a full list of my duties. Remember that this was the consultant that they had chosen and that they had also written him a letter which I had given him before the examination.

The meeting seemed to get off to a good start with Maurice acknowledging that he had his duties as a good employer and that he was bound by legislation, but how wrong could I have been? Now this latest consultant's report, saying that I was fit to return to work, wasn't good enough. I had never had a list of duties nor a job description, but suddenly I was ill and the club needed to draw up a list of duties for a coach.

I had been doing the job from July 2003 until April 2004. The side had had 11 consecutive wins, I had taken them to a Grand Final and a Challenge Cup Final at Cardiff. I think people would say I'd done quite well, that I knew my job. I provided Maurice with a list of my duties as I saw them, but Maurice said that wouldn't do; he had to write it and he didn't want the list to go to the consultant at Hope. It was Neil Derrick who put it in a nutshell. 'You are giving the impression,' he told Maurice, 'that this doctor's opinion is not the one you like.'

I couldn't understand why Maurice didn't want us to see him with a jointly agreed list of duties. The man was one of the best in Great Britain. It seemed as if Neil had hit the nail on the head. The meeting was stuck at loggerheads. Maurice and I were supposed to sit down and draft a list of duties but, like the proposed testimonial, it never happened.

A list of duties arrived from Maurice on the 29th of October. I examined them and they were an unacceptable version of what I did. On the 1st of November I received a letter from Maurice informing me that I had an appointment at Charing Cross Hospital in London on the 5th of November. It was short notice and what they were doing was trying to squash everything into such a short space of time so that I wouldn't be able to come up with my own list of duties. We had it checked out by two senior coaches at the Rugby Football League. Joe Lydon also had an input and we also went to Sport England, who monitor coaching in all sports. They came back saying that the list of duties did not reflect accurately what a head coach does. The whole thrust of the list of duties that Wigan came up with was physical demonstration. That was so unreal and in my mind I questioned why they had gone down this path, knowing of my impairment.

Sport England said that when dealing with elite athletes you do not do directive coaching, that would be really bad practice. So Wigan had drawn up a list of duties for elite coaches to use coaching methods which did not accord with best practice. I was head coach at the Wigan Warriors, a fully qualified coach, former England Academy coach, a former Great Britain captain who had been on two British Lions tours. I wouldn't say to Andy Farrell: 'Here, I'll just show you how to pass a ball.' You just don't do it, but there were people out there who didn't understand rugby league. If you are dealing with a seven-year-old, you have to show him how to pass, kick and tackle. But not with someone who is playing for the first team and may have played for Great Britain.

Wigan's quick turnaround plan didn't work because we worked like blue-arsed flies and got my list of duties and a job description from the Rugby Football League. We sent everything to the doctor who was to examine me and to report to the Wigan Warriors management.

Erica and I travelled down to London on the 5th of November for the appointment; we wanted to get back in time to take the children to a bonfire. Wigan made all the travel arrangements. We arrived at Charing Cross Hospital armed with our bundle of documents. I presented them to the doctor and he began to ask me about my medical history from when I had been bitten by the tick. When I started talking about the duties of a head coach, he cut me off short and said that he would do his clinical assessment, look at the documentation and come up with his decision on my capability to do the job.

He was completely different from the previous consultant and it was a very closed conversation from that point on. I thought 'I just have to get through this.'

He did all the tests the previous consultant had done –

reflexes, walking on my toes and co-ordination. He then did a test I hadn't had before and stuck a piece of paper in each eye. I had no idea what that was about. He told me that he thought it was a form of motor neurone disease. At no point did he ask me about my job and didn't seem remotely geared up to the practical side of determining if I was capable or not. I had mentioned borrelia, but he wasn't interested. There was no way that he should have been so dismissive, but I had that gut feeling during the appointment that it was a foregone conclusion.

We came out and Erica, who had been very insistent that we should get a copy of his report, even though he seemed worried that that would create a delay, burst into tears because of the way he had been with me. To me the process was degrading and to my mind the examination hadn't been humanely done. I just thought it was a complete waste of time and Wigan would end up getting the report that they wanted.

I received a copy of the report on the 10th of November and it was stating the obvious in saying that I had an upper limb weakness.

He said that I wouldn't be able to demonstrate the skills of catching or be able to implement skills drills, but he was missing the point because I wouldn't have to. If he had spoken to me about it perhaps he would have been aware of that but he didn't bother. The report agreed with Wigan Warriors; the doctor diagnosed MND and dismissed borrelia out of hand.

Neil Derrick looked at the report differently and said that the ball was in Wigan's court and it was still up to the club to demonstrate reasonable adjustments.

According to the Disability Rights Commission, if you have a disability or long-term health condition and you apply for a job or become a member of staff, the employer has a duty to make 'reasonable adjustments' to employment practice and premises if these place you at a substantial disadvantage.

In some circumstances, it is appropriate to make some

adjustments as a general response to the needs of all disabled people, such as ramps and easy access toilets. In other circumstances it is important to take into account the individual's needs. The DRC stress that it is important not to make assumptions about what someone needs in the way of reasonable adjustments but always ask the person, rather than trying to guess what reasonable adjustment would be most appropriate.

The DRC stress that as an employer you have a duty to make reasonable adjustments as soon as you know that someone defined as disabled in the terms of the Disability Discrimination Act may need them.

I felt encouraged that there were organisations and legislation out there to protect my rights as an individual and an employee. Surely the next meeting with the Club would to be to address these issues, talk about reasonable adjustments and for me to return to my dream job.

The next meeting was on the 26th of November which Erica, Neil Derrick, Dave Lyon, Maurice Lindsay, Carol Banks and I attended at the JJB Stadium. Dave Lyon came to the meeting as he had just finished a coaching role at the Wigan Warriors. Dave had worked with me at the club and when I was head coach of the England Academy in 2002 so he knew how I worked and how I structured the coaching staff under me. All the information was to hand to enable me to return to work and now I wanted to know what adjustments the club were going to make to facilitate that. The Charing Cross doctor hadn't said I couldn't return to work. He had outlined the difficulties I would have, so the whole onus was on the club to make adjustments. The meeting didn't really last long.

Maurice began by saying the situation was tragic, that I had MND and I was terminally ill. I felt like writing my obituary there and then. I was sat there, no different from when I took the team to Cardiff earlier in the year, I wasn't contemplating death then and I wasn't now. Perhaps I should have said 'You know Maurice life is a terminal illness, do you know how long you've got?' In fact people with MND may live up to 20 years or more and there are professional people with motor neurone disease who are still working. People still have lives, still have dreams and still do jobs; yes, they do have some issues and all they need is some help. But Maurice's views just seemed stereotypical.

I said: 'When you employed me I brought ideas to the field of play. We were quite successful; we got to two finals, which was an achievement. Your list of duties does not reflect how I work, more how you would coach juniors. I don't have to demonstrate tackling techniques. The way we coach is through empowerment, giving Dave Lyon and Nigel Ashley-Jones duties and surrounding them with good people who can do their jobs.'

Dave made comments agreeing with my explanation of how I coached and said that I would still be able to do that and continue being head coach. Maurice, who had briefly been out of the meeting, came back and said: 'Well, you know we've had to put an action plan into place with Andy Farrar.'

Maurice had just confirmed what we had read on Teletext the previous day – that Andrew Farrar was going to join the Wigan coaching staff. It had been discussed when he had been in England in August for a wedding. On the 11th of October he was formally offered the job and on the 25th of October Wigan had applied for Andrew's work permit. Never once had the club talked to me about their plans with Andrew Farrar.

By now I'd had two capability assessments; one had sat on the fence and one had been favourable toward me returning to work. Maurice had acknowledged in a previous meeting that he was bound by legislation to consider reasonable adjustments, he should have said 'Right Mike, how can we help you return to work?' That was the next step that should have happened but when it didn't I knew then that there was no chance of me returning to work at Wigan, even though we had provided him with considerable information to back up that case, even if it had been a three-month trial period. But whilst I was battling and going through all the distress of previous meetings, the club had approached Andrew Farrar. There was nowhere for me to go, I knew they didn't want me back. Had they wanted that they wouldn't have made it such hard work over the previous six months.

On the 14th of December I received a test result that showed that, even though after all this time on IV Therapy, I was still positive for borrelia. Our doctor in Bolton said that no-one could argue with it, I definitely had borrelia. I was disappointed with the result but I continued the treatment to fight the disease.

On the 22nd of December I received a letter from Keith Hollinshead, head of personnel at the club, stating:

'Maurice and David Whelan are away from the office at the moment and I have been asked to deal with this matter. In the absence of agreement they have asked me to convey to you their decision to continue with the present coaching arrangements that have existed at the club during your absence. You will continue to receive your salary in the normal way until the 31st of October 2005.'

I was put on gardening leave – a great Christmas present. I had jumped through every hoop, given them all the information and the club didn't know what to do with me. They knew they couldn't sack me as it would go to court and be in the public domain, but they wouldn't let me back to work. People may look at the whole episode and say that at least I've been paid. Yes, I've been paid because the club by law had to pay me and because the GMB were onto them. What that letter indicated was that they still weren't prepared to enter into what Maurice had already identified as their legal obligation as a good employer. That was so insulting because they had robbed me of my dream. I had gone into these meetings and they had scoffed at me. I had been belittled, insulted, bullied and humiliated, but I had kept quiet and didn't react because I wanted my job back.

Sometime later I became aware that the Disability Rights

Commission was following my case and spokesperson Patrick Edwards of the DRC said 'You'd think that the contribution Mike made to Wigan's success would merit better treatment, but far too often employer's are more keen to show disabled people the door than make the adjustments necessary to keep them in work. Mike's case is another example of how employers' refusals to meet their duties under the law is making a hostile environment for disabled people and those with long term health conditions to get in and get on. Wigan like thousands of other employers in Britain need to raise their game in this crucial area'.

Leading up to the subsequent tribunal I had been sent a series of written questions by the solicitors representing Wigan because it had been agreed that I would not be cross-examined and that I would give a written response. One of the questions I was requested to answer was: 'What additional adjustments do you say ought to have been made in your case? Please specify exactly when it is alleged the adjustments ought to have been made and the exact nature of the adjustments contended for.'

I answered it as follows:

'This is not a simple answer, nor can it be reduced easily. I anticipated a process of re-integration into my duties and a period of experimentation and trialling. Rather than merely being locked out and now left to prove that which would have been obvious if the respondents had complied with any of their duties. I understand that in such cases as these, employment tribunals will recognise the difficulties of proof in respect of adjustments and their practicality, and in this case I say that it is the respondents', Wigan's fault for removing me from the workplace before any detailed assessment of my abilities in the job and an assessment as to how I could be accommodated. The respondents' barrister now stands back and asks me to prove a case which has been made more difficult as a result of the respondents' actions. However, I believe that the evidence in this case is overwhelming even though the respondents' acted as they did. In essence, my case is this, I think that the respondents' should have begun a more meaningful engagement with me about the duties of my post and those parts of it which could and should have been adjusted. My case is contained in a bundle of documents in here. Even more importantly, the respondents' should have assessed my abilities and inabilities and then seen how to overcome these hurdles. Instead they held to a rigid list of duties and did not engage in a process of considering adjustment. My problem with the respondents' is their perception of me as a physical cripple rather than a skilled head coach with many achievements, who was able to fulfil the core tasks of the role with appropriate adjustments to enable me to access the work place. I ask that I be judged as Mike Gregory, rugby league professional, captain of Great Britain and skilled and successful head coach who has physical difficulties.'

Our solicitors were already involved and we commenced filing for discrimination against disability, because I believed and still do believe that the club had frozen me out. I had to fill in a disability questionnaire, then I had to inform the club that I was taking legal action against them. It was a busy period during the rest of 2005 and 2006 as the case papers were prepared for the action against Wigan. In addition the GMB asked the two senior coaches of the RFL that we had previously approached to be witnesses on my behalf. They were prepared to stand by their views as to the role of a Head Coach. However, when I asked one of them to confirm his availability he told me there had been communication between Wigan and his boss at Rugby League Headquarters and that 'it had really made the situation very, very difficult'. I have great respect both professionally and personally for both these experts and I did not wish them to suffer any hardship because of me.

In February 2005 Erica and I went to Colorado to see Dr Martz and Dr Harvey, the original doctor we had seen in Houston the previous year. They believed that my symptoms were the same as Dr Martz, who had had borrelia but had made a complete recovery from it. Once again we came home in a positive frame of mind.

Maurice Lindsay became aware that we had returned from America and on the 8th of March got back in contact with us saying that they would like to meet me for a medical update. By this time, I had no trust in them. After that, the club was saying in the press that I had refused to be examined. But I'd had enough and I knew they weren't going to offer me my job back. Very soon afterwards Ian Millward was made head coach with Denis continuing as his assistant.

I was still under contract to the club and couldn't say anything to the media, unlike the Wigan management who disclosed confidential medical information without my consent. I felt this type of behaviour just typified the disregard my employers had for me as an employee. When it came to the end of October it was a blessed relief. Much as it had been my dream job when I was appointed, because of what had happened to me it was a relief not to be connected with them any more.

At the last minute the Wigan Warriors tried to offer me a settlement. This was on the Thursday prior to the case going ahead the following Monday in Manchester. A lot of work had gone into the case preparation and I was ready for the battle ahead. What I was offered was an insult. I know it sounds stupid but they could have offered a gold pig and I wouldn't have wanted to accept it. My premise was to get the whole story out into the public domain. If I had accepted their offer, there could have been a gagging clause and you wouldn't be reading this book now.

My solicitors advised me that we should carry on, the GMB, who were stumping up the cash for the barrister were saying go on. We turned down the Wigan Warriors' settlement offer and I prepared over that weekend for the tribunal.

On Monday the 20th of March Erica and I arrived at Manchester for the tribunal and we were introduced to my barrister. My barrister at that stage stated that though I had submitted my written responses the other side had stated that I was to be cross-examined over the eight days of the hearing! The legal representatives for both parties had to go for a meeting with the chairman of the tribunal. I was nervous but ready for whatever the Wigan Warriors might come up with, especially after I had turned down their settlement offer. When our barrister returned, he said that the chairman had recommended that Wigan considered their position.

I had taken Wigan to the tribunal for injury to feelings and aggravated damages. It sounds really trivial doesn't it, injured feelings? But I was advised that was what their actions were classed as. I was advised a likely award could be upwards of £25,000. In some quarters it was reported that I had settled my dispute with the club and had withdrawn any claim against Wigan, who had agreed a payment of £17,500 settling this dispute after being advised to do so; the payment was a sum to reflect an award under the Disability Discrimination Act. If they had been so strong in their convictions that they had done nothing wrong they would have gone ahead with the proceedings.

Maurice Lindsay said 'Having seen Mike at the hearing we realised that his health had deteriorated further. We instructed our barrister that under no circumstances was he to cross-examine Mike in the witness box. We would not have been comfortable with putting him through that stress. We made a payment of £17,500 although it was officially confirmed that Mike was making no claim for the loss of earnings. We had honoured every penny of our contractual obligation. Now the matter is officially ended we wish Mike all the luck in dealing with his sad illness. He and his family have our utmost sympathy.'

The legal action I had taken against Wigan had nothing to do with loss of earnings and Maurice omitted to explain why they had to pay this particular sum. Settling out of court I could not understand Maurice's explanation given publicly at all. As I stated earlier, I had been advised I was to be cross-examined by the Club's barrister.

Wigan Warriors made an offer of £17,500, which reflects awards that the courts reserve for cases where serious disability discrimination has occurred. After advice from my barrister and solicitor, I accepted the offer believing by implication that discrimination was admitted. Also there was no gagging clause and I thought great. We had come to the end of the road; Mike Gregory with invaluable help from Neil Derrick of the GMB union and Charles Hantom of Whittles Solicitors had stood up to the world-famous Wigan Warriors. Now people could decide for themselves whether I had been treated fairly or not.

That was what the Wigan Warriors and Maurice Lindsay didn't say at their press conference after the tribunal and in their press release. The club's explanation was significantly different, claiming that they had taken pity on me, but that was just another spin.

15

WITH A LITTLE HELP FROM MY FRIENDS

It seemed to Erica and me that we had achieved an awful lot at the tribunal, but I still wanted people to understand what the club had done, or not done as the case may be. Now I was free to talk about my experience and I felt compelled to be interviewed by *The Independent*, *The Daily Mail* and the disability press, because I felt I needed to put the record straight.

There are people out there in the work place with chronic illnesses and disabilities who are covered by legislation. My own fight to go back to work will hopefully make people aware that they are not second-class citizens. By doing what we did with *The Independent*, who supported us when a lot of people were running scared, we could give our side.

It's not the club I have fallen out with, but only two men. They have even inferred that it's my fault for the poor start to the 2006 season, which just about sums it up. I want the club to do well and win silverware. I love the club and being a Wiganer, I've no wish to see them at the foot of the table. Even though there are new players there, I have worked with a few who remain at the club and I know their ability. I'm sure my mate Brian Noble will get it right if he is left alone to sign his own players. I'm a Wiganer and you'll never take the Wigan out of me.

There were times when I was furious with Maurice Lindsay and Dave Whelan, however, it's time to draw a line under it now, although it was superb being head coach of Wigan. I had lived my dream, but life goes on – with a lot of help from the people of Wigan and beyond.

Whilst I was fighting against Wigan, trying to come back to work after my first trip to America, there was a groundswell of events organised on my behalf. This began with the 'Hike for Mike' which set up a trust that is still running. Unknown to us, a committee had rallied around to do a sponsored event on my behalf. Word had got out that I was privately funding the cost of the medical treatment and that I wasn't receiving any financial help from the Wigan Warriors or anyone else. It was August of 2004 when the event took place – a sponsored walk from Haigh Hall to the JJB Stadium, the club's only connection with the event being that it was the finishing line. I arrived at Haigh Hall early with Erica and there were about 200 people milling around the grounds. At the start time, one of the organising committee asked me if I would like to say a few words to the people who had turned up for the event. As I walked around the corner I was completely overwhelmed – more than I ever was in my playing and coaching career. I was met by what I can only describe as a sea of faces; there must have been 3,000 people gathered in the grounds of Haigh Hall. The surrounding area was completely grid-locked. I couldn't believe what I was seeing. All these people had turned up to be involved and tears welled up into my eyes and I had a big lump in my throat. It was a truly amazing effort from everyone concerned.

I went in front of the sea of faces at the starting line as an emotional wreck and said 'A big thank you to everyone who has turned up and everyone who has put their time and effort into helping me one way or the other.'

I would have liked to have named and personally thanked the people on that committee who organised this and the continuing events for the trust fund. All those people know who they are and they didn't become involved to get a name check in the book, but I would like to place on record my heart-felt thanks to every one of them for everything they did and continue to do. The response from them and from the rugby league family country- and world-wide demands a very big thank you. You don't know how much this means to me, to Erica, to Ben and Sam and the rest of my family. I'm truly amazed at and appreciative of what was has been done for me. A phenomenal amount of money has been raised on my behalf and spent on my medical treatment and expenses both at home and abroad. No matter what happened with Wigan, this gave us some peace of mind.

There have been so many events since the hike began it all. My former club Warrington have been exemplary in looking after one of their own. They have hosted two dinners for me, one on our tenth wedding anniversary, so that was really special.

Following the fiasco with Wigan over a testimonial, Warrington arranged a benefit game for me after my contract with the Warriors was up. The game was played on Sunday the 16th of January 2006 at the Halliwell Jones Stadium and it was a local derby between the Wolves and Widnes Vikings. The Warrington club couldn't do enough for me and my family for this game, and involved both of my boys. They had both been through so much since my illness and I really wanted them both to know what their daddy had achieved as a player and what the people of Warrington and Widnes thought of him.

As I looked out onto the stadium I thought there must have been a thousand people scattered in the ground and I thought 'God bless them for turning up.' We went to do some things with the boys and the Past Players Association, which was wonderful. I was busy but the next time I turned around there was a big crowd inside the ground and I could barely believe it. Sam and Ben led the teams out as mascots wearing the Warrington colours and a crowd of 6,124 saw a game which was won 21-20 by Warrington. I had the onerous job of selecting the man of the match and finally plumped for Chris Bridge of the Wolves and he was presented with the Harry Bath Medal, the Australian legend's memento from Warrington's 1948 Championship success.

The Widnes captain, my mate Terry O'Connor, who played under me at Wigan, had some nice things to say about me; he must have been thinking about it for months. That says a lot about Terry O'Connor.

I thought that it doesn't matter what happens in our lives now; Sam and Ben have got this day to remember and cherish. Erica and I and the rest of my family had this memory. I can't thank the club and the crowd enough for making the day so special for all of us.

As well as my former club, the Sacred Heart Church, the Beech Tree pub and Wigan Rugby Union Club have all put dinners on for me. The Great Britain Rugby League Lions have been fantastic, organising a 'Tribute to Mike' and sending in donations periodically. There was the Tribute Night at The Monaco at Hindley, at which the presenters were Graham Lovett from the local radio station and Eddie and Stevo from Sky Sports. John Oakes of Micron produced a DVD of the night and it was unbelievable the way they managed to get all those tributes from overseas, including the likes of Peter Sterling and Shaun McRae, plus the past and present players and coaches who attended.

Then recently there was a bike ride from Whitehaven to Newcastle, when friends of mine were in the saddle for three days. Without those people I would not be able to pursue the avenues I am pursuing, one of which is stem cell therapy. One thing that Erica and I knew that we weren't going to be able to cope with was the building work to adapt our home. So one gesture which was an absolute godsend came from Jackson Lloyd who offered to do the extension and adaptations. They were absolutely wonderful about it; they came in and project-managed it, working closely with the architect. The other option would have been a care home, which had the facilities I now needed, and that wasn't an option I was going to take. Erica and the boys are my family and we are going to stay together as a family.

People knock the Social Services, but for me they have been absolutely superb, as have all the team involved with my care and medication – the occupational therapist, physiotherapist, speech therapist, doctors and nurses, you name it. But for these people Erica and I would have been completely lost and perhaps out of our depth, because there are so many ramifications to someone becoming disabled. Life changes in a way that it is not possible to imagine, not just in a practical way, but emotionally. Without these people we would have folded as a family. They are what kept us together.

My family, extended family and close friends have all been there for me, no matter what the task, and for that I am eternally grateful.

People I played rugby league with have come forward as well, like Rob Turner who played at Warrington. 'Rocky' has his own firm, Carefree Lifting, and he has been an absolute wealth of advice and helped us in so many ways.

When you're striving on the medical front, going through all the changes that disability brings and trying to keep the family together, it is easy to see why people just give up. Without all this help Erica and I have received from all these people, I would probably have given up.

As adults we didn't ask for the changes in our lives, but it's our two boys who most need to be protected from all of this. Through all these people we have been able to protect them as much as we can, so how can we pay someone back for that?

I had been very optimistic when I came back from Houston that I would improve. When I returned home I could walk all right. I had problems with my wrist rotation and my speech was a bit slower but apart from that everything was okay. People could understand what I was saying, but unfortunately over the next 16 months my voice, speech, and limb movements got worse. Recently I haven't been able to walk or lift and these factors have been very difficult to accept.

It has been upsetting as a dad reading books to Sam and Ben in the evening before they go to bed. What brasses me off is that I can't take them to bed now and I can't read to them in their rooms. But now Sam is a good reader and he reads to me. With Ben being only four, the books he has are only one sentence and he understands what I say even though my speech has deteriorated now. I can read to him but very slowly. That has been one of the biggest alterations in my life, as well as not being able to run around with them. I want to and I find it very frustrating as I was always a very physical and outgoing person and very tactile with my family. Up until the illness, I took for granted everyday things like lifting the boys onto my knee, which I am unable to do now. Last summer I was having problems moving my arms. The movement was getting gradually worse. Ben is the type of boy who is always saying, 'Come on daddy, play football/cricket/rugby,' but I can't do that now. I compensate in different ways and it does make me laugh and I suppose cry at times. Because as I am now with limited movement both Sam and Ben will crawl up to my knee and jostle for the best position. Erica, the boys and I will also lie in our enormous bed watching television.

I feel guilty at times that I can't provide physically for the boys. It has made me feel at times the way that Wigan had made me feel during the battle with them – unworthy. I wanted to be a dad and do things with the boys that dads do and I knew I was struggling. Time doesn't make it any easier, but I am trying to adjust because I have to and now I'm doing things differently. Children are very adaptable and they are also acutely aware of what's going on. They accept it but that doesn't mean they don't clock it. I was very hands-on with them, but the illness has robbed me of that. Now I show Sam and Ben in different ways how I love them. Erica many times has said to the boys: 'You need to know how brave your daddy is being. The only thing making your daddy fight this illness very, very hard is you two.' That's true and Sam and Ben know it. I'm sure that they wish I could get up and run, but daddy is still daddy. I still feel at times that I have failed them because of the illness although Erica says that I haven't.

Mentally, it really cuts me up. It's hard to accept that I can't do things that I take for granted, like going for a walk or scratching my nose. If I need to go to the toilet, Erica or one of my parents or in-laws has to lift me and walk me there. It's usually Erica who gets the short straw; it's a dirty job but someone's got to do it. At home I have an automatic bum washer and dryer. It's very deluxe and cost a mere £2,000. We didn't know these things existed. It is quite revolutionary, but since my illness I've cut down on my curries!

With being inactive I've had to be careful with my weight, so I've continued going to Royce's Gym three mornings a week, which is a godsend. I used to go there before this illness and knew everyone so it was no different. Everyone has been so helpful and understanding, especially when things were moved out of the way to accommodate me. Royce Banks, who owns the gym, and Freddie Ralphs have been especially helpful. I trained with Freddie before and now he takes the time out to put me through my paces and I can't thank him enough. Fred works during the night, has a bit of a sleep, trains himself and then he'll be in the gym when I get there to look after me. Without putting myself through it as I had done before my illness, my psyche would have gone down. Royce has been great with various pieces of information and putting us in contact with people who may be able to assist me.

Due to the illness, I twitch a lot. The worst time is during the night when I'm trying to keep still and go to sleep. My body is twitching that much that I don't have a proper night's sleep when I have this problem, so I'm more ratty than normal. I guess it's very minor in the context of everything else, but now I know what an insomniac goes through.

I had been to Houston and had been on the antibiotics for quite some time and I felt I was making progress in some departments. Erica and I had been talking with our consultant in America and he felt that it would be beneficial for me to go to another clinic he was involved with. The clinic was in Denver, Colorado and a Dr David Martz worked from there. He'd had symptoms very much like mine and he had been identified as having borrelia as well. He had the antibiotics and had started to respond well but when he stopped them his neurological symptoms came back. So antibiotics were an important factor and I felt it was a good idea to go to Denver, where a multi-disciplinary group was going to scrutinise me as a case study.

I went out in February 2005 together with Erica, the boys, Erica's mum and some friends to help us look after my sons.

Dr Martz met us at the airport, although I couldn't believe it could be him, as it had been well-documented in America that he had been in a wheelchair and like me had been told to say his goodbyes and come to terms with his life being cut short. His arms had wasted and his breathing had started to be compromised; yet I was looking at him and there was no sign of any illness. We have met some very special people along this journey and he touched my heart, especially with him having had a carbon copy of my symptoms. Dr Martz had turned everything around and he could have gone back to being the highly-paid consultant he was before he became ill. Instead, he decided that he was going to help people who had the condition he had recovered from. Dr Martz is living proof of recovery from borrelia. He now dedicates his life to helping other people push the boundaries back and using all his contacts within the medical world to fight borrelia.

Before we went to Denver I hadn't been able to move my arms a lot, but suddenly I was able to rotate my wrists. First it started with one and then the next wrist began, then I could control and rotate them simultaneously. I don't know how or why it happened but I thought the treatment was working and it would kick on during our time in Denver. We had seen these improvements, they had been seen by Dr Martz and his team and this does not happen with motor neurone disease. We flew back from the trip full of confidence after seeing Dr Martz. Here was living proof that borrelia could be beaten, as he had been like me.

On coming home I got something that I just thought was

flu. I don't know what it was, but it completely wiped me out. Erica, my mum and my sister Christine, who is a community nurse, looked after me 24 hours a day. I had something like pneumonia and Erica has since told me that she and my sister thought I was dying but didn't say anything to each other about that until I had recovered. I lost nearly a stone in ten days and they stopped all my treatment from America. There was a theory that it was the bacteria under attack releasing toxins. I recovered from this bout of illness but I have never been the same again since I came back from Denver. It was a devastating blow because we had come back full of hope.

I had been on the antibiotics for some time and I had this massive inflammation in my body and figured it was because I'd had a chronic infection. I began feeling disheartened and I told Erica that the treatment wasn't working. We went for more testing in October at the doctor's in Bolton which showed that I still had the borrelia infection.

I knew we couldn't go back to America again because the length of the flight would be too much for me. It had been very scary coming back from Denver and I didn't want to go through that again. We needed to start looking for a doctor in Europe who could complement our team through this battle. That was what took us to Rotterdam for stem cell therapy. We came across a Dr Trossel and what really interested us was that he had another approach to killing infections. It's not that I had stopped the intravenous therapy. This thing was bloody aggressive, I wanted to be aggressive against it and I wanted to run things in parallel.

Dr Trossel told us that for the 25 years he had been working with people with degenerative diseases he had often found that they have had infections which have caused their bodies to go haywire or they have been exposed to some form of heavy metal.

We needed to use a multi-pronged attack. One of the prongs involved using magnetic resonance and this therapy was the strangest thing I had ever seen. I was on a bed where there is a magnetic frequency to blast the parasite. It penetrates everywhere, so if the borrelia is in the liver it can get to it and if it's in the brain it can get to the brain. I also had ozone therapy, which was intended to go into the blood and destroy any parasite which was there.

The idea is to try and eradicate the infection and then introduce the stem cells. The ones that I was going to have are taken from a woman's placenta after child-birth. The placenta is very rich in properties which mimic your own immune system, your own antibodies, your own defence mechanism. It also has these spare stem cells and the principle is that I would be injected with these tiny little cells which have been pre-treated to become neurones. No-one fully understands exactly how this happens but these stem cells would be injected into certain parts of my body to encourage repairs to the damage that has been done.

I had to go on a special diet before I had the stem cells. I had to get rid of my mercury fillings, because mercury is toxic to stem cells, so I visited John Roberts, a specialist in Huddersfield. I also cut out caffeine for the same reason. This was to get my body in peak condition to be receptive to the stem cells so the body could utilise them as best it could.

In the meantime, our doctor in Bolton tested me for malfunctioning mitochondria, which is something that people suffering from chronic fatigue have. It's like little power stations in your body that produce the energy for every single movement and I found out that part of my mitochondria was blocked. All the time, Erica and I were finding new things in the battle to cure me and now we had a three-pronged attack.

There have been times during this journey when I have thought we were on the wrong track and that it wasn't working. I find it very frustrating at times but Erica and I have come a long way since discovering I was suffering from borrelia. We have come up against a very complex situation.

The statistics say that after stem cell treatment 80 per cent of patients make a significant improvement, but we will have to wait and see. Erica and I weren't given any timescale; it could be anything from straight away to a year. They can't quantify it either, they can't say 80 per cent of our patients will definitely walk. Instead, we might find that the improvement is to my voice. It doesn't mean I am going to get up and walk out of there. We have no idea what to expect but the stem cell treatment is not there to address everything. Just because it doesn't work after one attempt that could be because we haven't detoxed my body enough and the stem cells have been nullified by something.

Stem cells are part of the big picture, but my situation is complex. The infection has taken hold of my body and caused my immune system to become out of kilter, which has had a knock-on effect on different things. It needs to start functioning again and hopefully the stem cells will replenish and kick-start that regeneration. People might think Erica and I are stupid or in dreamland. All I can say is that until they can come up with something we will strive to find a cure for my illness and prove everybody wrong. In theory, according to some people, I shouldn't be around now but I'm here to tell my story.

There are many case studies we have researched, including one girl from Glasgow who had multiple sclerosis. Once she'd had stem cells, she just said she felt the energy surge through her body. She got out of her wheelchair and just stood up. Some people would say that was psychosomatic, but if someone's legs start working I defy anybody to convince me of that.

I have recently stopped the intravenous treatment and I am having the line taken out because it has been in for two years and we don't want the line degenerating within my body. So we have decided to take it out and give the stem cells a crack because they might be influenced by the antibiotics. If it's not working we will have to say that this is not the answer and Erica and I will continue the search for the cure. At the moment we are focusing on the stem cell treatment in Rotterdam. It doesn't mean that I have discounted the treatment I had in Houston and Denver, but it's another avenue. Erica has been magnificent with the hours and hours of research she has done, but ultimately I have made the decisions and they have been made for all the family. I am fully aware of what I have been doing and if things go wrong, then so be it. If I had gone down the conventional route I know where I would be now.

POSTSCRIPT –
ERICA, SAM AND BEN

I first met Erica during the close season in 1991. To be quite honest, I can't remember much about it although I certainly made an impression! I was in the Springfield pub this Sunday with quite a few of my friends including Joe Lydon. It turned out to be a mega-session, there were a lot of players in the pub and a good time was being had by all. Nicola, Joe's fiancée, came to pick him up and she brought her best mate Erica with her. I don't recall what happened, but Erica later said I came up to her, grabbed her by the lapels and gave her a kiss. She said that I stank of beer. I would, wouldn't I? But I can't remember that first romantic moment. Apparently when they left the pub, she asked who I was and Joe said, 'That's my mate Mike.' Erica said, 'He's awful.'

I saw her a few times after that because she was Nicola's friend and I was living at Joe's whilst my house was being built. We would speak to each other but it was purely platonic even though I was attracted to her.

My next close encounter with Erica came the morning after Joe's stag night. Erica was there with Nicola and they were making coffee. Erica came in looking for cups and she had both hands full. I got up to give her a hand, although she told me I had a mischievous glint in my eye and she thought I was going to grab her somewhere inappropriate. Hand on heart, I only wanted to help her with the cups. I walked towards her and I hadn't said anything when all of a sudden she dropped me like a bag of spuds by kicking me in the knackers. As I went down, I could feel these two lumps at the back of my throat.

It wasn't like playing in a game anticipating there might be a crack. I wasn't expecting it, I was a bit hung-over, my reaction time was a bit subdued and my gonads were defenceless. The other lads were very supportive. They were pissing themselves with laughter and I would have probably been laughing myself if it hadn't been for the ferocity of the kick. Erica didn't say anything; she screamed and ran out. I couldn't say much because I couldn't breathe, it was so bad. Anyone who has been kicked there will tell you what an indescribably sick feeling it is so I went upstairs for a shower to revive me. I then went into the bedroom and dried off and I heard a knock on the bedroom door. I put the towel around me and Erica was standing outside the door. She came into the bedroom and apologised. I gave her a big hug, told her not to worry and purposely threw her on the bed. That ploy didn't really work. Erica just got off the bed, went out of the bedroom and back downstairs. I don't think she trusted me. So a great start; twice I'd been either pissed or hung over and first impressions weren't looking good. But I was even more impressed with her.

Erica was the chief bridesmaid for Joe and Nicola's wedding the following week. I was Joe's best man so I would get another chance to impress Erica and I would definitely be sober. I had just finished with a previous partner and Erica had invited someone to the evening reception at the Kilhey Court.

During the wedding and the reception we had a good chat and we were getting on really well together. I was flirting with her and I got the impression that Erica was responding. I was putting right what I had done wrong before and she was seeing me in a sober light. Unfortunately, as the day turned into evening I was getting a bit worse for wear. I know it sounds as if I'm always drinking but, believe me, that's not the case. It was only that I saw Erica mainly at functions. Anyway, I was pissed. I got the priest who had married Joe and Nicola to bless my mum and dad three times. I vaguely remember that I got him in a head-lock and I would like to apologise to him now.

To complicate matters, my ex-partner turned up and whoever Erica had invited arrived as well. It was a nightmare. Erica and I were making eyes at each other and seriously flirting by this stage. I knew that she fancied me and Erica later admitted to me that she did. She didn't know whether she could handle me but thought she could. Erica knew by now that I was a rugby league player although she thought that it was a strange job. I had got so drunk that night and my behaviour was so bad that evening that Erica sent me back in a taxi to Joe and Nicola's to look after the wedding presents. The following morning I was asleep in the front bedroom when I was disturbed by a noise at the front door and realised it was Erica shouting. I jumped out of bed and brushed the curtains open and stood there in the buff posing like a Greek Adonis, showing off my torso and assets. Suddenly I clocked Nicola's mum and dad walking towards the front door with wedding presents. First impressions strike again. They must have seen me at the window as I opened the curtains to the watching world. I threw something on and opened the door for them and their body language said it all.

We kept in touch with one another and my first proper date with Erica was when we went for a meal with Joe and Nicola. We saw each other for about six months and then I broke Erica's heart. She told me I had to grow up and we went our separate ways and met other partners, although I wanted us to get back together.

I had just had a knee operation and was on crutches, but I decided that the only thing I could do was go to speak to her mum to test the water to see whether there was any chance of a reconciliation or whether I should forget it. I rang her mum up first to make sure I was welcome, and call it Dutch courage or whatever you like, but I had a few drinks. Erica's mum said that she wasn't speaking for her but that the guy she was seeing was really nice and wouldn't hurt her like I had done. 'Look, I'm not saying stay away from Erica,' she said. 'She's her own woman and she has to make her own mind up.'

At midnight I phoned Erica and told her that I had been to see her mum. She was pretty taken aback by that, but we had a long talk and I told Erica that I had grown up since we had split up and I wanted to see her again. We got back together but in fits and starts as she wasn't for trusting me after the last time. I knew I had to change a lot and I was prepared to do that because I loved Erica. The second time round our relationship was more on a level footing and I can honestly say today that I did change for the better.

The first time I was going out with Erica I asked her father for his permission to marry her and he told me no because she was finishing off her finals. The second time I asked her father again and he gave me the nod, as we had been seeing each other for quite a while by then. It was Valentines Day and that evening I asked Erica to marry me. The rest, as they say, is history and Erica and I got married on the 24th of June 1995, just before the start of the World Cup, in which I was involved as the assistant coach of Wales.

Erica has given us two lovely, caring boys and during her two pregnancies we went to the maternity suite six times with four false alarms. Because of coaching commitments with St Helens in 1997 and then with the Great Britain Academy in 2001, I was away for weeks soon after both their births. We had both always wanted children but we didn't think we would conceive as readily as we did – it was supposed to be difficult for Erica to do so because of polycystic ovaries – but both births went according to plan.

When Ben was born they said in the maternity suite that Erica would be a while before she gave birth. I left the maternity suite to tell both sets of parents that we would be there for some time yet. I had only been gone five minutes maximum and was walking back towards the suite when I could hear someone screaming and recognised the scream as being Erica's. They had security doors on the suite then and I could hear this screaming and nearly knocked the door off its hinges. Don't forget I was fit then. Erica was in labour and we didn't even make it to the delivery suite. Erica had Ben in the maternity unit and, although it's five years on, I apologise if I frightened any of the nursing staff or mothers but I didn't want to miss the birth.

Following the birth of Ben I was away for six weeks in New Zealand and Australia as coach of the England Academy. Ben was poorly when he was born and it was a bloody nightmare. It was really tough for Erica having two small children. When I came back I was up every night and morning giving Ben his bottle and doing whatever I could. I have always been absolutely smitten with Sam and Ben. The boys are our world and everything we live for, notwithstanding the pitfalls of what I can and cannot do now because of the illness.

Given Erica's medical condition, we felt very lucky and grateful for our sons, as some couples like us experienced protracted problems trying to conceive. We have had these two little miracles and we still find it amazing.

Over the last two and a half years, we have been through some tough times and Erica and I have had to have this resolve to battle on and fight this illness when things have looked desperate and dire. Somebody said to us that it's like heartbreak hill, when marathon runners hit the wall, as they call it. Their lungs are screaming for oxygen and their legs are burning. The lactic acid is being pumped out and they just feel that they are going to collapse. During these last two and half years, Erica has been unjustly criticised in some quarters for being stubborn, obstructive, unhelpful and confrontational. This could not be further from the truth. Erica has been my rock and whatever she has said and done has been for me. We are one in this, not two, and any unjust criticism of Erica is a criticism of me. We could have just laid down and let powerful people and institutions trample over us. We have fought the fight calmly, openly and fairly and but for my wife I wouldn't be where I am today. She is always searching for an answer, not leaving any stone unturned in our quest to find a cure for my illness. Her passion and drive is unquenchable and at times when I am down it's Erica who lifts me up and returns me to the fight. As well as this, she has the extra responsibility for everything else at home. At times I wonder how she does it all and always keeps a smile on her face and a positive attitude. We are, as The Three Musketeers say: 'All for one and one for all.' Both of us have felt like that all the way through this last two and a half years, even at times when the pressure has been immense.

Despite everything that has been thrown at us, Erica and I have created a happy home for the boys. We've kept them on an even keel as much as possible, even though both of us have been absolutely screwed up inside. It's testimony to what they mean to both of us. The whole point of this book is for them to know that, if the worst does happen to me, they were conceived in love and they have been cherished. Even when the world has been seemingly falling in on Erica and me, we've just carried on fighting. The reason why we've fought so hard is for those two boys of ours. I want them to have known their dad, even if I don't get better.

I want to hold them and play with them as I used to. I live for the day when that will happen and I hope that my love has shone through to the boys. This is not an obituary. I am far from dead and there are people all over the world worse off than me, but, if the worst happens, they will always be in my heart, my head, every fibre and ounce of my body. They will know that I tried for them. It is a father's fight for his wife and his two sons and that fight goes on.

Sam and Ben are my pride and joy and the greatest gift and reward I have ever received. They fulfil my life and I thank God that I have been here to help them. They are both so special and unique, yet in both of them I see parts of me in their looks, actions, mannerisms, traits and thoughts. You can't help but fall in love with them and lately that love, that bond has grown stronger and stronger. I've got to win the fight to get well for them.

They have both had a lot to put up with because of my illness and they have been truly amazing through that adversity. Like me of old with my setbacks, they have just got on with it. The hardest thing for me now is that while I can live with my arms and legs being poorly, it is hard to accept not being able to talk easily to the boys and tell them what I want them to know and remember. I intend to keep on fighting this illness for them – until the fat lady sings and there is a long song to be sung yet. I'm not going anywhere. I'm here for the long haul and I will bite back. It's not goodbye.

Erica, my wife, is a remarkable woman and words can't really say how much I love her. Whatever happens, I want the boys to know that their mum and dad love them more than we can express and that whatever they do in life I will be there for them and watching them.

MIKE GREGORY
TRIBUTES ...

PAUL CULLEN

The moment he walked into Wilderspool he was always going to be Great Britain captain. He was never going to be just another player, quality was written all over him.

There were faster, bigger and more skilful internationals, but no-one wanted it more or worked harder on all aspects of the job than Mike Gregory. He was smart, tough, honest, and ambitious, prepared to get to the very top by taking the hard route.

There are not many Warrington and Great Britain captains in the history of our game; it is an elite club for special players, special men. He did not chase the money or the glory elsewhere; he simply put his hand up and had a go with us.

His energy and enthusiasm was an inspiration at every training session and in every game. He was prepared to push himself to exhaustion and beyond and drag everybody else with him; his class was a bonus, his game was built on character.

Nothing surprises me about Mike, the guts that took him to the top are the ones that enable him to fight this cruel disability. They were evident the first day I met him as a 16-year-old; it was the way he was brought up.

During 17 years as a professional, he was the only player that I ever asked for help and advice. My game had hit a wall, my indiscipline was becoming a liability to our team. He said

'I couldn't have another 12 of you in my team but I couldn't have a team without one of you.'

I remember it like it was yesterday, every time I see him or talk to him or think about him, that conversation clicks straight back into my mind.

He has conducted himself with grace and dignity during his illness, he is a credit to his parents, his family, his club and the game he gave so much to. I have been humbled by the way he battles his adversity and I am very proud to call myself his friend.

JONATHAN DAVIES

When I left union to join Widnes in 1989, Mike Gregory was a league giant and one of the players I looked at with a gulp.

He played for our local rivals Warrington and represented a standard of skill and commitment I never thought I would be able to match.

But, although he was a fierce competitor on the pitch, I found him to be a genuine sportsman and always glad to help anyone. I grew to respect and admire him as a human being and a friend as well as a player.

My first playing experience with Mike was with the Great Britain squad which toured New Zealand in 1990. A lot of the superstars didn't go and, as captain, Mike had a big task in leading a team that wasn't given much of a hope.

But we won the series and a great deal of the credit for that was down to him. He was an inspiring general and the respect we all had for him was a great motivating force.

Even when he was unable to play he was a great asset to the teams he was associated with, such was the power of his presence as a role-model.

I'm so glad that I eventually played under his captaincy at Warrington and was able to get to know him better. It didn't matter whether you were a star or a beginner, any member of his team would get his total support and encouragement.

His whole-hearted, honest style as a player brought him many injuries and I think lesser men would have packed the game in, but his love for rugby was relentless.

There are many reasons why I'm grateful for the long spell I had in league and one of them was the opportunity to meet great characters like Mike.

He has been a great ambassador for the game, his club and his country. It is my fervent wish that one day he can return to coaching and continue his contribution to rugby.

I hope, too, that whatever clubs people support – and I know how fierce those loyalties are – everyone in league will band together to show their respect for a great man and support everything being done on his behalf.

SHAUN EDWARDS

Picture in your mind lining up for the national anthems and facing New Zealand, a team hell bent on winning a series in which they are already one-nil up. Your stomach is turning and a million things are rushing through your mind. You then look to the end of the line and you see our captain. Ball in hand and ready for battle is Mike Gregory – all of a sudden you feel a lot better.

Rugby league is a breeding ground for great characters and a game that tests your skill, bravery and competitive edge. Mike Gregory excelled at this highest level in the game he loves, leading his country to two magnificent series wins against the Kiwis and going toe-to-toe against the best the Aussies could muster.

I've had the privilege of playing with and coaching some tough competitors and great captains. People like Wayne Pearce, Ellery Hanley, Dean Bell, Graeme West, Lawrence Dallaglio – and up there amongst them as a captain and leader is Mike Gregory.

During his heyday, the thing that always stood out about Mike was his incredible work rate. He would be going at the same pace at the end of the game as he was in the opening exchanges. This sort of attitude and desire was obviously passed on from Mike to the teams he coached and, in particular, transformed Wigan's season in 2003, taking them from mid-table all the way to the Grand Final at Old Trafford.

Mike is facing up to his recent battle with the same determination and bravery that he personifies. I wish him all the best in his recovery. Let's hope he's back on the coaching field sooner rather than later, because you feel a lot better when Mike Gregory is on your side.

ELLERY HANLEY

Wigan was playing St Helens in the Challenge Cup Final at Cardiff in 2004 and Mike Gregory was head coach. I only had one intention in mind that afternoon and that was to find MG and present him with my winners' medal from the 1990 final, when I played against his Warrington side.

I found him half an hour before kick-off outside the Wigan changing room. I held out my arms – no words needed to be exchanged – and gave him my medal. We embraced and hugged each other tightly. I wanted him to keep my medal as a mark of the huge respect I have for the man. If there was ever a player who had deserved the Lance Todd Trophy that day it was MG.

Some people use words so easily, but I say this with all my heart and strength. I would give all the honours I have achieved for MG to recover fully.

As time goes by in our busy lives, it is easy to forget past players who served club and country so nobly and proudly. Let me give you a small indication of how MG played the game. He wouldn't take a backward step for anyone, he was physically hard and would be the first to make the hard yards coming out of his own quarter. He was mentally tough, courageous through pain and an inspiration to others. He was a legend you could not keep down; you knew he would compete to the end.

Mike has not only been my fierce competitor, but also my very good friend, whom I hold in high regard and honour. A champion, a winner, a front-line soldier, a man who led by example and would always compete regardless of the result and always wear his heart on his sleeve. His shirt was his badge of honour.

Truly brave men only come along from time to time. Mike Gregory, you are one of those men and a great human being. You will live in my heart forever, Mike.

HUGH McGAHAN

I first came to meet Mike through Joe Lydon when Joe was on one of his appearances at the Roosters and Mike was playing with Cronulla. Mike, being very close friends with Joe, was brought into the circle of guys at Easts and fitted in so easily.

Never pretentious, always friendly, Mike was comfortable to be around. His nature is to be collaborative, which showed in his leadership of teams. During his tenure as captain of the Great Britain Lions, Mike led from the front, vocally and physically. He never expected his team to do what he was not prepared to do himself and teammates liked playing alongside him.

Captaining New Zealand during Mike's captaincy of Great Britain, I found Mike to be a thorn in our side, as he was a player you could never lock down to be in a certain position at any point in time. Video analysis on each player was easier with some players but Mike was difficult to pre-determine. He was a menace to most attacks as he threw his body at the line with little self-preservation, but then in attack he was always around the ball and probably would have made a good loose forward in rugby union. He was a talker on the field, which was great if you were on his team, but for his opposition he was relentless in his constant chatter. Annoying is an apt description of his presence and it was not surprising that he always spoke with a little rasp in his voice, as he never shut up and he always yelled.

But off the field Mike is a gentleman and a pleasure to call a mate; many a laugh was had with him on tours, except for one particular incident after a Test match. It was the third Test played at Central Park, Wigan on the 1989 Kiwi Tour;

the series was squared off at 1-1 and needless to say feelings were tense with both camps confident of winning the decider. As on the 1985 Kiwi Tour, when Elland Road was the venue for the decider, there was a similar tension brewing. Fights broke out and at one point the police came onto the ground to separate players. That match ended in a draw (6-6) to level the series. This third Test was just as emotional, although without the fighting, and either team could have won. As history shows, Great Britain did win although the referee, the Australian Greg McCallum, made a couple of contentious calls late in the match which led to their win. It was a very tough pill to swallow and the Kiwi team held their heads up and moved on to the function following the match. At the function, we were trying to enjoy it as best we could, but predictably we were angry with ourselves because of the loss. During the speeches, Mike got up as captain to accept the trophy for winning the series and during the few words he spoke he mentioned how tough the game was and close the series was and that either team could have won it and praising all the players for their commitment, blah blah blah. He then finished off with words to the effect of: 'To the Kiwi team, after such a close series there is only one thing that I can say ... tough shit.'

Well, you could have heard a pin drop and you could feel the hair rise on the back of the neck of each Kiwi in the room. It left a bitter taste in the mouth of everyone but Mike didn't mean it literally; he was trying to make a tense situation lighter by making an off-the-cuff remark in the hope of raising a few laughs, but as you can imagine it did not go down well. Joe Lydon and I speak of it now and again and of course we laugh at it, but at the time it was not funny. Mike always regretted it, but once it was said, he couldn't do anything about it. It made no difference to how I felt about him as an opponent, but more importantly as a person. He is still the larrikin most of us know him as and always will be.

Mike deserves his accolades just as much as he deserves our support and friendship. He is a man who has endured more than any of us would want to in a lifetime and he has done it with the determination that made him successful as a player. Fortunately, Mike has the support of a close network of family and friends who stood beside him during his legal battle with Wigan and I know of his torment throughout that period. But with grace and aplomb he stood up to make a point; he is one who treats loyalty with honour and cannot understand how others could not afford him the same in return. It is a pleasure to call Mike Gregory my friend.

SHAUN McRAE

I first met Mike Gregory in February 1996 when he was appointed as my assistant coach at St Helens. I remember making reference to the 80-metre try he scored in the third Test of the 1988 Ashes series in Australia. Mike's response was one of a humble man who preferred to talk about the team performance and, even though the series was lost, the effect that win had on the morale of the touring squad.

Mike doesn't speak of his magnificent playing career, doesn't boast about the ultimate recognition in captaining his country. He'd rather use his knowledge and experience in helping others to achieve their goals and objectives, to encourage aspiring athletes to live their dream.

I spent three years at St Helens with Mike as my assistant, as well as the 2000 World Cup campaign with the Scotland team. Mike was a pleasure to work with, because he knew when to flick that switch to go from serious to relaxed and back again whenever necessary. He was a tremendous support for me, because he understood the pressures, he understood the system. He was a hard worker, he wanted to learn and become a head coach. He did become head coach, and a good one.

Mike is a very dedicated family man, a wonderful husband to Erica and a doting father to Sam and Ben. He'll always find time to spend with the loves of his life. The game of rugby league at the professional level can put a lot of pressure on families and friendships. These can be strained if the balance is not right. Not only has Mike appreciated this but, possibly more importantly, Erica has always been supportive and understanding.

There is so much more to say, yet if I told you stories of Mike Gregory and expressed views and opinions I'd have to write a book myself. My friendship with Mike and his family spans over ten years – and yet I feel like I have known him all of his life. Mike Gregory is loyal, trustworthy, sincere, honest, a man full of grit, determination and character. He has been a credit to rugby league, a credit to his family and to himself.

I was asked one day to sum Mike up and I thought of those horrific stories of war, where someone had to be first out of a bunker, a sacrifice runner maybe, somebody who could make a difference – I reckon that's Mike Gregory!

BRIAN NOBLE

The first time I came across Mike Gregory was at a chilly Wilderspool when, as an ageing Bradford captain, I can remember giving one of my famous 'under the posts' team-talks, suggesting that if someone didn't get a grip on the blond loose forward for the Wire it would be a long day at the office. It was a long day at the office.

Mike Gregory scored a try, made two and inspired the Warrington side to victory against a much fancied Bradford team. It was obvious to all that Mike would have a successful and inspirational career. Who could ever forget his iconic try against Australia to win that fantastic day for Great Britain.

Mike and I have mirrored each other along the way. We both captained our clubs and country and both had stints in the ARL with the Cronulla club in Sydney, under the legendary coach Jack Gibson.

We both came up through the junior coaching ranks to become head coaches. It is not common knowledge that I tried extremely hard to entice Mike to Bradford to be my assistant coach, just months before he became Wigan's head coach. He obviously made the right decision that day in that coffee shop in Prestwich.

Everyone is aware of the magnificent job he did at Wigan and the inspirational effect he had on his home-town club. If I am held in as much esteem as Mike when my tenure expires at Wigan I know I will have done a great job.

I am proud to have Mike as a friend, as an inspiration, respecting his courage, sheer doggedness, the hard work and effort that made him such a successful rugby man.

Many words are used in the modern era to describe what we are supposed to be all about. Here's what I think Mike Gregory stands for: Honesty, Integrity, Respect, Passion and Desire. Much overused in everyday parlance, each one – and many more – could apply to Mike.

His challenges in life have been documented in this book. He now has another challenge, one which he will face like everything else he has done in his life – head on.

A modern-day warrior in every sense. Those of us who know him stand with him.

MALCOLM REILLY

It's a pleasure to have been asked to contribute to Mike's autobiography. I have just recently watched a video of Mike scoring two tries against France in 1987 at Headingley, both followed by Mike's beaming smile. His enthusiasm on and off the field rubbed off on other players and people in his company. He had great enthusiasm for the game and life in general.

One of Mike's strengths was his ability to organise players around him; he never stopped talking on the field. I have the utmost respect for him; he is held in high esteem by everyone in the game that knew him. He toured and played with some outstanding players and they all share the same sentiments – players like Ellery Hanley, Kevin Ward, Garry Schofield, Joe Lydon, Kevin Beardmore, Shaun Edwards and Andy Gregory.

The international side whilst I was involved was more like a club side. The camaraderie and team spirit was exceptional and it's because of players like Mike that we were successful. He scored many tries in his career but none more important than the one in the third Test against Australia in 1988. A patched-up GB side minus seven or eight first choice players ended a record run of 15 consecutive Australian victories over Britain with a 26 -12 victory. It was testimony to the belief the players had in themselves and Mike played a huge role in that success. It was a tireless effort from everyone and Mike that day would have normally been ruled out through injury but played because of our crisis. On sheer adrenalin he scored the try to seal the game after his namesake Andy beat three or four Aussie players inside his 20-metre area, giving the ball to Mike, who ran 80 metres to score, ignoring the speedier Martin Offiah on his outside.

Mike captained the 1990 touring team to Papua New Guinea and New Zealand. The team was a young, inexperienced side with not many people giving us any chance of winning a Test. Mike's leadership and motivational qualities played a big role in us winning the series, beating a very strong New Zealand squad. One of the best things about Mike is that all his achievements and success in rugby league never changed him. Such a likeable character, he has always had a big friendly smile. Mike has been a great ambassador for our game, a game which is fortunate to have seen him play.

Other sporting titles by Vertical Editions can be
ordered from bookshops or our website at:

www.verticaleditions.com